FREDDY B

*A Semi-Autobiography of a Young Man
Named Frederic Walton Harris, Sr.*

By

YVONNE STEVENS WALTON HARRIS

ARPress

This book is dedicated to his children:

Frederic Walton Harris, Jr.
and
Kiarah Yvonne Harris

and to the memory of my son:
Frederic Walton Harris, Sr.

ARPress
45 Dan Road Suite 5
Canton MA 02021

Hotline: 1(888) 821-0229
Fax: 1(508) 545-7580

Ordering Information:
Quantity sales. Special discounts are available on quantity purchases by corporations, associations, and others. For details, contact the publisher at the address above.

Printed in the United States of America.
ISBN-13:   Paperback   979-8-89330-824-2
                   eBook   979-8-89330-826-6
                   Hardback   979-8-89330-825-9

Library of Congress Control Number: 2024902598

Contents

PREFACE

To have a child is truly a beautiful thing. To lose a child is a devastating horror. I wrote this book about my only child, my son, Frederic Walton "Walter" Harris, Sr. as a tribute to him. I assembled the papers of his life and his journal entries he left behind when he was incarcerated to give full meaning to his life for me, my family and those of you who have chosen to read this book. These are his words, his insights, sometimes filled with anger, foul language and sometimes filled with love. I now know in his early years as an only child he felt alone and he felt he had to have others to watch his back. It was a pseudo-family. So, he went along and became a "thug" in order to survive his environment even though his father and I were right here all the time reaching out to him every day. It is ironic he survived the "streets" only to find when he eventually came back to us, his true family, a cruel destiny awaited him at a high school friend's house one night.

Coming into this world on August 22, 1979 at 10 pounds, 15 ounces, my son was always a joy to me regardless of his shortcomings. It has been said Freddy inherited his personality from his maternal great-grandmother's side of the family. His maternal great-grandparents, Sally Elizabeth Stephenson Boone and Edward Boone, brought 11 children into this world. Sally was a beautiful, tall mulatta with long wavy black hair and Edward was a handsome man of Native-American and African-American mixed heritage. The couple's children were all shades of the rainbow. On the surface some of their children looked Mexican, others Native-American, then some appeared African American and even Caucasian.

The Boone Clan siblings lived in a two-story house my grandparents bought in Norfolk, Virginia. They often fussed and fought.

Some had run-ins with the law. Poverty stricken when Edward and Sally separated while the children were still quite young, Freddy's great- grandmother who never held a job did the best she could to raise her children. She was affectionately known as "Big Mama," Freddy's grandmother, Mabel Annette Boone Walton, the eighth child in the Boone Clan, often told me of the many days she went hungry. Some of the Boone Clan did not go to school and the ones who went, only went to the sixth or eighth grade. Eventually, one sibling graduated from high school and worked her way through nursing school. Another made a career in the United States Air Force. Later, he retired from a government job in Tucson, Arizona after many years of service. One might say, my son, Freddy, inherited his temperament from the Boone Clan.

Part I and Part III of *Freddy B* was taken from Freddy's own autobiography he wrote when he attended Indiana University Purdue University Indianapolis ("IUPUI"). He wrote his life's story in his English Composition class. His writing in Part II is remarkably different. His bad language and grammar gives us insight to Freddy B, the "thug" when he was incarcerated a year at North Central Juvenile Correctional Center (NCJCC) in Logansport, Indiana. Some of the "code" language includes SEG for segregated or separated from fellow juvenile offenders. SAT means satisfactory, UNSAT follows for unsatisfactory and 211 for the "time-out" room.

Part IV are poems my son wrote while incarcerated at Logansport unmistakably pointing to his loneliness and low self-esteem he suffered from 1996-1997. His "Mother's Day" poem is especially touching to me because he made a beautiful and colorful card filled with his love for me. Freddy always remembered our birthdays, our wedding anniversary, me on Mother's Day and his Dad on Father's Day. He was very thoughtful on special occasions.

I am writing this book on the tenth anniversary of the passing of my son, Freddy B. He was caught in a domestic dispute between a friend and her former boyfriend who simply did not accept the ending of their relationship. Freddy was shot and killed along with two other friends. Another friend was shot and survived.

Freddy was raised up at Eastside Missionary Baptist Church from conception until the age of 15 years when he strayed away from his Christian membership. After being incarcerated, he found he had a testimony to give about Christ and began a ministry with other juvenile offenders at NCJCC. His testimony gave him strength to withstand the test he endured during the time he was there. He became a changed and model citizen and returned to his true family.

I believe **Freddy B** will open the eyes of young men and women—"There are consequences to your actions in life." My hope is this book will continue his ministry to others. His struggle may help parents realize, no matter how difficult, to find a way to break the wall of silence that teens frequently suffer when they think their parents do not understand.

My only child referred to his passing many times in Part II of his journal entries as if he knew his life would be cut short. I can only say his children, his father and I love and miss him dearly and remember the warm times we shared together.

Freddy B leaves a son and daughter to carry on his legacy. So far, they are doing well in my son's absence and on their way to having well-adjusted lives.

I would like to thank my sister, Ayanna Nsenga Flechero, who gave her time and advice in the preparation of this book. Her love and support has meant everything to me.

Yvonne Stevens Walton Harris

PART I

INTRODUCTION

When I was younger (every since I can remember), I always used to get into trouble. Almost anything you can think of, I've probably done it or attempted to. As a child, I did things like getting into little fights, stole bikes and clothes, got suspended and expelled from school, etc. As a teenager I have been affiliated with gang activity, been in shoot outs, gang wars, hood wars, robbed, jacked, burglarized and been locked up.

It does not sound like any of this is significant to me. However, that is not the significance. The significance is after being locked up numerous times, the last one really impacted me. My last encounter with the law got me a trip for a one year stay at a Department of Corrections Facility.

However, the previous times I was locked up before I never stayed incarcerated for longer than two months. That means I would go in and get right out. Juvenile Center was a joke to me, especially if you had a lawyer with common sense, then you usually got off pretty easy. So, whenever I would get locked up, I usually took it as a slip-up on my part of getting caught. I never experienced it as a period to change, or to look at my wrong doings and work on them. To me they were just times I slipped up or a cop got lucky and caught me.

Well, as for the last time I got incarcerated, that is when things changed. They treated you like an adult and made you take full

1

responsibility for your actions. You had to actually work on your problems and try to focus on how you were not going to make the same mistake again when you got out.

In the beginning, I went in with a closed mind of not changing. That only got me extra time. As I continued to get in trouble, the duration of my time only extended.

As I Look Into My Life

As I look into my life, I'll tell you what I see
I see this young black man by the name of Freddy B
He'd always seem to get in trouble and end up in Juvenile
And every time you'd give him an inch, he'd always take a mile I don't understand his problem, he was really bright not dumb
He lived his life just like a game; his thinking mentality was quite young As I look into my life, I'll tell you what I hear
All my nizzaz proclaim my name, and all those scandalous hoez
Incarceration hasn't stopped the rumor and talk about his name And even though he has sorrows along wit his name comes fame I also hear no mercy, love or no fear
But deep down inside he says Momma I ain't happy here As I look into my life, I'll tell you what I taste
The bitterness of defeat and my teenage life to waste
I can taste the tears upon my lips of all my bad mistakes
But it always leads me back lookin in the mirror wonderously At my face
As I look into my life, I'll tell you what I feel
I feel that all this crime, dirt and fame wasn't even worth this tear My life as a thug and gangsta wasn't even worth my while
And although I'm sad and sometimes cry, I try to hold it in and smile
Even thugz have feelings I guess society just don't know
When people see a nigga cry he gotta be a bitch or a punk ass hoe I'm tired of trying to prove myself of what the world wants me to be I'm goin stop livin in society and live my life as Freddy B
But no one hears me; No one can feel me They act like they fear me.
What's in store for the things to come My future looks so dim
I'm lost and blindfolded all alone My options are so slim

I know there is no future for the things in life I've done A professional car thief, or burglarizer
Or take everything wit my gun
I know that sounds strange and even a little funny
But way back in the day I did anything to get my hands on some money That shits old, I gotz to get out the game
I've been livin too long for the hoez and the fame. As I look into my life, I'll tell you what I smell
The punk ass government and police tryin to set me up to foul
I smell envy and jealousy floatin in the air Sometimes life ain't easy, but who said it's fair?
I smell the struggle and strain of a young black brother tryin to maintain
And the smell of his pain lets me know the world's such a dirty game
As I look into my life, I'll tell you what's on my mind
I'm tired of reading the paper to seein brothers kill they ownselves
The Bible speaks of family against family and friend vs. friend
And although it's 1997, the world's comin to an end Sometimes I feel it's too late. What's the point to even try Whether I succeed or fail in life it doesn't matter.
I'm ready to die; I lift my hands to God beggin for forgiveness Praying he'll accept my repentance.
As I look into my life, I'll tell you what I've learned Just live yo life to the fullest to no one else's concern
Life ain't a breeze or easy; you'll learn that along the way
You could be fine and healthy right now, but be gone the very next day Don't trust no one in the world; sometimes not even your brother
The only ones I've depended on were God and my mother Your life is your only one, as precious as a flower
But the corruption of the world will try to devour your soul Wit money, greed and power
Listen to me–the words I teach are truthful and full of wisdom I've seen it, did it, lived it and through the system
These are just a few visions of my struggle and my strife
I'm just telling you the deal and spittin the real as I look into my life.

Freddy B

PART II

INCARCERATION

<u>Wednesday, July 10, 1996 – F. Harris – Journal</u>

Today's a new day and a new attitude. Yesterday when I was in group, a few suggestions came up that I think might have helped me with yesterday's problem. A couple suggestions were write a note to whom you want to talk to or express your feelings and when you write, instead of sending, just keep it or rip it up. It will feel as if you talked to the person one on one. So yesterday, I wrote a few lines to my mom and dad, a couple of friends, and my girl. I intended on writing to my grandfather, but I just wasn't in the mood or mind state to write my grandfather; but, I found that maybe if you write your problem a little better, you can look over, research some of your problems and see if you can find a solution yourself. So, I'm feeling a little better. Also, I go to treatment team today, and I'm 99.9 percent sure I'm going to get a SAT. Well, that's all that's on my mind today. *Freddy Harris – #966846*

Mrs. Martin – Teacher and Confidante

You've amazed me. You've already figured out what the journal is for. This is it – write it down

– weigh your options – talk it through. It does usually help you to figure things out. It sounds like you have a good group – get all you can out of it. You're doing a good job!

F. Harris – Thursday, July 11, 1996

Well today I'm in a pretty good mood. Yesterday, I received a SAT review on my treatment team and the next review will be on the 24th of the month.

Mrs. Martin

Good for you!

F. Harris – Continued Journal Entry – Thursday, July 11, 1996

I think I've been doing pretty good since I've been here. I try to complete my work and actually apply myself to the assignment. I'm not just doing it because I have to. I'm doing it because I want to. Day by day, I see more maturity and respect in myself than a lot of other guys in here. What I mean by that is a lot of guys just wanna clown, fight, argue, all of that type of stuff, just because they're upset and ready to go home. I feel if you're locked up (which we are) you need to make the best of it. For instance, right now we're getting a free education and a lot of people don't understand that, they must think this is just to waste some of the day, and these aren't real teachers, but the teachers I have are well qualified and have credentials (degrees in their skill). So while other people are drawing pictures and talking back to their teacher or whatever, I'm in the back quietly working on my work or studying on the G.E.D., that's what I'm getting from this. You get what you put in, so, if you put in nothing, you get nothing; if you give or put in something, you'll get something in return.

Hopefully, I'll be able to get my G.E.D. while I'm in here, because I'm working real hard towards it. Thanks for reading and giving me comments and suggestions about my last two entries.

> **Mrs. Martin**
> I think you are doing a fine job and I also am sure you are going to benefit from being here. You have to make the best of your situation to learn and grow, so that you can move forward in life. If there's anything I can do to help you – I certainly am available. Keep doing well!

F. Harris – Monday, July 15, 1996

Good morning. It's Monday which is usually a bad day for some people because it's the beginning of a new week. Today is really no different. I'm in a fairly good mood, but it's hard to be in a good mood when your wing is constantly in trouble. Sgt. Martin tells us everyday what he's going to do if we mess [up] at that time. Everybody acknowledges him because he's in and out the wing, but when he leaves, it's chaos. Nobody wants to do anything that he told us earlier. Kids arguing with staff, talking, in line movement, talking in the dining room, etc., etc. It starts to get kind of aggrevating after a while when we constantly get in trouble from the same play babies. Mr. Martin is cool too, he tells us straight up what he's going to do, then when people get banked (or caught) they want to start crying. Martin is the only one who be trying to give us hygiene items and trying to wash our clothes every night he can. Other staff will make us wear the same clothes for weeks, maybe even months. Everybody don't really realize how cool he is. Other kids think he's mean because he threatens to take our stuff, but he has no other option left. I'm not trying to make it seem like I'm perfect because yesterday I got a minor, and sometime I fall off mission, but I know how to correct my mistakes and to avoid things or situations that got me the minor before. Well, the bell's about to ring. I'll write you tomorrow.

Mrs. Martin

Everyone makes mistakes and bad choices – that's why you are here. We want to work on that, and for you to recognize it when you're doing it is a BIG step. Keep working!

F. Harris – Wednesday, July 17, 1996

Well yesterday I made another bad choice and it was my fault and my bad decision. Yesterday, we were outside in rec. playing a game. The rules were there were 2 lines of 15. 1 person out the line competed with the other by passing the ball to the other 14 members then run to the basket and score. Now a certain member thought it would be funny if he threw it at my face. When he did, I barely blocked, threw it away and said stop playing. From there, we exchanged dirty looks and words until rec. was over. When we lined up, he was mumbling under his breath saying stuff; about then I said say it in my face which I <u>should not</u> have done. We confronted each other as if we were going to fight, then some student broke it up. When we went upstairs again, we exchanged dirty looks, then he said "was up, what the Fxxx you lookin at?" I said "you." He said "was up then Fxxx the back. Let's take it right here" (paused) "ooooohh I when MF'S be talking sxxx I swear to God I'm going to hit you" then I made the mistake of confronting him. I got up, went over there, he made a gesture which I took as a swing and I hit him. Mrs. Jones was right there. She told me to stop, so I did. Then she said unball my fists, so I did. They separated us and Mrs. Jones said she appreciated my cooperation and she understood the gentleman was edging me on. I told her I apologized for my actions and accepted any responsibility. Since I cooperated, I didn't go to SEG, but I did get a Major. I understand I was in the wrong and that words mean nothing, but it seems my temper won the best of me. So could you give me a little advice so an incident like this won't happen again (I pretty much learned my lesson). I just wanted to know how you could've gone about solving this problem?

Mrs. Martin

> It certainly is very difficult to brush those kinds of things off and not respond at all – but – your main concern has to be – going home. Keep working on it. Patience is something you <u>learn</u>!

Fred Harris – Thursday – July 18, 1996

Good Morning. Today's Thursday and it's getting close to the weekend so I'm feeling pretty decent. Well the incident that happened yesterday is pretty much solved; me and the young gentleman had a conversation, apologized and pretty much smoothed out our animosity between us. Now the major problem to be avoided now IS the Major. And I think I solved that problem as well. For one, I've been told that a report hasn't even been written and staff only has so long to write it and so long to serve it. For two, I haven't really been in trouble excluding this incident right here. So I spoke with Sgt. Davison and from what he said he made it seem if I got a Major or didn't I really shouldn't worry about it. So hopefully, my previous good behavior could maybe cover up that one incident. But another thing I've discovered is when your locked your main focus should be going home. If you try to think about all the bad things like family problems, hurricanes, tornadoes, etc., you tend to be more concerned about other problems than your own. Plus, you tend to get upset, aggrevated or maybe even stressed which could cause you to take your anger out in a negative way or on a person or staff which I did and shouldn't have, and I take full responsibility for that. So all the negative input and words that I hear now I must worry about it later because I'm incarcerated. I couldn't do anything if I wanted to. So from this point on is focus on my priorities, not anyone else and negative input goes in and outs.

9

Mrs. Martin

What good processing! This has got to be difficult to do – try to take out some of that frustration in your journal – it's a good way to start every morning. I know you can do it – put your mind, soul, and self into it – I have faith in you.

F. Harris – 7/23/96 – Tuesday – Journal

As to your last comment I appreciate your faith in me, but the problem is I'm losing faith in myself. I have a lot of support from teachers, students, family and friends. But the faith within myself is dwindling down to nothing. With all the problems in the world in my (neighborhood/community) family and myself, when I try to look at the good I find none. Every week, every time I talk to my momma there's some bad news; if it ain't a death in the family, it's something else like someone sick or something or the topic that puts me over the edge is the police are trying to put new charges on me and waive me over to adult court. That was what really made me click, but also my name was in the local newspaper for a charge I haven't committed or been charged with. Now my family thinks I'm a hardened criminal. Oh, I forgot, the charge they're trying to get me for is auto theft; me and four other guys were in the paper. One of the guys stole my aunty's car, and she thinks I had something to do wit it, not only do they think I'm a criminal, they also think of me as a disgrace. My mom also stated that if somehow they try to convict me, I may be looking at some years. This is why my attitude has increased and my tolerance decreased. Yesterday I saw the psychiatrist. I take ritlin at breakfast and lunch. He said I do so well at school, but at the "J" Building, I tend to change. He said he would start giving me medicine in the evening because he thinks it wears off after school; hopefully he's right. There's one thing I want to apologize for, and that's making myself seem perfect when I'm far from it. When people look to you as a role model, it's hard to sustain that role because of the pressure. I will continue this tomorrow cause the bell rang.

Mrs. Martin

> Criminal or not you are a person and I think you do a good job at that. One day you will too. Please don't ever feel like you need to apologize for how you are. You are doing a good job of acting how you want to be – now you need to <u>feel</u> it! No one is perfect – we all have our issues and problems – we need to work on your self esteem – think of some ways to do that.

Fred Harris – Wednesday – 7/24/96

Today is treatment team day, and as I've said in the last entry, things are looking no good from 8-4 shift. I'm a perfect angel, no complaints, but from 4-12, things start to get out of hand like I said yesterday it could be the missing dose of medicine in the evening. I'm not trying to blame the downfall of my behavior on my medicine, but that could be the problem yesterday. I took an evening dose and no one had any trouble with me. Now that's just one day out of many more to come, but if this continues, hopefully, I won't have any trouble on treatment with custody sergeants, etc., etc. I can actually feel the medicine impact when it kicks in, but it wears off slowly and gradually, so I really can't feel the decrease, but I do tend to see more aggressiveness and less tolerance, but when I do realize it most of time its too late to change what I've said or done. Like I said before, I must learn to control my tongue, and my mind, but I'd rather think bad thoughts and not say them, than think bad, say bad, act bad towards other individuals. I have buddies in here, but only 2 true friends. God and my buddy, Billie. He's been in the system, and he knows what it takes to get so he tries to give me helpful hints to progress towards my release. But I need more than just him. I need the community's help. I'm sure a lot of people will pay more attention to 70 people than 1, and that's the problem instead of fellow students trying to stop an argument or fight. They provoke one to see who's bad that's what I need to block out. I won't see any of these people on the outs, so I don't need to do anything to try to make a good impression to any of them. So what I need to do is practice what I preach. I know the rules and expectations and all that; now I must abide by them starting today.

Mrs. Martin

Good Job!

Fred Harris – Thursday – 7/25/96

Well from the look of things I've been doing O.K. for the past few days, although yesterday, I did get an UNSAT, but I'm not even worried about it. I'm focusing on the next team, but as for my evening behavior it has been decent for the last few days. My name hasn't been on any lists, and I haven't had any paperwork. Now I know it's been only about 2-4 days, but usually my name ends up on a list or they're continuously saying my name, but I haven't had any problems at all. A minor misunderstanding here and there, but other than that, it's all good. I've started to communicate with staff more. For instance, yesterday, I asked custody (Ms. Johnson) what do I need to do to better my behavior, and we talked and she gave me advice on what to say, what not to say, and when not to say it. Then I told her what my concern was in my own behavior, and she acknowledged me saying "That's good you know, understand, and admit your problem. Now all you got to do is fix it." And that's what I'm working on. I need some correction, this is a correctional facility, so now I must want to get corrected, which is what I'm doing, but my anger, temper and attitude try to hold me back. But I'm starting to learn how to dispurse my anger. That's all today. Thanks.

Mrs. Martin

You are well on your way to helping yourself. Staff will help when you show effort and interest. What happens in the day room compared to school – try to list the differences and conflicts and evaluate them so you can start to work on them,

Fred Harris – Monday – 7/29/96

Today and every other day since the last week has been terrible. Every other day we have conflicts, stealing, fights and disrespect. On Sunday we spent 3 hours with Cap'n Herron talking about people stealing from one another. **(Mrs. Martin – "I hope it helps.")** How to for the day room, and how to help the community out period. Anyway we felt it did some kind of good, so we told him we would do better. Then today this fight happened and Graves went to the hospital. The Saturday before this Sunday (27) the reason Cap'n Herron came in was because 2 guys were going to fight and the whole dorm was acting crazy throwing things at staff and students; everything just plain crazy. During this whole period in time I've been doing O.K. I did have a few problems but everyone does, but I think the major problem is Sgt. Butler.

Mrs. Martin

Try to finish your thoughts!

7/30/96

Every second shift he works, I get in trouble. I'm not trying to blame my conflicts and problems on him, but he said I'm making or have made the front page so he tries to bank me if I sneeze wrong. He constantly picks and nags on me waiting for me to click on him or just say 1 thing to take me to SEG. I have went to SEG for being ill-tempered and having an attitude, and since then I try to bite my tongue before I make the same mistake. Another thing is he tries to make me the bad example or the big, bad wolf. Saturday night, he tried to use me as an example of being off focus, off mission and the number 1 bad guy of the community. Then almost everyone got up and used me as a negative example in every scenario. I got very upset and addressed the community and Sgt. Butler for making negative remarks. Butler was getting so upset because I fronted him out in front of Lt. Holmes and the community, and I had support in some of my awarenesses. I said he showed favoritism. I had support on that. I said he never listens to you when you need support or help, and I made a few more comments which I had support. Then I told Lt. Mills about the favoritism Butler was showing to certain students, and he (Butler) and Lt. Mills had a talk about that. That Sunday Butler didn't pick, fuss, or say anything to me and I did pretty good. He hasn't worked the wing since Sunday, so I have to wait and see.

Mrs. Martin

Pointing that negative awarenesses were being made at a constant was a very good thing. You know (because I read it) what is happening. The next step is to work on either avoiding the situations you get into or dealing with them differently. What are some ways you can work on that – if I can help, I will. I appreciate your hard work and behavior in my classroom – I know you can transfer that over to the other building. BELIEVE!

F. Harris – Thursday, August 1, 1996 – Journal Entry

August 1, the beginning of a new month. This month is my birthday, my father's birthday and my best friend (one of them) Billie Harrell. My birthday is on August 22 (79). I'll be 17. Billie and my father's birthday are August 25. Billie will be 18 and get this; my dad, my real dad, Frederick Emmitt Harris will be 65 years old; that's kinda old, he's old enough to be my grandfather. Some of my buddie's grandparents and great-grandparents are younger than him. But, it's O.K. cause he's a good father and he provides for me. I have three brothers, one sister, one sister-in-law, a nephew and a niece (we all have the same father, but different mothers). My brothers are Troy–35; Larry–32; Danny– 23; sister Lois–34; sister-in-law Charlotte (married to Troy); nephew Jerry – 11; niece Marie – 8. I was planning on spending summer in Dallas where my brothers and sister live; but things didn't work out. Anyway, my brothers and sister are supposed to be coming up for my father's birthday, so hopefully, they'll be able to come visit me around my birthday, **(Mrs. Martin – "Yes.")** but I think the limit of visitors is five so we'll have to see what I can do to try to get all my family to come. At first I was depressed about spending my birthday in here, but I won't let it get to me. Maybe me and Billie can clown together on our birthday. So I think I'll be O.K. this birthday; but another problem I will address in another entry is Billie and this month. I can't write it now because the bell is about to ring.

Mrs. Martin

My father is a lot older than most too – if you enjoy him as your dad – that's what matters – not age.

Fred Harris – Monday, August 5, 1996

Well again my temper and attitude have got the best of me. See on Thursday evening, my mom told me that I have to go to court (on

15

August 15, Thursday) for pending charges. It's in Hamilton County. Then I got a subpoena from Marion County Court to testify against someone I know. These 2 court hearings have made me very upset and irritable. I snap on the quickest thing. Anyway for some of those reasons up above (upset and angry, etc.) I was placed on loss of privileges which made me really mad because I couldn't call my mom inside which caused me to unleash it in a negative way which was fighting. But this whole situation could've been avoided if we both wouldn't have provoked the fight. Me and this gentleman aren't the best of friends, but usually when we talk we argue and you know this young gentleman, he's cool, but he knows what to say at the wrong time. This young man's name is (Mr. Graves) yes the one in this class we got into it, then someone told. Sgt. Butler was going to send me to SEG for battery, but he failed to realize that Graves did physically retaliate. So, they were going to charge us with fighting, but Lt. Mills being the good man he is gave us an option that we would be on the buddy system for 4 days, write a 10 page report, me and Graves together and present it in a townhouse meeting after the community meeting and do everything together or get paperwork, automatic UNSAT and 5 days SEG. Well of course, we both chose option 1. We didn't like it at first, but I can already tell that 4 days of being his buddy won't hurt. We'll probably be friends, still after that, but this wasn't really a learning experience because this has happened in the past. I was supposed to have learned from it, then this was more like a bad choice of judgment and decision on me and his part. I'm not learning anything. If I make the same mistakes like I have in the past. I will elaborate more on this topic tomorrow. The bell is about to ring. Just read this part and comment on it tomorrow when I get finished. Thanks

Mrs. Martin

What can we do – so you don't pick this choice when you're angry. Can you write like in a journal and put it in your folder? Extra work sheets. Let's talk.

Fred, I think you are learning more than you realize – you need to work on putting all of your knowledge in action and learning from your mistakes.

You know where you need extra work – now <u>do something about it</u>!!! Quit sitting on it.

I think Lt. Mills offer was fair and you are right – it will do you some good! Make the most out of it and go on. Good Luck!

F. Harris – Tuesday, August 6, '96

As I was saying yesterday, my temper continuously is rising, but not just because I'm mad for no reason, it's because I have a lot on my mind like I said before in a journal entry (on July 23, Tuesday), the police were trying to bring up new charges against me, but, from the look of things, they have. On August 15, '96 of this month, this year in less than two weeks, I'm going to Hamilton County to get questioned. I know it's not a for sure thing they will try to charge me with anything, but a few of my so-called friends put my name in the story. Anyway, me and my family don't have the kind of money to get a lawyer or money for bond, plus, I don't want any charges against my adult record. Then, say if they don't waive me they'll send me back here for an even longer time, probably till next year. My faith and hope have <u>quickly fallen.</u> **(Mrs. Martin – "Don't let that happen.")** My determination and desperation and thoughts of going home are all wiped out. If it wasn't for this school right here, I'd probably be in SEG or something. School is the only thing I've got and/or want and need if they told me I couldn't come to school and learn, I'd probably go crazy with all this stress and choices and decisions. I'm about to crack like a peanut. From deaths, to family trouble, financial problems and court procedures, I can't take on these decisions and problems alone. I hardly use the phone, and some things you just can't talk to a teacher or staff about. I got a friend, but we can't even talk without getting paperwork or L.O.P.(Loss of Priveleges). My friend is getting very thin, and I'm about falling apart. My medicine is like a toy now. I'll be cool or relaxed for a short period of time, but after a while, I tend to get restless. I read the Bible and ask for the Lord's help, but nothing's happening. I just don't know what to do or how to control my actions anymore. **(Mrs. Martin – "He works on His time, not ours.")**

I haven't even told you all the other problems I've had. If I did you would understand a little more better. The problem is I'm only 16 with the responsibility of an adult, and I don't know if I'm ready to handle it; but I have to and that's a few of the reasons of my attitude. You see some staff is cool. They'll try to see what's wrong with you and help you out, but others want to do nothing and see you fail and could care less about any of your problems and conditions. When certain staff treat me like that or talk to me like a dog or give me no respect, that provokes me to treat them the same way, and I think it might lead into other shifts (meaning, if I treat one staff like that, I'm going to treat them all like that). The attitude I have right now is, "It's just me against the world." No one seems to understand me, and if they try to they still can't relate to my problems or situations that I've been through or about to go through. I just can't think of anything that can get me on mission or on focus. As I said before, I'm losing hope and fast. I just don't know what to do anymore.

Mrs. Martin

There are some out there on your side. I suggest that you seek some outside help – I am very available and willing to talk to you anytime – your counselor would be too. I think you would be surprised that one of us might not be so hard to talk to. If I can help, please let me know. Keep the faith and don't give up.

F. Harris – Wednesday, August 7, 1996 – Journal Entry

I appreciate your offer for help but as you can tell, my trouble is not in school or in the morning. It's in the "J" Building after school on 2nd shift. (**Mrs. Martin – "If you'd like to talk after school, I'm free."**)

My counselor (Ms. Scott) is too busy and the only time I see you is in the morning, and if I have or had a problem, it would've been the previous day, and that's in the past. It will only upset me to bring it up again, plus me and my counselor got into a little argument, and I really don't think she has something to say to me, and I feel the same way as well. We had a disagreement during our group yesterday, and I made a negative comment, but said it in a positive way which resulted in a minor argument and Sgt. Davison overlooking the situation, he told us that we discussed it, analyzed the problem, now it's over, get back on mission. (**Mrs. Martin – "The two of you will need to talk this out."**) But a certain member wanted to continue the conversation after Sgt. Davison left which resulted in another argument, and my counselor got upset and put us on dead mouth, then another group of hers combined with our group because their teacher left when they entered, they didn't realize we were on dead mouth; a student came in joking around, my counselor got upset and snapped at him. Then the student began to talk about her which resulted in making her cry, and the summoning of Sgt. Davison for some strange reason due to the arguing earlier, she said I participated in the negative behavior and Sgt. "D" chewed us out back at the "J" Building. I'm not sure what the Sgt.'s going to do, but him just yelling at us was not the end. As for me seeking outside help, I can't for (1) one month L.O.P., (2) you can only use the phone two times a week, (3) one visit out of these three occasions due to the behavior of west wing. I only talk to my mom on a visit because we never get a chance to use the phone. The only person I'll listen to out of this whole world is GOD and my mom. My dad is half and half. Sometimes I listen, sometime I don't; but the person who I'll do anything for, I mean anything for, is my mom, Yvonne Stevens Walton Harris. She has done everything for me, giving me everything she can, supported me through all my downfalls, all that, my mom means so much to me. I'll take a bullet for her, after all the wrong I've done, and all the pain I caused, she still looks at me like momma's little boy. She's the only one who understands and knows how I feel. She never looks at me like a thug or criminal, or that I'm heartless or wrong even when I'm guilty, and she knows and I know I'm still her innocent little son. I'll finish up tomorrow, the bell rang.

Mrs. Martin

Unconditional love is a wonderful thing – be thankful and appreciative. You've got a great mom.

<u>Fred Harris – Friday – 8/16/96</u>

Hello Mrs. Martin. I'm finally back. I've been gone for about 4 days. But I'm back, and I intended on coming to school everyday for this past week. I've been in constant trouble. I've been in SEG 2 times, I have loss of privileges for 4 days (today's my last day), and I think I have received 2 Majors and 2 Minors. It seems like I fell off the deep end. I haven't been to school in 3-½ days and the bad thing about it is, is that I like coming to school and I was doing something that no one else could do, take away and that's my education. I really showed how smart I was. I thought if I debated or argued over the situation I would win, but I lost and everytime I argued I was off mission and I thought of it as I didn't care, but I did. That's why I was arguing the point of going to school. I don't know why, but it did take me 3-½ days to get back on mission. I think some of the reason is a staff, her name is Mrs. Johnson. She's cool and all, but I'm not used to taking orders from women (unless my moms or Grandma), especially getting threatened by women. But my mistake was taking Mrs. Johnson's authority as a joke, but it wasn't funny when she put me on 4 days of L.O.P., gave me a major, sent me to SEG, made us do 7 hours work detail and 2 minors, being she's a woman. I took all these as a joke, but when everything she gave me landed, I got upset and argued and debated wit her, but we finally had a talk and smoothed things out (hopefully). So I really shouldn't have anymore problems. Also me and Sgt. Butler are patching things up so hopefully I'll be able to stay on focus.

Mrs. Martin

I'm glad you can see some of these things for yourself. Taking orders is difficult, but you need to realize where you are and that staff does have the authority, no matter what you're used to. You've come a long way – I'm proud of you.

F. Harris – Wednesday, 8/28/96

Was up Mrs. Martin? I haven't talked to you in a long time. Since the last time we've talked, my time here and behavior has been shifting up and down like a roller coaster as you know (because you were there). I was going to SEG like I was going to the bathroom every-day and every other day I was going to SEG, getting majors left and right. I wanted to change on the outside, but I was confused on the inside. I was so used to my old behaviors and actions that if I wanted to change, I wanted to change on my own and not be forced into changing especially by people I don't like or want to listen to, and those times when I did change or wanted to and let staff talk to me however they wanted, I didn't want to accept the fact they had authority and could tell me what to do; so the inside was like HELL no, nobody talks to you like that, but my outside and half my inside tried to maintain it, but usually the bad would win because I didn't want to look like a hoe in my eyes as well as others. Whenever I thought that that's when I got out of control and started running off at the mouth. All of this happened before the 21st of August. My last treatment, of course, I didn't get a SAT; I didn't deserve one, but I knew and understood that. But lately, about three weeks ago, I started going to Church and Bible Study everyday I could, and I really started getting into the word. I read special verses on anger, faith, and difficult times. When I read these verses and applied them to myself, I started to find myself avoiding trouble. I used to carry my Bible everywhere I went because whenever I flipped my lid, I would read certain verses to relax me and calm me down. Then after a while I started to do it on my own calming myself down relaxing my thoughts by going over Bible verses in my head. Since my last UNSAT, I've been on mission. I haven't even been on an off mission list, and I intend to continue on staying on this path. I know I've said this before in last entries, but I'm true to this before I said I wanted help, and I was unsure and alone, but now I know I do, and God is on my side now. Also, for the past few days I've been witnessing to other students telling them about Jesus Christ and God, and how the end of the world is near; how we must repent and so on and so on. Some people listen and don't take heed, but others sit wit me at rec and before bed and fellowship wit me and discuss issues that they're unsure about, and I try my hardest to answer or lead them to an answer, but I always try to influence them to continue reading and try to get a better understanding of Christ. Before I was a little concerned of people's thoughts and opinions, but now I'm doing what I gotta do for the Lord and myself to keep us both on mission and help others learn about what they must do. Since all of this I've had a new inner peace with myself and God. Every night before I go to bed and pray, I felt a lot better. I cast all my worries and troubles and gave them to God. My temper has dropped considerably. Now I can go to bed stress free, worry free, anger free; all that anything that bothers me, I give it to God, and it's over wit. So I feel that the rest of my time will be a peaceful one. Although I'm locked up I feel like this is a summer camp now. So I feel pretty much on my way to success now. So pray for me to stay on mission, and I'll pray for you as well and to help to stay on mission in case you see me slippin. Well, that's pretty much all I have to say. Thanks and God bless you. *Freddy Harris*

Mrs. Martin

Wow! I'm so impressed with you. I hear you talking, sure of yourself and that's very important. I'm very excited for you in your new peace and journey. I'm always here to support you.

F. Harris – 8/29/96 – Journal Entry

Was up Mrs. Martin? Yesterday I helped Cap'n Herron move yesterday. We worked all day. It was strenuous work at first, but when we used teamwork, we got it done quick. It was six eastwingers and two westwingers. They only helped us twice. Anyway, helping the Cap'n is a privilege. So that means I was on mission. Plus, since yesterday was my birthday, Mrs. Malone got August birthdays a cake, plus, we got commissary for helping Cap'n Herron. Although it was hard work at first, we eased into makin it easy and helped out the community and our Cap'n and as well as that, Sgt. Butler put me on elite group of 16 people who will be in the privileged room. Like I said, everything is on the up and up because of my faith in God has been looking out for me and the way things look, I might not even go to court. Hopefully, I won't, but I'm just gonna continue to stay focused and on mission so God will continue to bless me. Thanks

Mrs. Martin

Happy Late Birthday

Fred Harris – Tuesday – 9/3/96

Was up Mrs. Martin. Today isn't looking so good. Earlier me, Sgt. Howard and Officer Venable got into an argument. I'm a permanent laundry worker and yesterday I did an inventory list on everything in the laundry room. We had enough and a little extra, but all that stuff is supposed to be saved for later on when we quail. So when we stripped our beds, some people threw their clothes away along wit their linen. This made Howard and Venable mad and at that particular moment, I was doing something I shouldn't have. I went to someone else's room (even though they were there) without staff permission. So when Howard saw me he chewed me out, but I accepted it. Then he chewed me out again for not having my pants or shorts again. I was upset, but accepted it. Then when we went to the dayroom, I asked Venable why were they trippin. Then Venable chewed me out. I tried to maintain and I did, but I did use a little profanity to vent my anger, and that's when me and Venable had a verbal disagreement, but I still maintained, and I talked to Howard and Venable and we figured out the problem. So they put me in L.O.P. until shift change (8:00) so I can calm down. Other than this incident today, I've been on mission and focus, and I'm proud of myself for handling this situation without going to SEG or getting paperwork or a sanction. I'm not going to let this mishap get me off mission.

Mrs. Martin

It's great that you are seeing these things as they happen. Keep it up!

F. Harris – Monday, Friday, 9/4/96 – Journal Entry

Hello. How are you doing? Although my body is kinda sore, I'm half and half. Well you probably know about the incident wit me and Mr. Crowe that was dirty. He tossed me around the hall like a rag doll, and I was helpless. I couldn't do anything. A 5'10" 185 pound. 17 year old compared to a 6'7" 260 -270 pound 26 year old correctional officer. I couldn't do anything if I wanted to. (Mrs. Martin – "Good for you!") That incident on Friday, 6th, was the only time in my whole life when I got beat up and didn't react to it. He didn't beat me up fist wise, but, him slingin me around and throwin me against the

24

wall and doors without me resisting, I wouldn't call that a standard Prt (physical restraint technique). It got to the point where he was throwin me against the walls so many times and constantly jabbin my right shoulder against the wall and slamming me, I had to try to get loose with all that, plus the prt it felt like he broke my arm. When he was finished, my face was swollen and my two shoulders were badly bruised especially my right. I had a laceration on my right shoulder as well. They were going to take me to the hospital, but I didn't want to go. When I saw the nurse, she said I pulled a muscle, and it might take a while to heal. After all this prt-ing and slammin happened, he cuffed me face down on the floor when I felt my face throbbing as if it were swollen and saw the blood of my lacerated shoulder on my t-shirt. I almost went crazy. I was yellin, cursin, disrespectin him all that, plus I threatened him. I wasn't goin to SEG, timeout, or getting paperwork. **(Mrs. Martin – "Was this a good choice? What could you have done differently?")** I chose to go to SEG because all my mind was filled with was bad intentions about C/O Crowe. So, I requested to go to SEG. After about 2 hours, I came back to the wing and Sgt. Butler and Lt. Holmes took pictures of my arm. So, I'm not sure what's going to happen. Well, that was the first issue, the second is terrible. Yesterday, I got a major for **BATTERY ON STAFF**, and I don't understand how me and a fellow were arguin; she told us both to be quiet, we both did until he muttered something disrespectful. I got upset and argumentative again sayin a couple of profane words. Mrs. Robinson started yellin, spittin, and pointing in my face. I asked her numerous amount of times could she please give me room and stop pointing in my face, but she only provoked it by yellin louder and getting closer to me during this time. The student I was arguing wit before was havin a good time watchin me getting chewed again. I said some wrong things to the student which I think Ms. Robinson thought I was referring to her. Then she got more aggressive and angry and getting closer and closer. I tried to space myself from her until she cornered me where then I shielded my face from her poking me and that was about the end of it. She said I pushed her away forcefully 2 to 3 times, and I balled my fist at her. I have a lot of witnesses sayin I didn't. I can't really even ball my fist up (my right, anyway) plus, I'm right handed. So, even if I did (which I didn't) I wouldn't have been that forceful plus I think I have common enough sense not to get into a situation like that possibly getting prted again. I could've got my arm broken. Ms. Robinson seems to have a vivid imagination, I'm not even concerned about this cause I know I didn't do it. I admit to the <u>verbal abuse towards the student,</u> not the C/O, but the other stuff I almost couldn't do plus if I did with 2 officers supervisin (2 female officers) and a big guy like me pushin them don't you think I would've been in SEG or got took down. Nope, none of that, just a timeout and a major that doesn't make sense. I just can't seem to understand it. Oh, well, like I said, I'm not letting this get to me. **(Mrs. Martin – "How can you work on this to avoid <u>all</u> of the mess next time?")** Oh, I forgot to say, I don't know if you know him, he was here before about 2 months ago. Raymond Twyman. Anyway, he's my cousin, and his grandpa died about 3 to 4 days ago. Also, my grandma's sister, Martha, died (my grandma, Bertha, her sister is deceased as well. R.I.P. God Bless her soul). This incident has had a little effect on me but not as major as my grandpa. I wasn't too close to neither one of them but I loved them anyway. Well, like I always say, just pray for me and continue helping me so I won't get off track. Bye.

Mrs. Martin

I'm sorry about your family members – It's hard to lose loved ones.

What happened yesterday in G.E.D.? Are you losing your focus and direction? Let's work on it!

<u>Fred Harris – 9/5/96 – Thursday</u>

Was up Mrs. Martin. How you doin? I'm doin alright. On Tuesday, I helped the Cap'n move beds in the new buildin. At first we were going to move the whole wing on Thursday, but as we were working, we told him we felt we could work all day until we got it done and we did. We worked from the end of lunch until about 11:15 and the end of lunch was somewhere from 12:30 – 1:15. We worked the whole day, hard too, it was a lot of stuff to move; couches, tables, chairs, desks and drawers, beds, mattresses, pillows and a whole lot of other stuff for the counselors. After movin, we had to get quelled and make our beds. I thought I was going to pass out, but I made it. Yesterday was cool too. At first I didn't like it, but it's getting better and better as we go along. I really hated eating those sack lunches yesterday, but other than that I've been doin fine. Oh well, that's all I have to say for today.

Mrs. Martin

What hard work! Wow – you probably slept well that night. Thank goodness the sack lunches were a one-day deal – they had to move the kitchen. So sometimes we must suffer!

Fred Harris – 9/11/96 – Wednesday

Hello. What's goin on Mrs. Martin? I know you're wondering about G.E.D. class yesterday, so here's the story. Ms. Hester's class joined us and the population increased to 24 people which made it cramped and noisy. Then she goin to turn on the radio even though people were still talking. Before class started, she said due to the number of people in the room, she kickin people out wit 0 tolerance. But she wasn't doin. Then it just got louder wit the radio When I started to tell people to be quiet, she sent me in the hall. I told her I was telling someone to be quiet, she said she know, but she'll handle them. Then I said well you ain't doin what you said you was going to do and she said what's that? I said sending out people who talking so she got mad cause she thought I was tryin to tell her how to do her job. So she said you want me to do what I said. I said, yeah, so she sent me down the hall. When I was in 211 they told me I could get an UNSAT or extra time so I got mad. When I came back, I was very upset. Then when I came back we were still not to be talking. People were still talkin. I made several statements sayin send them to 211 like you did me. Then I made a few sarcastic statements directly and indirectly towards her. She still wasn't kickin no one else out for talking in the room. Then I made the remark about not doin what she said she was goin to again, and she told me to go out in the hall. At that point, I didn't want to speak wit her. I tried to get my books, but she wouldn't let me until I talked to her. She asked me where did I want to go after lunch, 211 or her room, so to get things over wit, plus to get my books and out of anger, I said, 211 after lunch. I changed my mind, but she had to talk to me before I returned back in school. Every time I asked her why, she sent me and no one else. She never answered me and I got upset again and left. So my name was on the list again. But the reason for my actions is because it seems I'm not sayin it is but it seems like everyone wants to find a reason just the littlest thing to bank me for the smallest most petty reasons. It seems like they want to see me fail, and it's just makin me mad because I've been doin so good over the last 3 weeks, and I don't want to lose it in a week, but even the smallest, most petty things in here will give you an UNSAT. I'm just getting frustrated. I can tell I'm getting better maintaining, but I must keep my composure. What I think is I'm losin sight of God, the word. If I start reading it again and getting in it again, I'll bet I won't get in trouble. Just watch, today, I'm getting back in it. But that's all I have for today. Talk to you tomorrow.

Mrs. Martin

You need to keep <u>your</u> focus and not let what other people are doing push you in the wrong direction. Are you still reading? Find some time this weekend to do it for you!

F. Harris – Friday – 9/13/96 – Journal Entry

Hello. Today is Friday, the 13th, not a good day, but it's been goin pretty good. Last night I ate commissary cause I sleep in the privilege dorm, and we were on mission. So we ate commissary. My boy, Robert, is in SEG for I don't know what, but, I know he's sick. We were talking yesterday and I said, "Man I'm gonna be bored witout you, but, I don't like seein none of my dudes locked," so I said, "Be cool so you can leave and go home." I don't know what he did, but evidently it was bad enough to go to SEG. But hopefully he'll be able to leave next FRIDAY. So, I'll just pray about it today. I'll be startin my Bible reading again, so I can get back closer to God. My arm is almost all the way healed. I can stretch almost like regular now. So, I think I'll be fine. Well, that's all for today other than that Coleman, Mr. Adams incident. So, I'll write you on Monday. Bye, bye.

Mrs. Martin

I'm glad you're refocusing – it takes a strong person to be able to do that on your own. Keep up the good work – the privilege dorm? I'M IMPRESSED!!!

9/17/96

No entry – Pinballs work – O.K.

9/23/96

No entry – SEG

Fred Harris – 9/25/96 – Wednesday

Was up Ms. Martin? I haven't wrote you in a while, well, since Friday, 13th. I got a SAT; I'm on level 2 now, went to SEG which got me kicked out the priviledged dorm and fired off the laundry team. But qualified for my G.E.D. so 2 outta 3 ain't too bad. First about my SAT, I was so happy, it felt like my birthday. I just wanted to celebrate plus my new program is getting my G.E.D., and if I do that will most likely be my releasement. I take the test October 1 (Tuesday) and go to team the 16th if I even attempt to get it. If I pass or don't, I might still be able to go home. Now that brings me to SEG and my G.E.D. Ever since I went to SEG, staff been pickin wit me. I went to SEG for arguin wit Ms. Woods and Wells thinkin I threatened him (but I didn't. It was a misunderstandin and we got it straightened out.) So I stayed in SEG from Sunday shift change at 4:00 to Monday shift change at 4:00 at my Cab. I only got a 1 page apology report because I rarely get paperwork and hardly ever go to SEG, but since then I've already went to time out again for arguing but wit a student not a staff. Since I've been to SEG, I've been upset because I sleep wit a bunch of play babies, and my job as a laundry worker is gone, so I don't have anything to occupy my time in the evening. Well finally I passed my Pre-Test, so now all I have to do is take and pass the test. But if I keep actin a fool whether I pass it or not, I might mess around and get an UNSAT, but I ain't havin that cause I promised myself and my mom I'd get a SAT. So I got to be a man of my word, so I'm going to forget about the 24 and back and focus on the 25th and beyond. So pray for me and help me when you see me in the wrong. Thanks Ms. Martin *H – 966846*

Mrs. Martin

Fred – You can do it! You know what you need to do – ask for extra work to practice for your test or get a book – don't let others push you wrong – be strong – and be proud of yourself. Make your mistakes of yesterday your lessons for today.

Fred Harris – 9/27/96 – Friday

Ms. Martin, I need help. I'm slowly but surely turning back to the Fred of the past. Everytime I make an attempt to be good, they fault me for my effort. Not the fact that I don't do anything wrong, it's just the punishment I receive doesn't justify the crime. I don't understand what's wrong wit me. I mean I want to be good and do good as well, but my will power and enthusiasm is fadin away. And the real bad thing about it is I could possibly be goin home next month. But I haven't even really cared about it. I complain about it and complain about bein here and now when I have an opportunity, I'm not takin advantage of it. Ms. Martin I know it's not much you can do about it, but positively lead me in right direction. Even the Sgts. like Big Mart, I should've got a major, but Big Mart looked out and gave me a minor. I still messed up. Butler let me slide a few times, I still messed up. But once again before it's really, really too late, I need to buckle down and get on mission. I made promises and commitments to too many people, Sgt. Martin, Butler, the Cap'n, Sgt. Ellis, myself, God and my parents. So now I need to stop rappin 'bout it (talking about it) and be 'bout it, ('bout it means stop talkin and be about it – street slang).

Mrs. Martin

Thanks for the explanations. Happy Face Sticker

Keep <u>pushing</u> forward no matter how hard people are pushing you back. I know you can do it! The one thing I see is that you haven't <u>decided</u> what's important, if you don't care about going home – you won't. REMEMBER THAT!

Fred Harris – October 9, 1996

Was up Ms. Martin. I've been in a few problems. The day before my G.E.D., I found out about my court cases. I was supposedly goin to court today. But I asked my counselor yesterday, and she said she had no transport papers for me. So over the weekend, ever since the 3rd (Thursday) it's been on my mind. That's kinda why I went crazy Thursday evening and went to SEG. I had so much stuff on my mind I just had to talk or write to somebody. So at first I tried to talk to Big "Z" (Zuckerman, Hal). But Butler told me to go to bed because he thought we was just clownin. So instead of explainin or arguing, I went to bed. Then I still had to get it off my chest, so I was writin it on paper (which you can't have in the dorm) Butler put me on S.A.S., and I tried to explain, but all he did was antagonize me even after I told him about my G.E.D. So in my frustration, I took it out in the Day Room by throwin chairs and tables. But I did that because I chose to. I was just tired of holdin in my anger and I wasn't losin anything anyway. But I chose to do it on my own free will. It was a bad decision, but I had to do something. I could've done a lot more things than that, but I just kinda in a way wanted to tell them to stop messin wit me. It was like a message to them if you keep on messin wit me, I'll go crazy. That's not the image I want to have, but I hope it at least make them think to try to talk to me instead of just tryin to bank me. I know this is the wrong approach, but this seems to be the only method I can use to get heard. I don't want attention, I just want to be heard and recognized wit respect when I need to talk or be heard. At that moment I was gettin neither. But this behavior I chose to do before will not always be done. I just had a lot on my mind. These staff think we don't have any other problems other than being in here. I guess I should take things day by day instead of lookin into the future if it's goin to happen it's goin to happen. I still would like for you to give me some constructive criticism.

Mrs. Martin

Explain. Let them help you! You are recognizing your behaviors. That's great! You can't lay that responsibility on them – you need to ask for help!

Fred Harris – October 18, 1996 – Friday

Was up Ms. Martin? You probably already know, but if you don't, I went to court and I found out that on November 7th, I'll be getting waived to the county. It's kinda good in a way, but of course it has it's downfalls. The good thing is I could get out on bond. In fact that's the only good thing. The bad is it's gonna be on my adult county time which is a lot longer than juvenile and lawyers and bonds are a lot more expensive. Plus, since my incident was recorded in the newspaper, I was told by my lawyer that the state prosecuting attorney is gonna try to make my case a publicity stunt. He's gonna try to give me a lot of time. Even if it is a bond set, most of my money is going to my lawyer, so we probably won't have enough for my bond. So that's why I pretty much been so down and keeping to myself. All yesterday, I didn't talk to nobody, but my dude Thomas, and at first I brushed him off. I know it's better for me to confront my problems, but if I do, I'm just gonna get upset and click on somebody. Especially dudes talkin crazy to me in the past (and present), and I didn't do nuttin about it. Another thing is when I get my sentence from Marion County, Hamilton County is pressing charges on me too, and I heard Hamilton County is prejudiced. But whether they're prejudiced or not, they want to press charges on me as well. I've been handling this situation by keeping to myself, writing notes to my family, and that's how I intend to keep handling it until November 7th. After that I'll be considered an adult. But if any controversy in between happens, I ain't even gonna lie, I think I'm gonna make some bad decisions because I ain't got no time to be playin or messin around wit anybody in here. I would appreciate your input, but I pretty much know what I'm gonna do.

P.S.   Next Wednesday I go to team, but it really don't matter because I'll be gone on November 7th regardless.

Mrs. Martin

It never hurts to get a <u>SAT</u>! Keeping to yourself is fine – just don't shut out people that can help you. What can I do?

Fred Harris – 10/22/96 – Tuesday

Was up Mrs. Martin? I've been stickin to my advice of not talking to anybody. The only way I talk is wit a paper and pen, and sometimes I do hand gestures and sign language. At first I didn't think I could do it, and I really didn't want to, but now I like it. People leave me alone because they know I won't respond. Staff are noticing whenever the wing is being bad, Harris ain't involved because he don't talk. The only reason I shut it in is a couple of reasons. One is if I talk about it, I'll only get frustrated and upset. But if I just analyze it in my head and keep it to myself, I ain't got to worry about nobody asking me all kinds of questions like did you do it, why did you do it, what's going to happen, etc. That don't do nuttin but aggrevate me. The other is if I start talkin I'm going to start clownin around and get in trouble. Then my whole attitude will change. When I start getting in trouble, I'll just be like "<u>F</u>" it. I'm gettin waived anyway, I might as well clown. So I like the approach I'm takin now. Thanks for offering me help, but I'm O.K. If I need help believe me I'll tell you. And as for a SAT or an UNSAT, it's not the fact I don't care, its just that it doesn't have any effect on me. But that doesn't mean I ain't trying to get one.

Mrs. Martin

_{3 Little Fish Stickers}. Good to hear.

34

<u>Fred Harris – 10/28/96 – Monday</u>

Was up Ms. Martin? Today has been pretty good so far. I just woke up really so it just startin up. But as for the weekend I've been doin a lot better. Friday evening was like the first real day I talked. The reason I did so is because on 2 occasions me and an officer C/O Brown were about to get into 2 physical encounters. The reason was because like everybody said I shouldn't bottle in my anger. All the times the staff and students were upsetting me and making me mad. It would all come out when somebody ticked me <u>off</u>. Plus I got an UNSAT on Wednesday which made me mad plus on Thursday, we had to stay back from school. Until I started talking, I wouldn't have been abe to contain my emotions, but now since I'm in better spirits, I think I can handle it a little better. But I still pray and go to church for extra strength, but I could still use your help.

Mrs. Martin

3 Little Palm Tree Stickers. You've always got my support – I know that you can make it.

<u>Fred Harris – 10/30/96</u>

Was up Ms. Martin? How have you been doin? I've been doin fairly. I've been tryin to stay cool, but I slip up every now and then. I let actions of the past affect the present. Ms. Gardner, for instance, the sweetest counselor in the world does my anger management. I intentionally made her kick me out of group. Why? Because I felt she was a reason or cause to my UNSAT. When I was goin through my mute stage I didn't talk or participate in group, and she was very concerned about me. She tried to talk to me and everything, but I brushed her off. Not because I didn't like her, just because I didn't feel like it. So then that Wednesday when I got an UNSAT, one of the reasons was because I didn't participate in group. So I was very upset. So the next group out of my frustration, I made her kick me out (my group's are on Monday). So then yesterday, she made a comment, "Fred, do you still hate me?" I was like damn after all the stuff I've done to you and she's worried about how she made me mad. That made me feel guilty. So then I told her I wanted to talk to her later on this evening. So we talked, and she said she'd let me back in the group, and if I had to she'd make it up wit me personally. Then we discussed my problem. Then on top of that, she helped me out of a verbal disagreement wit me and a staff. I felt and still feel so stupid. I don't know why I reacted like that. Other than that I've been doin O.K. I need to process thoughts and actions before they occur.

How I feel about bats I don't like them, they're too mysterious. I don't believe all that Dracula stuff but 'lil rats wit wings flyin around in the middle of the night freaks me out.

Mrs. Martin

3 Little Butterfly Stickers. Me too! I'm glad you've found someone else to support you in Ms. Gardner. Please let her help you and learn in your group that one in particular group make some changes.

11/1/96

No Entry

Fred Harris – 11/9/96 – Tuesday

Was up Ms. Martin? How have you been doin this past weekend? I've been doin alright. A lot better than in the past. First of all, you don't know how much you coming to the building and helping me finish my test means to me. I appreciate Ms. Kennedy, Simmons, Ms. Howard, and my counselor Scott's help. (**Ms. Martin – "I was glad to help you Fred."**) That test took a lot of pressure off my chest and relief to my mind. You remember how I was tellin you how I didn't want to let ya down by failing on my G.E.D. test. But now I'm not really worried about how good I did because I did the best I could, and I had a lot of stuff on my mind, and I had to cram 3 ½ days of testing in a 1 ½. Those hours were hard to work wit too. Three to four hours straight just lunch was the only break. Then at the building, then I had to get up at 5:30 after getting no sleep hardly at all the night before. The first time I had plenty of time and enough rest and everything. And I may have passed part of the test. But I failed at keeping myself outta trouble. So I can at least be proud of myself that I at least finished it. **(Ms. Martin – "Good for you.")** I still want you to pray for me that I passed my G.E.D. I just came from parole board, and they said wait until we see what happens in courts. Now there's possibly a positive and a negative to this. The positive is, is that if a witness doesn't come to court 3 times, the case gets dropped. So far I've been twice, the 16th of October and the 7th of November. So on December 4th, if he don't show up that will be the 3rd no-show, and they're supposed to drop it. 95% for sure, I think. Anyway the bad is that if I do get lucky enough to avoid Marion County, I've just found out today from the Parole Board that Hamilton County wants me to come to court. I think around the 5th. So that means I'll be in here a little longer than I anticipated. Hopefully, I'll handle this as well as before, but pray for me for the extra help to deal with this. I hope I can make it before the 5th if I do possibly pass.

Mrs. Martin

You're going to make it! I'm sure – once you get through all of it, you'll get your chance to start over.

Fred Harris – 11/21/96 – Thursday

Was up Ms. Martin? Yesterday was horrible, but the strangest thing is I got a SAT. The reason why it was horrible is for a few reasons.

One, although I gotta SAT, I was still upset because I was supposed to go home this Friday, but since I gotta go back to court, I'm being held as a temporary hold. If I would've got an UNSAT I might've handled it better because I would've just been like, "Oh well, that's another 30, but it don't matter cause I gotta go to court." But since I got a SAT, I'm a little angry because I would've left. But now I'm just in here for no reason, and I'm gonna miss Thanksgiving again for the second year straight due to being incarcerated. I know, I know it's my fault, but I'm just upset. But at least I'm still constantly striving and reaching my goals. Two of them getting a SAT and taking my G.E.D. were 2 I've already done. So those keep on releaving me of added pressures. But when I thought of missing Thanksgiving again, and I could've been out, but I ain't, I got upset. Back in the A-Building, I was clicking over silly stuff and almost got put on S.A.S. (Student Administrative Segregation). But I excluded myself from the others and went by the time- out rooms where Mr. Healey counseled me and when he kept asking me what was up, I just couldn't hold it. I started crying, not like waa waa waa, but tears were coming out because I'm fed up with all this bull crap. After Mr. Healey, Mr. Lyons talked to me too and after that incident, I felt a little better, but I was still upset. Then the whole last night everybody was clownin and then the incident when Thomas and William went to SEG. It was all just bull crap. So I'm still trying to be good, but I'm just startin to wear and tear a little bit. How can I handle this better? I don't want to start actin stupid again. I need your support.

Mrs. Martin

> You're doing it! Taking time-outs when you need them – locating and talking to staff you can relate to – writing in your journal – ASKING FOR HELP! You've learned so much since you've been here. I'm sorry about your situation, but you will have to find the best way to deal with the consequences of your actions. HANG ON!

Fred Harris – 11/27/96 – Wednesday

Was up Ms. Martin. How have you been this week. I've been doin O.K., but, I've been slippin a little bit. Over this past week I've made a new enemy, Ms. Robinson. I hate her guts. I know I ain't supposed to hate nobody, but she don't be doin her job. I ain't tryin to be disrespectful, but its true. Any time she sees somebody talking or playin, all she does is say "What's wrong wit this picture"? She gives no awarenesses or nuttin. Then she'll punish all of us by making this little stupid lecture over something 2 other people did. And when I make an awareness to her about it, she thinks I'm trying to tell her how to do her job. So she puts me on S.A.S. All the time she'll let people get away with stuff, then if or when I say something, I get put on S.A.S. She even tries to tell the other shifts not to give me a vote. She can't do that. Every time I try to talk to her about it, she always says I'm arguing or not accepting because I always catch her in a lie. I know you're like wait til it calms down, but that doesn't even work. Today I now declare her as my arch rival. I'm just going to try to ignore her as much as possible. But I get so frustrated when she lets people playin around slide. An example, she'll see someone talking or can tell that it's their voice, she'll walk right past them or stand in that area and ask the stupid question "Who's talking?" like they're really going to tell who was talking. She tries to be too cool, but most of the time, she's being a pain in my neck. I need some ways to avoid talking crazy to her or block her out.

Mrs. Martin

Do what <u>you</u> need to do – don't focus on <u>anyone</u> else. <u>You</u> are in control of <u>you</u>. I know you can do it.

Ms. Scott - 12/20/96 – Counselor

Write your Life Story!

<u>Freddy – 12/20/96</u>

Was up Ms. Scott? I'm kinda shaky, shaky about this book. I mean I like to write a lot and stuff, and I have my own personal journal anyway, but I haven't really wrote something down like this and gave it to someone to read. I'm cool, but personal, personal stuff I don't think I'll feel comfortable about writing. But I am at least going to give it a try. So here it is.

When I was a little kid, I used to get in all kinds of trouble. From the age of birth til about 6 or 7, I had different behavior patterns. See my momma had a job and she went to school at the same time, plus my pops worked hard, long hours. So my grandmomma being the loving woman she was (God bless her soul) stood up and decided to help in my up-bringing. The only bad aspect of it was, she lived in a bad neighborhood, Haughville. That's the name of the hood and from 0 to 6, I rotated back and forth from my parents house to my grandparents. Although this was helping out our living arrangement, it wasn't that good for my attitude. The reason being is for a couple of reasons. My moms is the nicest, most sweetest, kindest, gentlest, caringest, friendly, lovable (you get my drift) person or mom in the whole wide world. However, my grandma was so sweet, yet firm, a very strong dependable woman, someone who I respect very much. Anyway, the point is my mom used to let me get away with a lot of stuff. On the other hand, my grandma, cool yet firm and strict, believed in discipline first. Also, my parents live in a good area and neighborhood, while my grandma stayed in a bad area. This influenced me two different ways. It was like I had two different attitudes, two different identities. It was like Dr. Jeyhell and Mr. Hyde. I come across as a well-mannered kid, then the real truth is I'm doing all kinda stuff when yo back is turned. So as a kid, I had a real anger problem, plus off the barrelhead, my parents are kinda old. In fact, they are old enough to be my grandparents. So it was like we were in two different time zones. I'm in the present, and they're still in the past. So when I stayed with them (especially when I was older) I used to always get into arguments and disputes. But I've always had a little anger problem, and I've always been mischievous. But in Middle School is when stuff turned all around. Sixth grade was the first time I got suspended. I met all kinds of people. I started hanging with crooks and criminals. In my 6th grade year, I think I got suspended 6 to 8 times. In 7th, 10 times. And in 8th, I got expelled. Some of these reasons were again like I said, my buddies. In 6th, my buddy (ex-buddy) Jerome moved in my neighborhood. He had 2 brothers, Tim, he was about 16 then and Bobby, he was about 1 year younger than us. Anyway, they was from a bad neighborhood. So I kinda hung with them because his older brother tried to teach me the ropes. Plus another kid (that used to be here before) Billie Harrell was my dude til the end. Well when they moved in, all kinds of stuff happened. I started getting in fights (this is what Tim was teaching me). He taught me how to box. He tried to get me to gang-bang. Well not really gang-bang, but represent what he was. I started stealing. Tim taught me how to crack-up a car. I rode a cracked-up stolen Cherokee in the 7th grade. Tim was like my idol. I learned so much from him and his brothers. But we kinda fell out because me and his brother got in a fight. We was still cool, but it wasn't the same. Anyway, oh I also was sexually active during this time period which also contributed greatly to my downfall. My life's been so crazy (not that crazy, but strange) that I'm sure I'm gonna leave a lot of stuff out. But anyway, when I got expelled in 8th grade, I hardly ever stayed at the crib. My folks really couldn't do anything because I was so rebellious, so they kinda talked to me, but nothing real serious. But they did do all they did and could to help me. I started stealing bad from stores, people, bikes, anything. Me and Billie both got expelled, so we would always clown. In 9th, all my buddies moved, so I hung wit a new crew. And to me it was a lot worse. As usual I got expelled from North Central High School. Then I went to Washington High School. It wasn't nothing but thugs in there. Once again me and Billie both got expelled from North Central; then we both got expelled from Washington High School. When I went to Washington, I stayed on this street called Highland. As I said before, I wasn't actually in a gang, but I didn't like a certain one (because they shot my cousin). Anyway, they tried to jump me at any opportunity they could if they saw me on the streetz. So I hated them and their gang, but eventually I got expelled and didn't worry about them. But in that time period, I started kicking it with the thugs and the crooks. I started stealin cars because I wanted to show off for the chicks I had met. So I'd steal a decent car so I could roll to their house to visit 'em. Don and Fraser and me was the do dirt crew. All we did was steal anything we could. Then when I was in 9th, I hung wit some 8th grade pimps, Ralph, John, George, we was the Click. Them was my "down for me niggaz." Any fight or battle I got into they was right there wit me. Then there was this dude named Paul, who I called my cuzin because we was so tight. But Paul lived in a placement home so we didn't kick it that much. Anyway, the Click used to get into wit it all the time because they was (L's and we lived all North Side. All it is is VL's on North Side. So when I came back in 10th grade, I used to get in all kinds of fights because when the 8th graders came to high school all they wanted to do was gang-bang. But I was cooler than that. I was all about girls. But since we was the Click, I had to be down for the Click because they was down for me. I know you're like I didn't have to, but I did. See look, you've seen my parents, they're kinda old, so all my family is old too. I got 1st and 2nd cousins old enough to be parents. I got nephews close to my age. I don't really have close, close relatives so that's why I was so eager to look up to someone else like a brother or a cousin. Because when I was younger, I didn't have nobody like that. So when I got older and hung around dudes that fought for me, watched my back and crib when I didn't, gave me scrilla (money), all that's stuff that made me close to my dudes. That's why I'd fight or shoot or rob anybody for 'em (that's in the past though). So in 10th, when the 9th graders came, everything was crazy. They wanted to bang (G this G that, then they said V.L. this, V.L. that. Luckily, I got sent to an alternative school where eventually I got expelled. Again I was runnin the streetz wit my do dirt crew cause they was outta school too. We stole cars a little, but I had a job so I chilled out. Just a little bit. I was still hangin with the Click, and they was still fightin, shootin all of that. When I went back to North Central, I ended up getting expelled again because me and my dudes got jumped by about 12 V.L.'s. It was on 3 of us. Boy, boy, boy.

That's when the shoot-outs, stabbings, people getting jumped, shot, and drive-bys happened. I was in it to win it all the way down until somebody from the other side got shot. That stuff made me realize if I keep fucking around, I'm gonna wind up dead or shot. Things was getting too deep. They had shot up a couple of my buddies cribs and shot up one of their rides (cars) So I kinda tried to stray away from that stuff. So I started to kick it wit the Do dirt crew and my nig, Paul. That's when I started catching my cases and getting locked up. I was so caught up wit money, girls and cars, I didn't care about nuttin else. In fact, I was so caught up in 'em that I wouldn't come home for weeks at a time. I was meeting grown women who wanted me to live wit 'em all that. So I felt like I had to start actin grown and driving so I could get to and from my house to they house. So to skip all the exciting fights, shoot-outs, and all the other stuff, it boils down to this. It runs into my court situation right now. Peep. One night at about 3 in da morning, police came to my crib. I looked out the door (the shade in front of the door) and saw it was po po's. So I ran out the backdoor. I guess the police saw me peeking out, so they started banging on the door. I cut out though. The police had a talk wit my folks sayin they wanted to question me about some stolen cars. Shit at 3 in da morning, I ain't stupid. Anyway when I came back, my folks told me, so I packed up my stuff and left. While I was gone, some people told me the feds was lookin for me. I didn't believe them though until this dude told me to watch my back because some detectives was lookin for me. So I figured since I had to go to court anyway to get off suspended commitment, so I figured it'd be best to just do my time and forget about it. So when I went to court, the judge knew I had ran away and a few other petty stuff (like curfew and something else I can't remember). So the judge asked me did I want to handle it right there, so I said yes. I probably could've avoided going to IBS (Indiana Boys School) but I chose not to. Then my buddies was still stealin, lootin, robbin on the outs. So then they got caught, they tried to put my name in some stuff that's why I be going to court now. Man, I'm telling you Ms. Scott, I could write a novel about my life, an encyclopedia if I wanted to from day 1 til now. And I know it would be real interesting. There's so much stuff I left out or forget to write. I mean, for instance, one time I had the F.B.I. tappin my phones and keeping an eye on me. I'm not proud of that. I'm just giving you come examples. Look, when the F.B.I. took me to juvenile, they said they've never been there in 20 years, indicating it's been a long time since they've dealt with juveniles. I've had guns put to my head. One time this dude did a drive-by on me right across the street from my house. I was out of the car and my mom was sittin in the passenger seat of the car. My momma almost got shot. Me and my buddy almost did too. I've been in high-speeds, chased on foot by police and their dogs. My life's been real crazy. I mean it could be worse and it could be better. But the thing is, it's my life and I wouldn't change a day or thing about it. Yeah, well I know if I could've changed this or that, I may not have been locked up. But who knows, if I was out, I could be shot or I could've shot someone else or I may not have earned my G.E.D. It's a lot of different consequences, but all of them in the long run will do nuttin but strengthen me and make me more knowledgeable. I bet I won't do nuttin I did before on the outs. I bet I'll think twice about a fight or gun. It's a lot of stuff I've done that I may have succeeded or failed at but I'm proud of myself for getting through all this. And I'm proud that I know I take on educational, physical and mental challenges better than I've ever done before. And it's all a result of my incarceration. When I first came, you know how I was. Sometimes I just sit and think. Damn who was that. Now, I say, I'm Fred Harris. And you know how I used to talk crazy and click and was so short-tempered. Well, I still have all those, but I can maintain them and it ain't cause of frontin. It's cause I changed. If for any reason, any of them things do come out, it's through my struggles and frustration, not my ignorance and stupidity. But as I said before all and all, I like my life and everything about it. I wouldn't change a bit of it. So I hope you like my extended 3-page condensed shorter than a novel version of my life story. Here are a few more final facts (don't tell nobody my middle name) Frederic Walter (top secret) Harris born to Frederick Emmit Harris and Yvonne Stevens Walton Harris. Favorites: Blue, pizza, Rap – E-40, 2-Pac, C-Bo, sports – Basketball. I luv GOLD.

I got 3 older brothers: aka Troy (Troy Harris, 34); sister–aka Lois (Delores Harris, 33); brother–aka Larry (Lawrence Harris, 30); brother–aka Danny (Daniel Harris, 23); Me– Frederic Harris, 17 (8/22/79–Leo); nephew–Jerry, 11; niece–Marie, 8; sister-in-law–Charlotte. I can't think of nuttin else. Sorry it took so long.

Ms. Scott Fred –

Wow! That was the greatest Life Story I have read! By the way, <u>Congratulations</u> on your GED! For your next assignment, write an essay on Respect. Observe it happening. What does Respect mean to you? Please identify the person you respect the most and why! Good Luck!

<u>Fred Harris – 12/26/96</u>

Respect

Respect is one of the most important things a person can have or give. Respect is usually taught to us when we're younger. Most of the time it interacts with our manners and stays with us until and through adulthood. Like every other person thinks, I feel you must give respect before you get it. A lot of people also think respect is just "no mam," "no sir" or saying "please" and "thank you." Respect goes a lot deeper than that. People claim to respect themselves, yet, they smoke, drink, overeat, and don't stay in shape. People claim to respect other people, yet they call people muthafucka, this, muthafucka, that, and talk behind their back. People claim they respect their families or their mothers and fathers. Yet they talk about other people's parents, fighting over names that the next man says about their family. See, even myself, I consider myself to be respectful, but on occasions I seem to always do one or two of these things. However, when someone else does the same thing, I see it as I don't have to respect them. Why should I respect somebody who don't respect themselves. But that's wrong; I still should respect people regardless if they respect themselves or others. So that's why sometimes I feel it's okay to disrespect because they've usually done something for me to lose my respect for them. So in general, I feel respect is a mutual thing, and I think that's why a lot of disrespect happens because some people don't know how to give respect. (**Ms. Scott** – "**Very True!**")

My respect in here is very little. I don't feel that some of these staff don't even deserve it. Staff at times seem to think they're better than us just because we're incarcerated. (**Ms. Scott** – "**Good point.**") That ain't even cool. Other staff at times abuse their authority. They'll talk to us any type of way cussing us out, trying to snatch us up for any little thing.

Also, some staff be holding grudges. Truthfully, I think it's all about favoritism at times. I know that's not always the case. I also know that staff do be trying to help us sometimes, like Thomas, me, and William might get away with some stuff others don't get away with. For the simple fact that they can sympathize with us being here so long. But it's not always a favoritism game, but I do see a lot of staff letting certain students get away wit stuff that they might not let other students. Overall, my respect for staff ain't never been the same, and it's not going to ever since that incident with C/O Crowe. When he abused his authority by whipping my ass, I ain't never really liked that many staff. If somebody (like staff) feels they can vent their anger at us because of something that happened before or after work, that's abusing their authority. (**Ms. Scott** – "**I agree!**") Some C/O's swear they care, but they don't give a shit about us. Especially this past Christmas, a lot of staff was saying this is just another day in the D.O.C. (Department of Corrections), or "Shit I don't want to be here either, it's Christmas." Yet, those be the same staff sayin "A Fred, if you need somebody to talk to, I'm here." The only reason they do that is so you won't trip. Not because you're risking your SAT or UNSAT, they just do it so it won't be any physical force involved. Also, staff talk to us like shit. They do everything we do: sit on lockers, cuss, play around, all that. But they want us to be on mission.

I mean we should be on mission, but how they goin be some hypocrites like that. **(Ms. Scott – "I agree – <u>We all should follow the same rules!</u>")** Some staff are worse than us. I be cool wit 95% of the staff, but the others, I just front it off. So as you can see, my respect for staff in here goes only so far. **(Ms. Scott – "You have made some good points – but you could be the <u>example</u>!")**

As for the outs: I'm a very respectable person. Not sayin that everyone respects me, but I do try to give people the utmost respect. I used to go to church on a regular basis. All the church people didn't understand how I seemed to get in so much trouble. Not just people in church, but people in the hood, and my parent's friends all spoke highly of me, how handsome and a very well-mannered and respectable person I was. But, that's in front of them. I mean I guess I never really looked at my stealing and fighting and stuff as disrespect. I just looked at it as looking, but for myself, I mean of course, if I actually stood in front of someone's car or house and thought, "Hey, what the hell do I call myself doin," of course, it would hit me. But on the outs, it's so much peer pressure and other stuff that influences people to do what they do. I ain't putting it on nothing else, but other stuff did help me out. As for other kids and students or whatever, I really only have main dudes I kick it wit. A lot of other people don't like me because of my fighting days when I used to fight for no reason, but just because my buddies fought. I really don't have much respect for that many other kids. The reason is, is because I know how backstabbing and kniving people can be, behind your back. So I usually brush others to the side. But at a time in point in my life, I didn't respect anybody but my folks. But that's changing though. **(Ms. Scott – "Great! Why?")**

The person I respect the most is Jesus. He died on the cross for us. He didn't do nuttin wrong, and the people he tried to help only hurt him. He knew all that before it happened, but he still did it. I just respect him for taking on our burdens and handling them for us. I really don't have any people on earth that I respect the most, but there are a few. Here's a few names.

Abraham Lincoln, Martin Luther King, Harriet Tubman, Ghandi, JFK, Malcom X, Helen Keller, Ryan White, Colin Powell **(Ms. Scott – "Me too!")**, all the soldiers in all the wars, Ms. Martin, my folks.

It's many, many people, but there's a few that I could think of off the top of my head. It's a lot more that goes along wit my respect ethic, but once again, it would fill up a gang of pages. Thursday – 12/26/96

Ms. Scott – 12/27/96 Fred –

Excellent Job on the essay – You continue to AMAZE this counselor, with your great essays.

You made some really great points with your essay on respect. I also was impressed that the people you said you respected were not sports figures or rappers.

Now write an essay listing all the crimes you committed, even the ones you didn't get caught for (No, this will not be used against you!) Also, explain the crime (Why!). Then, if you feel you should write a letter to the victims – (This <u>will not</u> be mailed) it will be used for this Treatment purpose only.

Good Luck – Ms. Scott ^{Happy Face Sticker}

F. Harris – 1/7/97

I'm not really comfortable talking about the crimes I've committed, especially telling people why I've done them. Also, listing all the crimes I've committed including the ones I haven't committed is kinda hard for me to do. Plus, there's no way in the world I could list every single thing that I've done. So, instead, I'm just going to list about 3 to 5 of my crimes that I have been convicted of. The reason being for this is because some are just too personal to discuss, and others are too long to explain, and I just don't want to go into too much detail. So I'm going to do about 3 to 4 of some of the crimes I've committed. The reason it took me so long to write this was because I wasn't going to do it at all because I didn't feel comfortable and I still don't. So I just decided to write a few of my charges that I've been convicted of. So here's 3 of some of the most troublesome charges that led to bringing me here.

Charge 1 – Auto Theft and Run Away – 6/6/95 Approximately

Being 15 in the summertime is live and adventure. You're so young and rebellious and dumb, you really don't care about anything. See, I had stole this 94'/95' Toyota Camry. It was damn near brand new. Anyway, it was green, dark, dark green like a deep dark emerald color. Anyway, this was only like the 3rd or 4th car I had had, and it was damn near the best I had had. So I tried to find all kinds of ways to keep it, but I couldn't. One day I was rollin wit my buddy, and he told me to stop at V.P. (Village Pantry). (I was wit this dude named Paul, a dude I considered to be my cousin. We also did a crime together which I'll discuss as well. I also mentioned his name earlier in my life story). When we went in there, it was these 2 chics in there. They was about 20 (this was about 1:00 a.m. in da mornin). Well, my dude, Paul, started conversation, and eventually we both ended up getting their numbers. When she asked me how old I was, I said 19; luckily she was the same. Before I left, she asked me whose car was I driving. I told her mine. So after she heard that, she was in love. I really didn't think we was gonna have a relationship due to her age. But we started talking and gettin to know each other. The only problem was I was getting in trouble at the crib because I continually kept coming home late. Most of the time I would pick her up and take her home from work. My parents kept telling me to be home at curfew, but I never listened. I wanted to keep this girl I had talked to (by the way, her name is Kathleen). So a couple of nights I came in at a reasonable hour, but then I just started right back at breakin the curfew.

Since it was getting close to summer, my parents had planned a trip. I didn't wanna go so they was gonna stick me over somebody else's house. I think it was my Auntie, but whoever it was, they wasn't goin for the late night rondevues. So one day me and Kathleen went to her Granny's house. It was so late I fell asleep (no bullshit), and when I woke it was like 3 a.m. goin on 4 a.m. Boy, I put the Camry to the test. I had to take her home, then go to the crib my damn self. I couldn't do it though; I was too sleepy. So I dropped her off at home and she got her car and took me to my house. But before I got half-way down the block to my house, I saw a sheriff comin out my drive-way. My heart was out of control, I couldn't even think straight. I wasn't sure if we got robbed, or someone got killed or what? I wasn't takin no chances though. I told them to circle the block, but the sheriff got suspicious and followed us. I said fuck it, let me out. I'm just around the corner from my crib. So I got out. Next thing you know, the police did the same. He asked me a gang of questions, then he started to flash his light in my face to get a better look. But I wasn't havin that though. So I cut out. The police tried to chase me for a minute. But when he observed that whole block distance we had apart, he quickly retreated back to his vehicle. After about 2 to 3 hours of runnin, duckin, dodging and hidin, I went back to the crib to see what was up. My mom said that pops had called the Po's on me. He thought I ran away. When I told him I was cool, he said it's too late. He wasn't changing his mind. So I left. I ran away. I was cool though, I had a little money, plus a car and a place to lay my head (over Kathleen's house). I figured I'd be cool. Plus my folks was goin outta town, so I was gonna break (or sneak whatever worked) back in my house and get my personal belongings. I usually called my mom to let her know I still loved her, and that I was all right. I never told her where I was or who I was wit because if I did I was good as jail bait. Anywayz I stayed wit Kathleen, and that's when me and her began to get sexually active. I'm not tryin to be disrespectful, but it seems like when you have sex with a female, they think yaw'll is married or something. Granted, I understand sex, or love either way is usually a much more special experience for women than it is for men. But she should've waited longer, thought stuff out and set things up for our relationship in the future. Anyway, she kinda started to actin funny, so I used to leave and be gone all day, then come back at bedtime. She started getting mad, telling me she'd kick me out. So I left. But you know how a couple gets in feuds. She really didn't want me to leave. But I did anyway. I decided to stay wit my cousin. My cousin was hookin me up wit all kinds of females. Once he'd say I had a 95' Camry, Emerald Green, power hole, power steering, dual srs, air bags, leather interior, cassett and disc player, wit a customized Rockford Speaker, air amp set, I'd always hear a yeah you can come get me or yeah, lets go roll. (I just want to explain real quick. A lot of people want to know why men refer to women as bitches, hoes and sluts? Here's a prime example. Not referring this to every female, but a lot of the one's I've encountered have been gold diggers. Just like females stereotype males as shovenist pigs, dogs, playerz, whatever. The same goes wit women, it's just those words like hoe and slut offend women. But some men take pride in being a player or dog). Anyway, one day I let my lil cousin drive my ride while me and another female were in the back. We were only makin conversation (It was broad daylight and I had just met her. Her name was Claudette). Anyway Kathleen saw me and Claudette kickin a conversation in the back seat. (She was in her car, and we was side by side). She got hot; she stopped and tried to turn around. I told my lil cousin to get ghost. So we left them. Meanwhile, she went back to my cousin's house. My cousin, Ronald, was about 17 then, so he player hated me something decent. He told her my age and everything. Even the female's name wit me in the car and who she was to me. So out of her anger, she started telling all these lies and stories about me to my cousin. When I heard, I decided I was goin clown. So one night I picked up Claudette and her buddy and my lil cuz and we was about to roll for a minute. But I had another plan in mind. I was gonna go by Kathleen's house and let her know what was up. Plus I figured I get a few p's (props) for letting her know in front of the ladies. (I was only 15; gimme a break) So I was driving all crazy, swerving all on the curb. Plus I had my system damn near all the way up. Suddenly I peeped a cop in the turning lane. We was in the middle of a 3-lane street, one-way, and we was a full car ahead of them. I decided to get nervous and actin funny behind the wheel. So the hog followed me. I whipped and cut and sliced corners until I just got far enough to jump out and run. So that's what I did. I told them in the car that I had passed my Granny's house and I had to run out real quick. Right after one time came around the corner, I cut but then I realized that my lil cuz and 2 other innocent people were in there. So half-way of getting around the corner, I turned back and said I had stole it and that they didn't have nuttin to do wit it. So they let them go and arrested me for run-away and auto theft. When I went to court, my parents didn't show up because they was still on vacation. So they postponed my court hearing until the following day. My parents still weren't there, so I was assigned a guardian Lightern (that is a person filling in for the missing guardian. The court assigns them to you.) They didn't want to delay it any longer than they had to. I was also assigned a Public Defender. So without any parental guidance from my real folks, I was basically bribed into pleading guilty to an auto theft. I'm sure I could've got it converted to a misdemeanor, but the p.d. (public defender) said I'd get out the same day if I'd plead guilty. So I did and I was convicted of a Class D felony of auto theft. The bad thing about it was the person I took it from was handicapped. In fact he was in a wheelchair, but he was a musician that played for handicap charity funds. In fact I talked to him over the phone and he said he wanted to spend some time wit me. He wanted to help me out and show me a little about what he does for the charity club thing. I couldn't do that cause you're not supposed to make any contact wit the victims. So I apologized to him and told him I wouldn't do it again. I do feel as if I was obligated to give him something or do something to repay him. I don't think it was through an apology letter though. I think I should've done some type of an activity that he wanted me to do. He was a pretty easy-goin guy. So I think an apology letter would've been to for real or old-fashioned for him. So I feel that the punishment and all the other projects and programs I had to do were good enough.

I think I did this basically because the peers around me were doin it. I figured if they weren't getting locked up, then neither would I. Also as you read, I think my hormones were giving me the extra juice to conjure up enough courage to do it. I know I was the person who did it, but I wasn't thinking about stealin cars until I was easily misled into doin it. Plus, I was just too young and naïve in general.

Charge 2 – Approximately 7/19-21/96

Armed Robbery and Auto Theft and Possession of Stolen Goods

A little over a month later and not much smarter, I was still up to the same old stuff (I forget to mention I was currently employed then at Mickey D's. Sometimes I would drive to work). This time I wasn't actually stealin them, I was just rollin out in them. I had damn near lost my job from the time before when I had run away. So I decided to chill out and just make all my scratch (money) from my job. But sometimes, especially on paydays, I would tell my friend, Paul, to come pick me up. So one Friday (on payday) I let my pops pick me up. We went straight to the bank. While I was in the bank, I paged my dude, Paul, telling him I'd be home soon. I got off about 4:00 p.m. I chilled to about 5 somethin. Then he picked me up. At first we was driving around to different stores to see if I was gonna get anything, but I didn't. So then we was just driving thinking if we could get into something. After about 8:30 to 9:00+, we had no plan for tha night, my buddy was like, shit let's do, do some dirt. I really didn't want to, but again I was a lil misled cause I didn't want to look like a hoe in front of him. So I didn't really say yes or no. I just kept on for tha ride. Plus he said he wanted to get another car and if he did, he was gonna give me his car. So I was like damn a free car. Why not, what tha hell. At first he was talking about stealing cars, then he got to talking 'bout beatin people up and taking they shit. I'm think-ing, he's just playin. I understand you don't play wit stuff like that, but I'd never heard him talk like that before. Anyway, less than 10 blocks from my house, we saw this old lady takin groceries in from her crib. I was like look that old lady taken in them groceries. She looks like she got some scratch (money). I wasn't tryin to tempt him to actually consider robbing her. In seconds he had formatted a plan.

He was like hell yeah. Today is Friday to hell yeah she got some scratch paper (money). That's when I realized he had a stun gun. The lady's house was one house away from the corner. Then he busted a u-turn and told me the whole ordeal. First of all I was gonna grab her, then we was going to either lock her in the trunk or in the closet. Then he was like I know ain't nobody there because they would be helping her wit the groceries. Then he said look it's only one car in the garage. So all that boiled down to she was home alone. I was like damn this muthafucka 's criminal minded than a muthafucka. It sounded pretty tight, but I wasn't physically or mentally ready to do this. I didn't want to rob an innocent old woman. But shit was happening too fast. My mind and heart was racin like race horses. He took one more trip up the street just to get the scenery and visual effect down. So he turned around, then got ready, he hit the lights, then parked on the corner. We had no gloves, no masks or nuttin. He turned off the car and opened the door. I was still sittin in the car then, he looked in and said, "Bring yo ass on." I was void. I couldn't think straight. Usually before something happens, I always think how I'm going to do it. Or I picture it in my mind what's about to happen. But I mean this time I was just goin wit the flow. My mind was completely blank. I didn't really even think it was goin to happen. To tell the truth, I thought we was goin to get up to the house and it was goin to backfire. I figured she'd shut the garage or would be in the house by then. But it didn't work like that. And this seemed like it happened on purpose. Right before we entered the garage, the garage light went off (you know how whenever you shut or open the garage, it has that timer when it shuts off so it won't run your battery or lights down). At first I thought she had turned it off. But she didn't. It was just perfectly a coincidental mistake that was just that encouraged us more to proceed on our mission. We rolled up and down the street to format the game plan and set up. When we did, we hit the lights and parked on the corner. We cut through the yard, sat on the side of the house for about 10 seconds, then right as we turned the corner the lights went out. When strange stuff happens, your mind goes blank. All I remember was screaming, thumping, grunting, electrical shocks, a lot of stuff. The only reason I even went was because I was right behind him. I'm not tryin to be funny, but it seemed like he hypnotized me. All that was on my mind was I'm down for Paul, Paul's down for me. Do what he says. Grab her, hold her. Get the scrill and lock her up. Wit those thoughts fresh on my mind I complied wit all of them. I really think it was what I was thinking. Shit was goin too fast. Plus I was young and tryin to show the big dog I was down. In the beginning, I know I grabbed her. Then when my buddy started to stun her I let go cause I thought it would stun me too if I was holdin her. Then she began to scream and retaliate. That's when I tried to grab her again, but I really don't know if it was her or my buddy. So I let go of whoever. Then I pushed away from them. Then I heard a body thud against the car and the stun gun fallin, then I heard a tussle. I was so void cause she was screamin at the top of her lungs, and we was only adding on by wrestling wit her. So I ran out. When I did, the motion light came on. I think that was when she got the chance to get our descriptions. My dude thought a car was comin in the driveway, so he finally snatched off the purse and ran. I had no clue of what was goin on. I quickly followed behind him. We got in the car and got ghost (outta there). First, we went to my crib. I had to drop off my scrill (money). While I was in the crib trippin a bit, Paul was in the car being shady. He went through the purse and took out some money. (I didn't find this out until the end). So when I came back, it was only 3 to 4 hundred dollars and some credit cards. He took the cards and the lute and threw the purse out the window right around the corner from my house. I told him to get it,but he wanted to wait until later like a hard head. So now we was both hype. Paul was lookin for another victim. I was just ridin. I didn't even want to, but I was just ridin (Damn, I was dumb as a kid). Well after a couple of hours of following people to the crib and plottin schemes on people drivin by. We finally decided to go back and get the purse. So we did and I went to the crib and told my folks I was spending the night at my buddy's crib but I was really goin to Paul's crib. Then we left and went to his apartment. He lived in some downtown cheap apartment (I forget to tell you that it was a cell phone in the car and purse so it was 2 in all). When we got to the apartment, Paul counted all the money and cards and stuff and was like come on in, we'll split it up. But I wanted to be an asshole. He had got out I was still in the car on the cell phone. Then I moved from the passenger to the driver's seat. When he saw I wasn't coming, he came back. He was like, man don't mess around out here, it's hot. I still didn't listen. So he came back and said, all right Fred, I tried to tell ya. The reason I wanted to stay was because he didn't have a phone. And the cell phone battery was almost dead. So it only worked in the car and Paul didn't want me down there by myself. (His apartment was more like the projects. They was bad too.) Plus he stayed wit his baby's momma and him and her got in a fight one time and she put his name on the restraining visitor list and she couldn't get it off once it was on. So he came back in and just sittin there. We both talking to some females. I had my head down and eyes closed. (The window was down too. The car was off). Next thing you know I heard a door slam shut. I opened my eyes and looked around, but nobody was around (I thought). Then I heard some footsteps. It was the security guard, but I thought it was 5.0 (Oh my fault I forgot to mention that Paul gave me his stun gun after the incident because he said that they didn't work like he wanted them to. He said he wanted to knock somebody clean the fuck out. So he let me have it, and I had it on me when the security guard was approachin me). My mind was blank; I kept on sayin what should I do. Should we get out and run or drive off. The parking lot was very small and almost full to capacity. So that wasn't really an option. And running wasn't any good because he was already up on the car. So I didn't do nuttin. Then when Paul finally did realize what was up, he said, oh shit and tossed the purse under my seat. I didn't have time to react too because by then the police was on the car askin me questions where's my license, registration, I.D., all that I didn't have none of it. Then he asked did we have any receipts or anything for the phones. I was like naw. Then he questioned Paul wit the same questions. After he didn't answer the questions either, he pulled out his gun and called for back up. He told me to get out of the car. I had the stun gun halfway in my drawers when I stepped a foot out, he said hands in the air. But I was too worried about getting caught up wit the stun gun, so I reached in my drawers and threw it on the seat.

Right when I did that the policeman's buddy and him was like, Freeze. Then they tossed me on the ground. Then they got my buddy out called for additional assistance from the real 5.O'. When they came, the guard claimed that I was gonna stun him but I was just tryin to get the weapon up off me. Then the police checked the car and us and found everything. Even the registration of the person's car it really was. Paul didn't tell them his name so he was a Jon Doe and sent to the county and at first I lied to them too. But when they said, fuck it, take him to the county to. He's old enough. I told them what was up. I went to juvenile and Paul went to the county. I didn't go to court until Monday. The strange thing about it was I only went to court for auto theft, but my arresting charges were possession of 2 counts of stolen goods, auto-theft and armed robbery. So listen to how crazy this is. I got out Monday on house arrest. When I went home, Paul called me telling me he got today to on Monday. He said they threw the case out; that's why I got out. But the next day on Tuesday, I got locked up again because they didn't charge me wit my robbery, so I went again on Wednesday. And that's when they detained me. They was goin to do all kinds of stuff. First, I heard them talking about waiving me, then they was talking about sending me to the school for a year. They was planning on doin all kinds of stuff. But on the other hand, Paul was still out. But he was on Bond, but I didn't know it. Plus, he was under another name. So I kept thinking that something funny was goin on. And it was. I found out that he got locked up and had approximately 70 outstanding warrants. Some of his were 3 counts of fraud, auto-theft, jumping bond, and missing courts. Those were just some of the charges. Anyway come to find out he was calling my house and telling my dudes and folks to take the charge and plead guilty. The thing about it was he had already blamed it on me, but he wanted me to jus go along wit it so it seemed like he was telling the truth. So when I found out I was like hell naw. So I told the truth. Then it was like a debate. We was both tryin to get each other. But since he had battery charges and violent crimes, and since this was only my first violent charge and second overall charge, they took to my side more. So he got sent to Boys School for a year, and I got out on house arrest. He was telling everybody he was gonna kill me when he got out. Another thing that helped us, but hurt us at the same time was the victim was a pillar of the community and well respected person. So that's why everybody was tryin to stick me. That was bad. The good was that she was so nice that she didn't want to press any charges. The state is the one that did that. I had to do a few programs, but I feel that the punishment was too easy.

House arrest was bullshit compared to what should've happened to me. I mean I'm glad nuttin bad did happen to me, but one month of incarceration and about 2 months of house arrest was bullshit. I really didn't learn nuttin. I felt so bad about what I did to that woman, especially when she was nice enough not to press charges. Plus she didn't do nuttin to me from the get go. So I felt that I should've got some kind of a more severe project or punishment or do some work hours for her or something.

Once again I was still in my young-minded years. It was only a month later from my first charge. I just wanted to impress my dude. I always said I was down for him and he always said he was down for me. So I guess I just wanted to prove it to him like I said in my life story wit no family, brothers sisters, cousins, etc., my age, I tended to look up to the older cats. And most of them tended to be on the thuggish, ruggish side. Once again, it wasn't just his fault. It was a spur of the moment thing, and I just seemed to go wit the flow. I didn't really start doing stuff on my own and actin silly for no reason until I was about 16. I had been expelled about 3 or 4 times. I just didn't care. My record was getting worser and worser every month. However, I feel that if it wasn't for those negative influences I don't think I would've been misled in the wrong direction. You remember how I was when I first came here. I didn't give a fuck about nuttin. That's how I was on the outs, only worse. It seemed like I yearned for trouble. I used to like high speeds and runnin from the police. But that's all changed now. So much stuff has been goin on that I had to deal wit in here. And I had to handle it in a positive way or else get another week. I'm very sure that when I get out that I won't come back (not even to the county). This is my last chance, and I'm gonna take full advantage of it. But a few of my other charges and crimes are listed below. I'd have to have 3 or 4 of these to complete them.

Possession of alcohol as a minor, battery, criminal wrecklessness, auto-theft, burglary, theft of a pistol, fleeing, runaway, criminal trespass, etc, too many to name. I would've done much better job if I wasn't sid-tracked wit other things to do. But I did at least work hard on it when I had the time. So now I'm finally ready for my next assignment. *Fred Harris – 966846 – 1/7/97*

Ms. Scott – 1/8/97 Fred –

After all of that – I must tell you good job – I wonder the reason you don't feel comfortable telling everything – is it because you feel guilty, or ashamed or because you just basically don't trust me?

O. K. Fred, if you feel the need to apologize to any of your victims, please write a letter to your victim(s) for your next assignment.

Ms. Scott Happy Face Sticker

P.S. If you need something let me know. Happy Face Sticker

F. Harris

I do feel I owe the victims in each and every crime an apology. In other cases, I owe them more than that. However, due to all the crimes that I've committed, it would be impossible to write each and every one of them. So I've decided to write an apology letter concerning all the victims.

To the victims of my crimes:

Dear Victims,

I want to take this time to express my sympathetic and apologetic feelings. The crimes that I've committed against all of you were wrong and unjust. I understand this now. Before, I really didn't comprehend the mistakes I was making and even when I did, as I got older, my heart still showed no love or remorse. However, that's changing. Right now, I'm currently incarcerated in Logansport at North Central Juvenile Correctional Facility. Here, I've been going through treatment plans and psychiatric therapy to help assist in my rehabilitation. I understand that my behavior and attitude were unsafe and uncontrollable in the community. My repeated auto-thefts and numerous other violent or unsafe crimes were not safe to my community or society. I caused insurance rates to rise, expensive damage fees, and the public to pay extra taxes to feed, clothe and transport me back and forth place to place. However, I'm a man. Yeah, I made some mistakes, and I accept that. That's why I'm now serving time in a D.O.C. facility. I realize that being 15 and committing armed robberies wasn't right, or being 14 and driving stolen cars isn't right either. That's why I feel that I owe the community, the public, and of course, the victims an apology. To all of "you" know an apology means nothing. The crimes have been committed and over with. But I feel it's my obligation to humbly apologize for my lack of respect to each and every one of you. See hearing I'm sorry for a "lost" little 15 year old child, with no direction is meaningless. On the other hand, hearing an "I apologize for my actions and own full responsibility for all of them" from a sincere 17 year old humble young man. It means a lot of difference. I feel that this incarcerated time period in my life has taught me a lesson and more than one. I've learned that if you make a wrong choice or decision, you must pay the consequences. A measly 8, 9, or 10 months of my life might not seem to be a "just" punishment for my past history. I would have to disagree though. I feel that a lot of time will only anger or frustrate a person. Although an incarceration time of reasonable length will determine the person to get out earlier and get the adequate rehabilitation so there won't be a next time. During my incarceration I have had psychiatric therapy, medicine, attended G. (group), G. (guidance), I. (interaction sessions), anger management sessions, and I've also received my G.E.D. These accomplishments would not have been fulfilled unless I have been rehabilitated in some matter. Hopefully, you've read this and actually considered on accepting my apology. If not, you're just as foolish and close-minded as I was when I was a teen. However, I've learned to forgive and forget, and if you've not, you're just as guilty as I am. So in conclusion, I really would like for you to accept my apology as a young man and forgive my young teenage nonsense. I thank you for taking the time to read this, and I apologize for consuming any of your time or any other inconveniences that I've done against you. Thank you for your time.

Sincerely yours,

Fred Harris – 1/9-10/97

P.S. This is in regards to a comment earlier about trusting you. I'm not guilty or ashamed. It's just that I rarely get a chance to talk to you. I would like to see you more often and have little chit chats here and there, but I understand you be busy. But, more and more each day and each time we talk, I start to feel more comfortable and start to trust you more. Plus, after 6 months and I've grown to like you, and find myself not wanting another counselor or whatever to talk to. Another thing is don't take it personal if you see or hear someone tell something I said. As you can see and tell, I'm better at writing it down or relaying it to another person. So don't take it as I don't trust you. Over these months, truthfully, I've grown to like you as a counselor a lot. I remember back in the day when we used to get into it, and I wanted a counselor change. I couldn't think of that now. You've grown on me like a horrible disgusting black, hairy mole (only prettier). So don't take that stuff personal, and if you don't understand something or you want to know something, just ask me because we might be interpreting each other differently. So now I'm just gonna say good night cause it's about 12:15, 1-10-97. Now it didn't take me that long to write it. I fell asleep and woke up in the middle of the night. Oh, by the way, "Happy Birthday." If you want to tell me, tell me if you don't don't. How old are you anyway. I think you're either 24, 25, 26, or <u>27</u>. You look young as hell, but I think you turned 26 or 27. I think 26. I ain't tryin to make it sound like you old, but you are (just kiddin). Anyway, I'll work on your card over the weekend. So you should get it Monday. So I'll just let you go before I end up writing 10 more pages. Freddy

P.S.S. Hey! Where's the stickers? Naw, you 27! Ha.

Ms. Scott – 1/10/97 (Radical Sticker!)

Bravo, Bravo on your assignment! Also, thanks for the note and the honesty. I'm glad things are going better between you and your counselor (me!). And I'm glad you didn't get a counselor change, because you have taught me lots!! I hope you have learned something from me too!

Your new assignment is to write words of wisdom to kids. Basically, it's kind of your public announcement or warning to stay out of trouble – I know it's weird – but the point is know your reasons for not getting in trouble.

A good way to start your assignment is: In life I've learned....

Good Luck

Ms. Scott Happy Face Sticker

P.S. <u>Thank you</u> for the birthday decorations on my door. ^{Happy Face Sticker}

<u>Fred Harris</u>

In life I've learned a lot of lessons and knowledge; some good and some bad. But whether it was good or bad, I'm glad it happened cause it's just making me smarter. There's so much I learned and obtained from being on tha streetz and incarcerated. Too much to write. So I decided to condense it into 3 major topics. These 3 major topics that I'm about to write about are the 3 most important things to the majority of the young black juveniles: money, women, and friends. See most young kids look up to their idols, and what they say. Most of the idols are rappers and sports players. So when rappers talk about grindin (sellin dope) or buckin (shootin) at somebody else, their fans start to mimic and act or want to act the same way. **(Ms. Scott – "I like this code.")**

Money – slang terms – scratch, paper, bread, doe, lute, shrill or skrilla, endz, dividendz, snaps, bills, etc., mail Money, the root of all evil. Money can make people do strange things. A lot of teens, my age now and race, do all their (or almost) crimes for scratch. Maybe what they do might not be money off the bat, but it's an either possible profit or to look like one. For instance, auto- theft ain't money. Stealing a car ain't no skrill. But they either stole it to chop it up (take it to a chop shop) or to make everybody think that the nice luxurious car they got is theirs'. Ballin (sellin dope). People do this to make their pockets fat. Everything costs (well, almost everything). Some people say emotions like love and happiness can't be bought. <u>Bull butter</u>. Just think on that first day if the man didn't buy dinner or a rose or somethin nice, how would you react if you was on a date? The dude didn't have no money, so yaw picked berries for brunch. I know you wouldn't give him another chance. **(Ms. Scott – "Who?")** Or say somebody bought you a ring for a quarter million? You'd love him just for spending all that scratch. Or say, when you're a baby and your parents didn't buy you nuttin but cheap baby food. No presents, toys, nuttin. But then yo auntie bought you Gerber and dolls and all that. I bet you'd love or want to love them more.

In today's society, money is the world. Sex, weapons, clothes, and cars are all bought with money. The thirst for money is constantly growing. In the hood, when one person has more money than the other, they got a couple of options. Compete to see who makes the most, rob the other, or just kill them and take it. Some people want or need money so bad that they do all kinds of stuff for it; like, rob, steal, murder, grind, lie, whatever. All kinds of scandals happen because of money. Credit card, counterfeit, illegal car trades and sellin, illegal clubs and bars. Man its crazy. I know people who've got killed because they took all of another person's money in a crap game (dice).

Greed is another thing. When a person starts seeing all that green, they get overwhelmed by it. Friends will turn their back on each other if the price is right. Money is like a bad addiction. Once you get some, you gotta keep it and get more. As much as you can. On the outs, if you ain't got no money, you ain't got nuttin. No girls, no ride, no gear (clothes), no buddies. I've heard people say this (exact quote) "I can't be hanging around no broke muthafucka" by boys and girls. One of the first things females (my age and race) wanna know is, do he got a job? Can he take care of me? Can he afford me? I know that this is not all females, but this is what I've seen and learned. If you want money, make it. Do it legally, but be prepared to protect yourself from others who want it. If you do it illegally, be prepared to take the consequences. If you got the heart to make it, you got the heart to take it (the consequences or punishment). Because whether you do it legally or illegally, people are going to want it and do whatever they can to get it.

Make your choices wisely wit money cause it can help you or hurt you either way. But you can make of your money what you want. The things that I've really learned about money are that it's taking over the world's economy and the people's minds. People will do a lot of twisted and crazy things for money. So watch what you do wit yo scratch cause it is the root of all evil.

Women – slang terms by youth today, brauds, ladies, dames, females, chics, and a whole lot of other disrespectful names I won't mention. **(Ms. Scott – "Thank you.")**

Women. You can't live wit them, and you can't live without them. The term is a well known one, the truth too. Most people think of it just sexually. But women are the building block or backbone of men. I've learned that without my mother I wouldn't be shit. Without a strong supportive female in our lives, most males would be nuttin. Most males feel insecure about telling or sharing emotions wit another male. We need that special female friend or relative who's sensitive to our feelings. It seems like women touch our inner feelings. God made the perfect match for man. Men usually have the strength, leadership, heart, and responsibility, but without the females caring, guidance, sensitivity, respect and support, most couldn't handle it. Females are great parents, people, and are very responsible. I wouldn't be the young man I am today without a few (includes you too) women.

However, to every up, there's a down. Today's women (of my age and race) are becoming back stabbing, kniving little …. Most females today are so hung up on money. In fact, I remember at a point in time, where if it wasn't for the car I was driving, I would not have had any relations wit that female. Most girls want their nails done, hair done, clothes he's bought, food, etc., everything. However, wit the young black male mind thinking another way, most relationships rarely start. To tell the truth, it goes back to that rap thing. E-40, he made this song called, "Captain Save a Hoe." It was basically talking about how a man shouldn't spend his money on another chic especially when she's doin all kinds of scandalous stuff behind your back, or when she's using you just for your money. Ever since that song, the thought that's on most male's minds is hell naw, I ain't saving no hoe or I ain't spending no money on that bitch.

On the other hand, females tend to think, well I'll wine him and dine him, drag the relationship for a while before I get him sprung (in love wit the sex), then I'll have him where I want him. Not all women act this way, but I think women are starting to care more about their personal welfare. A lot of females I've come in contact wit are actually modern hookers. They'll do whatever it takes to keep a rich man wit them, and if having sexual relations wit him is the only way, sometimes they'll do it. I said before this doesn't apply to every female, but like I said the numbers are increasing. Also, pregnancy is becoming a big problem. I'm not sure if it's ignorance to the point, or lack of responsibility, or they just plain don't care. I've seen women intentionally have kids just to get more money. You know what? Straight up wit no offense, women is some sneaky meniacal, twisted, sly, slick, crafty little people. Women know what they can and can't do. They know what their boundaries and limits are. If a woman wants money, food, clothes, whatever, they know what to do, and how to do it to get it. Whether it's sexual saducing or verbal, women have that kinda freaky power or way to get what they want. Positive or negative, if a woman want's you to cry or let out some emotions, she knows the right words or feelings to express to get you to open up. If a woman wants you to buy her dinner, a female knows the effective approach to get her needs met. You know what? Now I see how Eve saduced Adam to eat that apple (ha, ha, ha) **(Ms. Scott – "ha ha")**

(The reason this sounds and looks so shitty is because I am shitty.) **(Ms. Scott – "Mood! <u>Not</u> shitty person.")**

One more thing. Say if a woman get caught up in one of her schemes or scandals, women always play the calm, ignorant, I don't know what you're talking about approach, or they'll have a counter attack to back them up. For instance, like they might bring up a moment when you cheated on them because they need to cover up for the kiss you caught her and another dude doin. But of course, they usually play the calm ignorant role. And most of the time, they get away with it. Women are very tricky and complex things. Most people underestimate women thinking they're only mother and housewives, but gradually, women have been gaining honorable positions of prestige and have gained much more respect.

Overall, women are one of God's greatest gifts. But the way that today's (African American) young female generation is being raised, I'm not sure how much longer the African American families will last. If you notice, thee have been a lot of pregnancies, and with those babies, there's not a father or stable environment there. To rap it up, I don't really know or understand how females operate. I mean I guess I've learned a little from them, but I don't understand women period. (**Ms. Scott – "No guy does."**) It basically depends on the female. Women can be stuck up, conceited, gold diggers, all kinds of stuff. But they can also be beautiful princesses, capable of being the leader and taking charge, but sweet and nice and a person to relate to. I guess it just goes on, how you go about finding your woman. So if you go to a bar or a sleezy night club, most likely, you'll get a bar or night club sleezy type of chic. But if you happen to meet a nice down home church lady, you'll probably find a good mate, and a strong Christian woman. So it's basically at your discretion. (**Ms. Scott – "Good point."**)

Friends (hommiez, boyz, niggaz, partners, ace, and a lot of other stuff too.)

Friends. There's no one in this world that's your friend except for you (and God). Many people think, oh yeah, such and such is my friend or yeah that's my dog. But on the other side, they backstab, player hate, and scheme behind yo back. Do you really think a man is that true to you where if yaw two did a crime that he would take the fall. Or if you like the same girl and yaw supposed to be so cool, he shouldn't relate in any type of way wit the girl? Do you really think he'd turn down a date, kiss, or maybe even sex? I don't think they would. I found out real click, that I should never have friends, just associates. You can't trust a man's actions or words if he steals, fights, robs, or kills. What makes you think he won't do the same thing to you. You don't. **(Ms. Scott – "Good point!")** That's why I try not to get too close to dudes or people in general. Most of my friends are females. Like I said about females, they seem to understand men more better (well at least me). They're more trustworthy and understanding and won't clown you when you express your true feelings. But like I said before, just about everything has a price. And friends will betray you for material things, money, gold, cars, dope, whatever. If the price is right, you could lose friends in a matter of seconds. I've seen it all the time. Do you know what the friendship was over for? Dope. In order for this to get his papers stackin, he had to drop his old boyz and hang wit him so they could get on the grind. He took the dope and money over his friend. Another thing is me and my cousin, who grew up together, don't get along wit each other because he's in a gang that doesn't like my boyz who hang around gangs. That shits so stupid. How the hell is my own relative gonna turn his back on his own cousin? I'm not sure myself, but he did. In fact at a point in time, he was gonna help his buddies jump me. That's fucked up man. That's a crooked ass couzin. That's why I have no more buddies or boyz strictly associates. **(Ms. Scott – "People turn their backs because they haven't learned family is everything. What's the definition of an associate?")**

Also you should never do anything illegal or something you don't want people to know wit another person (you shouldn't do illegal stuff anyway). Ain't nobody goin do one minute one second one day or one year for another man. Yet, so many dudes claim to be so true to you. But they don't keep you outta of trouble; they just get you into it. Tell me this if you supposedly have best friends, they're supposed to help you not hurt you, right? But if you analyze most of your problems or troubles, I bet it's something you and them did. Or something they talked you into, or something of that nature. Your friends don't steal, rob, kill or shoot for you. They keep you out of those problems and situations before they start, or at least they're supposed to.

A lot of friends also get caught up in jealousy and envy. When you or your friend, for example, happen to run into a lot of money or a very attractive woman, you'll notice a change in behavior of your so called buddy. They'll start to show their jealousy by actin shady playa hatin or by tryin to make your strive to the top a long, hard tumbling fall. So people may even be only interested in your material possessions. There's a lot of tricky and complicated things about friends too, but my advice is to keep to yourself. It seems like when you start to have friends, you start to have trouble. *Fred Harris – 966846 – 1/15/97*

P.S. I don't really think I deserved an UNSAT today. (**Ms. Scott – "I agree."**) When I told Hughes, Campbell, and Thomas I got an UNSAT, they damn near flipped they're lids. I really don't think I've done anything to get what I got. The incident wit the priviledge dorm was not UNSAT type of behavior. If it was, most likely I would've got some paperwork or something. The only reason I did get an UNSAT was because Coleman was there. If Ellis, Long or maybe (I'm not sure, but maybe) even Riddle was there, I think I would've got a SAT. Since I'm shitty (so very shitty), I think I'm goin to refrain from talking again for a minute. I'll occasionally speak to you and maybe utter a few words to a select choice staff. But other than that, I ain't talkin. If I did I wouldn't have nuttin nice to say. But I was wondering if there's any way possible in the world that I could get a 2 week delay on my next team? I think I should get one if you tally up all the dead time and missed teams that I've missed out on. I think I should get a 2 week. I know that was in the past and it was dead time, but this past 30 days have been dead time too. Plus I'll damn near be in here for a year. I know it's my fault, but I feel I shouldn't be held an extra month just for wakin up late, and all those other bullshit ass excuses Coleman had to say. He knows I didn't deserve an UNSAT, he knows it. I don't know what he was goin on. He ain't even been on our wing a whole month. How can he judge me for a couple of weeks (or maybe even less) over a 4- week period. I'm not understanding that. It seems like them muthafuckas wanna see me click. They fuck wit me and pester me and I accept all the stuff they say. But when and if they can find a reason to persecute me, they do. That's bullshit. I've been doin all I can, and I get banked for some bullshit. I'm sorry for my language, but this is fucked up. I don't know how to explain it. If you do have time to talk to me about it, I would like for you to if you have time. You said you want me to tell you the truth and spit the real, so that's what I'm doin. I'm telling you truly how I feel. **(Ms. Scott – "Good.")**

Ms. Scott – 1/17/97

Fred–

Great job on the essay! Also I understand your feelings – you express your feelings very well! Sorry about Thursday – the snow was beyond my control. If you want to talk tonight or even call your Mom – you can!

Just hold on tight – You are doing a good job – You will be <u>sooo</u> perfect next time at Treatment Team, there will be no question! (Stamp of a Bear)

Next essay: Write on the topic of your support system (the people who help you through the tough/good times). Tell me how and why you think this happens.

AS Happy Face Sticker

<u>Fred Harris – 966846 – 1/22/97</u>

My Support System

Through my life, I have been through a lot of problems. I've been through some good stuff too. But over the years and through the trouble, my parents have been my one and only basic support system. God on the other hand is, of course, my first priority essential support system. But as for the people that are physically here on earth, I would have to say, it's my parents most definitely. However, since my incarceration here, I'm starting to really portray you as being my other support system. You know how our relationship used to be. I thought I could never tell you anything or trust you with my problems. But, of course, as you know now (how I feel about you), I've chosen to make you my other person of support (not totally, completely yet. I mean I trust you and all, but I'm still trying to get used to you.). I'm so used to conversing with my parents about different problems or issues, I'm not really used to talking to anyone else. But like you've heard me say many times before, my trust in you is continually growing. You're starting to be more like a buddy than a counselor. You're more chill and mellowed out. Not all uptight and stern like you were when you first came (that's my opinion). **(Ms. Scott – "I agree!")** You've even been with me during exciting and disappointing times in my life (Good). You were at my G.E.D. graduation and satisfactory reviews (Bad) Unsatisfactory reviews and escorts to SEG, were also bad moments you have been there. Also, when you were there to help tell me about my grandfather's death. Man, that was some deep shit. I haven't even been through some of that stuff with my associates on the outz. Some of those moments were unforgettable and may not ever happen again. That's why I think I'm never going to forget you. I've had probation officers, counselors, teachers; all kinds of things like that, but none may not ever be as memorable or important as you. Peep game (that means, listen up, or pay attention). You may think I'm bullshittin, but this is the real. I've damn near been here 7 months. In the first couple months of my stay here, I kind of didn't care for you that much. We both know it. No need to sugar coat it. We despised each other (or at least I did). I wanted to have nothing to do with you. But after a couple of UNSATS, I realized that I needed to work with you whether or not I liked you. So I straightened up my act and maybe even fronted a little to get by, but, I was just doing what I needed to to get home. Anyway, when my behavior changed, yours did too along with our attitudes towards each other. I was beginning to realize you weren't that bad at all; it was just me. But we didn't communicate that much because I was too stubborn to do one of these books before; also you were quite busy. But I didn't really mind much. Then it seemed like all of sudden, we came to some kind of mutual agreement unspoken. We would both speak nice to each other also about each other even though we hardly spoke. You began to see my effort, so I guess you put forth more of yours. You helped me get out of trouble, and counseled me through my frustrations. Even though we rarely ever communicated on a one on one basis. We both had a mutual respect for each other. I looked at you more as a counselor than as an employee. While I looked at you in a better perspective, you did the same as well. You started giving me the benefit of the doubt and tried to work to help me sort through my problems. After a while, I started seeing you as my only form of support (other than my parents). During all my downfalls, you did at least try to encourage me. And you'd support me whenever I achieved something good. With all that court shit on my mind too, you did try to assist me in handling that situation. And now, now that we communicate more often, and we both have new perspectives on each other as well as this test. We seem to be like old, old arch rivals who buried the hatchet and mended things up. If you really think of it, that is kind of true. At first I tried so hard at being stubborn and obnoxious. You seemed to be formal and real business like. We two totally different people could never get along with each other with those types of thinking, but, we both changed for the better. And since for damn near 7 months of being without my parents, I have considered you to be more my support system. Now I'm not going to be and say you've been my system for the whole 7 months. You've always supported me, but I think I really classified you as being my support system starting through all that court stuff. You began to be sensitive to my feelings. You could tell when I was sad, mad, or depressed. You always tried to make me think of the positive to care about my feelings. If you did or didn't, it at least you made me feel good. When I returned through all that drama (trouble or bad dealings or situations), you welcomed me back and started helping me even with more determination. To tell the truth, if you believe it or not, I don't think I would've even made this much progress (to level 4 or recommit or nothing this good) without your help and support. (**Ms. Scott – "No, I don't."**) You think I'm bullshittin, but I'm spittin the real. I can remember times you helped to calm me down or help me talk to someone about a problem or situation (like the time I went to SEG and Ms. Staley was going to try to charge me with something, but you and the nurse got me a time-out instead. (Also, when me and Ms. Staley came to your office for a talk). If you wouldn't have helped then, those same problems could be escalated or blown up by now. You all around have turned yourself around into one of the best counselors. That might not mean much from 17 year old convicted felon, but to me it means a lot because I've done things I thought I wouldn't do or have done without (get my G.E.D., actually do this journal type of stuff, alter my attitude, go to anger management class) You've helped me a lot over these 7 months. Thanks. I appreciate it. Yo job is being a counselor, but more and more each day, you seem like a buddy. Like I can relate to you, plus if you can put up with me for 7 months, you gotta be the greatest counsel or that ever lived. Plus I want to apologize for all that stupid shit I did and said when I first came. I don't think I have apologized to you before about my previous behavior. So, I'm sorry for being an asshole to you, present and past). (**Ms. Scott – "<u>Apology Accepted</u>."**)

How – I basically summed up all the points in that you go out of your way to provide any extra help or support I need to be cool. You help me to think about the real objective of getting out. You don't lie. You be straight up with me, and you a very fair person. You counsel me whenever I need it and give me positive way to deal with my problems. You just basically help me however you can.

Why – I think this is because you actually want to see me make it through this. I think you think that I've finally learned my lesson and want to see me move on with life. I also feel that you know I'm still young and have undergone some adult experiences. You know I can go out there and make something of myself. You realize that everyone makes mistakes, and I made a pretty big one. Young and stupid as it what I was, but know a little more wiser is what I got. I've obtained a lot of knowledge both good and bad, but I know what to use and what to throw away. My temper and tongue is still a very big problem, but not as bad as it used to and not for no reason now. At times I blow up over these last 7 months of anger, frustration and depression. I think you know all this. That's why you help me. Cause you care (I hope). (**Ms. Scott – "Yes, I do."**) But I think you really do. And knowing all this is the reason why I think you put up with me for 7 months,

Teachers

On the outz I didn't go to school that much. I was either kicked out, locked up, or in trouble. Most of the teachers wanted to help me, but, I rarely showed any interest or put forth effort in my work. Plus, I never was in school for a complete semester. There's a lot of teachers and principles who've worked with me to try to help me get through some of my schooling. But out of all of the principles and teachers my 2 bestest facoritest teachers are here. Ms. Kennedy and Mrs. Martin have done so much for me, they both pushed me to my limits. Even when I messed up and wasn't able to do my first test, they still pushed me to try another time. When I even didn't want to try to take the test again (because I figured I would mess up or go to SEG again). Mrs. Martin and Kennedy pushed me to it. So I did it because (I'm talking about the pre-test) my court date was coming up and I figured, "Hey it don't matter, I'll be in court during the test anyway." But while I was gone, I was hot because I thought to myself that I could've actually passed it this time. My one week departure was hell, my mind was in a jumble. Court, G.E.D. and sentenc-ing was stressing me out. I was going crazy. Finally I came back. My mind was still twisted. The G.E.D. popped in my head when I entered the gate and saw Ms. Kennedy. Then that's when I talked to you and found out yaw hooked up a way for me to complete my test. When you told me how I would finish it, I thought to myself "Hell naw ain't no way." A 3 and 4 day test in a day and ½, plus getting up at 5:30 to complete the rest of my test. I thought it wasn't possible, but it was. With the help of you, Ms. Kennedy and Ms. Martin. If it wasn't for Ms. Martin though, I wouldn't have done it all. I had a book similar to this one, and she always helped me out. She's a very good woman and person. That's one of the reasons I chose to be her student helper. I want to do as much as I can to help her out. Since we can't keep in touch with each other, I just try to repay her back while I'm still here. She actually volunteered to come in at 5 something in the morning to help me finish up my test. I mean anybody could do it, but look at the scenario. I'm a criminal, for 1, 2. I already had an opportunity to do it, but I messed up, 3. It was my fault I committed other crimes to get myself going to and from court, not hers. She didn't have to take that responsibility. I didn't even have faith in myself, but, she had faith in me. I don't know how to show my respect or gratitude towards you 3 females. But I do sincerely appreciate it. (Ms. Scott – "Good – That makes it worth it!")

How – All 3 of yaw have gone and continue to go out of your way to help me. My teachers lend positive support and constructive criticism whenever I need it. Just all around helped me to make my stay a little better. I consider Ms. Martin my incarcerated momma. She does everything in her power to help me. She even be telling Sgt. Martin to look out for me and to help me out. We was already cool, but we even cooler now. She tries to encourage me to spend my time wisely and turn my stuff around. Ms. Kennedy is cool too. She's more hip or whatever you wanna say. She usually joked around wit me to make me feel better. But, she too is a very good person, and I would do what I could to help her too.

Why – The reason is obvious. They believed in me. They knew what I could do. I just had to believe in myself first. That's another way they helped me. They made me change my mind about school and my G.E.D. When they observed my determination when I first came, I think they knew that I was capable of getting my G.E.D. So they did what they could to help me out. Also, it's part of their job. They enjoy helping others out. Especially kids. Teachers just love working and helping out kids. I just think that Ms. Kennedy and

Ms. Martin put forth special interest to help me because they saw I wanted to help myself.

Parents

My parents are my entire world and life. If it wasn't for Yvonne and Fred Harris, I wouldn't be here today. I'd either be dead, in prison, selling drugs, or on crime stoppers. I have so much respect and love for my parents. I don't want to do anything to hurt my parents. Although all this shit I'm going through now is hurting them, that's why I've been trying so hard to get up outta here. They spoil me to death. Not necessarily in money and material possessions, but love. I always know my moms and pops will eternally be wit me, always. I don't know how to explain my feelings toward my parents, especially my moms. She's been through a lot and her childbirth wit me was a tough one. She wasn't even supposed to have any children. Now that she does, I feel ashamed of myself that I ended up incarcerated and all this trouble. They visit me almost every week and make sure my commissary account is sittin pretty. All that stuff is cool, but the letters and cards also help me get through this. They always let me know they love me and care about me even if I have no friends or money or clothes or women. All that's bullshit. My moms and pops is #1 (except for God). My parents have supported me the whole way of my 17 years of life. Whether it be good or bad or achieving or failing, they've always been there every step of the way. Money's no object, material possessions are no object when it comes to our (me and my parents) love for each other. Man, it's not too much more I can say about my folks, But to me, they the best ones a kid could ever dream for.

How – Visits, speeches and punishments were a few approaches my folks took on disciplining me. As I got older, my dad pretty much let me learn from my mistakes. I guess I might not of ended up here if he (or she) would've been more strict. But this time is a lesson that I've learned and will never forget. I saw myself go from top dog to low life. I started to see that the dirty, cruel, crooked stuff I did wasn't even cool no more. My parents even knew about some of the behavior (well, really just suspected it). But my dad just took the casual approach. I'm glad he did too. He just set back and watch me fuck up. And even though I'm locked up now. I feel I deserve this because it's my last and final wake up. My dad treated me like an adult to make me realize that I didn't wanna be grown no more. I just wanted to be stubborn. Still, I still get visits, cards, letters walkmans, commissary money, etc. They still do everything they can to show me their love. But they don't even have to show it or prove it. They did that a long time ago.

Why – The same thing as the teachers except for they love me. They know I'm smart and fully capable of making adult decisions. They believe me in my ability. They know that I wasn't born bad. I just was easily misled into some negative influences. **(Ms. Scott – "Bingo!")**. They know that I'm going to really change; they trust and believe in me. That's why I do the same and love them wit all my heart. That's basically all of my support system except God. He's there for all of us, and we know what and how he did show and prove his love. I guess I'm my own support system as well. But recently I haven't been feeling too good about myself. I'm slowing, slumping into a state of depression, but hopefully my self- esteem will help me out. If you have **any extra support, why don't you fill me in. [what is this???]**

P.S. Why do you support me, or even try to help me? I know I probably said why, but I just would like for you to kinda tell me how you see it and why. I got one more question: what made you decide to be a counselor especially for bad ass juveniles. I know this is my book for me to do, but you know so much about me, and I hardly know nothing of you. I know I really have no need to know; I was just curious. It makes me feel a little more comfortable talking to you. *H.*

P.S.S. Do you know I average 11.7 pages each essay. Damn I'm good. *H.*

Ms. Scott – 1/23/97 Fred –

Why do I support you? Because I see a brilliant young man who is in a tough spot who needs support, emotional and a "friend" to lean on. I also see a young man who has stood up to his mistakes and took the consequences – Good/Bad. That, last but not least, I like your personality – you have grown and changed soooo much. O.K.!

Now I decided to be a counselor for "Bad Ass" juveniles. When I was really young I was in a tough spot? Like you I made really bad choices, and someone put faith and effort into me and helped me – believe in myself – besides I like kids – This is the only place I could where the kids had to listen to me – Yeah Right! (Ha Ha). Any other questions, just ASK! Your assignment <u>WAS</u> Perfect! Keep up the hard work – if you finish this book I'll get you a new one! O.K.!

I know I can't take the credit for the changes you have made, nor would I want to, but you have tried hard and succeeded. (I think that's a word!)

Be Good –

Ms. Scott ^{Happy Face Sticker}

Bear Sticker and Big "S" Super Sticker

<u>Fred Harris</u>

A Ms. Scott that was tight. I like yo little responses and story you wrote back. It was nice. I didn't even think you was gonna answer or respond to any of my questions. Ms. Scott, man, I don't know how to describe you. No, I don't mean in a bad way. I mean in a good way. I never would've imagined you used to get in trouble or a lot of problems. I guess I was stereotyping. I figured you was just a hometown country girl who lived life carefree. (**Ms. Scott** – "**My parents wished!**") I don't really know why I think, well thought that, but I did. To tell the truth, we aren't that much different than each other. Well, of course, physical features, color, gender, etc. But as far as our lifestyles, you made it sound like we were very similar. I think you said you never been locked up, but how did you get through your problems? (**Ms. Scott** – "**True.**") I know you mentioned that lady, but what did you tell yourself or commit to yourself for you to actually change or get through your situations? I also want to ask you did you stay wit both of your parents? If not, then why? And out of your folks, who did you relate to or communicate wit the best? And the worst? How did you resolve that barrier between you and that parent you didn't get along wit? I know that's a lot of questions and you don't have to answer them if you don't want to. *H 97*

Ms. Scott. Anyway about your questions – When I was younger and was having problems growing up, things were a lot different. Basically, back then (yes, I'm old!) people supported and encouraged me to hold on! Change for me happened when I got to college and was able to escape the old "self"! At college I was able to change and grow and try new positive things, at that time my parents just sat back and watched me – because I was away from all my negative peers, they were able to support me, the way your parents have you!

Ms. Scott – 1/23/97

Could you write about your <u>fears</u> (if you have any?) about changing – To me, it was completely scary to change my way of thinking and making choices –

Be Good

Ms. Scott ^{Happy Face Sticker}

<u>Fred Harris – 1/23/97</u>

Fears About Changing – I really don't have any fears about changing Change for me would only be better for me. I do have concerns, but they're really not that important because my mentality, along wit my attitude will (or should) change wit it. My only 2 concerns was really about my associates (so-called friends), and I guess you could say my reputation. But that's why I said my mentality will change wit it. Because you wouldn't care what everybody else thinks or says, because you're making a change for yourself, not nobody else. **(Ms. Scott – "The only way to make it work.")** That's why I said it's not a fear, it's just concern. See, I know one day somebody just goin test me or talk shit or something to piss me off. And all I'm going to think in my head is hell naw, if I was old school, Fred B that shit wouldn't've (conjunction for would not have) rided. **(Ms. Scott – "Thanks for the explanation!")** Then I'll basically just hype myself up thinking about all the crazy, devious, sick stuff I used to do, so that'll give me some type of heart or strength so I could do what I got to do. For an example, that time I got put on S.A.S., and I couldn't take my G.E.D., after I tried to reason wit Butler and he wasn't listenin, I took off my shirt. Then I started thinking about times when I busted somebody's shit or when people was shootin at me or that time when people was shootin at my momma. That stuff gets me hype. So then I let that anger and frustration build into adrenaline, then I use that to either smash somebody, or just plain go crazy. But see that's in here because on the outz, I just fight without getting hype or nothing like that. Now I really don't even want to period. Back in tha day, I used to love to fight. It didn't matter for fun, for real, for fake, for whatever. I'm totally off that. Fighting's not really an option no more in here. **(Ms. Scott – "Just in here or on the outs too?")** Well, it is if you wanna another 30. But I've gotten to the point where I at times fear fighting. Not necessarily the person, just the fact of getting caught or slammed. Now I really don't choose to fight. If I really wanted to smash Wagnor that 1 day, I would've, I could've, but I didn't. I don't know why I've reacted this way. Well I do. I've been locked up so long that I'm starting to fear anything that'll give me an extra 30. I think it's going to stay wit me for a minute and maybe even permanently. (**Ms. Scott – "Good reason if you need one."**) I done been disrespected so much and let it slide. Man, I think I'll be the same way when I leave too. Not letting everybody disrespect me, but just overlook certain things. (**Ms. Scott – "The little things."**) If I would overlook a lot of the silly stuff, it wouldn't even have to get big. That's what I'll do the same. Avoid all the little stuff and people who cause it. So my first concern is that my transformation may just turn out to be a fronted-flop. You know how you be making all those positive comments like I'll be sooooo perfect, and I ain't goin get in no trouble. I be getting shitty because I always remember that "You'll be soooo perfect" saying in my head. Then when I get in trouble, I feel like you lying, and I'm just bullshittin. (**Ms. Scott – "Perfection is a personal idea."**) If I make a change, I want it to be for good or at least far, far from what I used to be. I have changed tremendously. I just gotta work on some weak spots. As you can remember that time I was goin crazy in time-out, see I don't even want nuttin like that to happen, if so called supposed to be changing. That'll make me look worse than I was before. So my first is … If I make a change, it's gotta be for good and no turning back. (**Ms. Scott – "I agree – <u>ALL</u> or nothing at all!"**) The only fear of my choice making is making the wrong choice, then throwing it all away. (**Ms. Scott – "It's O.K. to make poor choices so long as it doesn't return you to your former lifestyle!"**) All my hard work would probably be wasted because I would be disappointed or ashamed to keep it up. But like I said, I have no fears, just merely concerns. (**Ms. Scott – "Good Difference!"**)

My only other concern is how I will be seen to others, or if my level of respect or prestige is the same. I don't really mean that, if I was the number #1 nigga in tha hood, would I still have that same honor or respect if my dudes see I'm tryin to change? I really don't care if they think I'm a hoe or a punk or whatever. But if you never called me a bitch or a hoe before, then you call me a bitch or hoe just because I wanna get my stuff together. Man that's some fluckery (fluckery means – liked fucked up, or actin shady or schisty or stingy. (**Ms.**

Scott – "I like this word.") It all depends on how you use it. In this case, it kinda stands for fucked up, or dirty) stuff. That's not a fear to me because I'm not really too worried about how people view me, its just a concern to me because I don't really want to communicate or socialize wit people who can't accept the new Fred B. I don't want to hang around people who just wanna see me fight or shoot or steal. I don't want Fred B to be seen as a hoe because I couldn't handle being locked up. I just wanna be me. (**Ms. Scott – "I agree to be – is a good state of mind."**) Changed or unchanged, but I shouldn't have to get my respect from being violent or rough. (**Ms. Scott – "I agree."**) And I shouldn't have to continue to act that way to maintain my respect. (**Ms. Scott – "I agree."**) Eventually, it'll all boil down to my first problem: turning back to my old ways. I'll be so pissed because everybody disrespecting me that I'll mess around and click on somebody. So I hope I'll still be considered the same respect-wise, so I won't have any conflicts wit anyone. (**Ms. Scott – "Your true friends will support you through any choices!"**)

My fears about changing is very limited. Change can't do nuttin to hurt, all it can do is help (if the change is for the better). Since I've been changing and continue to change. I've never really ran into any fears or problems. I do have a problem wit finding a positive way to vent my anger. Other than that, a piece of cake. But I haven't made the full complete transformation. I need your help to do it. So help me out a 'lil by giving me some positive feedback. (**Ms. Scott – "O.K."**)

Freddy B – 1/25/97

P.S. Since you about to leave us for a while, I would like for you to give me an assignment that will keep me occupied to 2/8/97. All right Ms. Scott, have a safe and nice vacation. *FH* (**Ms. Scott – "Fred – The next Saturday I work is February 8 – O.K."Happy Face Sticker**)

Ms. Scott – 1/25/97

I really liked your essay, <u>fear</u> is a difficult emotion to overcome. Your fears are very real, but when you face fear, you can overcome it. I agree, we just need to conquer your anger – so where do we put all that anger/frustration? We need to think!

<u>H/97 – Friday – 1/31/97 – 2/5/97</u>

A Mrs. Martin, was up again. It's been a long time since I've wrote you or talked to you one on one. That was my fault. I was pretty dumb to stop communicating with you. You're a great listener, and you have real good advice. Over the past few months, I've been in my F.T.W. (Fuck the World) mode. I haven't been wanting to talk to anybody. I also was a little upset because I got an UNSAT. I'm not sure if you knew or not. I couldn't believe I got an UNSAT. Out of 5 people, only 1 person gave me an UNSAT. The 5 were 1,2, & 3 shift. Then you and my counselor. 3rd shift was the only shift that gave me an UNSAT. I got an UNSAT due to me getting kicked out of the privilege dorm. That's bull butter. 3rd shift only spends about 2 hours of the whole day with us from 12 to 6 (on the weekends 6:30) from 6 to 8. We busy doing clean-up, hygiene and breakfast. So out of the 2 hours they do be wit us 45 minutes is about the average that we actually spend chillin in the day room. Sgt. Coleman has changed the way treatment teams are done. Now instead of 3rd shift voting just for 3rd shift, they evaluate you overall of all 3 shifts. I'm still a little hot about that. I had no paperwork or been to SEG. People whose been in fights and SEG got SAT's. Then this death been getting to me. Along wit being in here for 7 months and being concerned wit the twins as well as my momma's health, plus I gotta go back to court again, March 4th is when I'm supposed to go back to court in Hamilton County. The court dates in NAP are over, but I'm still going through a lot in Hamilton. This should be the last one before my release, but I'm afraid that they'll try to keep me here as a court hold again. Man,

I'm tired of this shit (Excuse my language). How much can a 17 year old young man take? From the looks of it, a whole lot. But, that's the point. I'm tired of taking. I'm ready to start taking or giving, but I'm afraid the only thing I'll be giving is pain, trouble. I'm not trying to do that. I've come a long, long way from that first entry on the 9th of July. I just took a little time to go over some of my passages, and I was shocked. I read and saw so much stuff I forgot and couldn't even believe I had done. I also realized how much I miss talking too. You're so nice. That's whatever I can do to help you out, just name it and I'll do it. I try my hardest to be the best T.A. you've ever had; the best student; the best whatever. I know that time is dwindling down to my release. And I know that our contact will probably cease to exist when I get out. So, to try to repay you, I do everything in my power to show you how much I appreciate it. Today, when that kid named Shawn asked you was you my momma. The reason he asked you that was because I look at you as my mom. He had said something referring to you and I said what you say about my momma? He was like that ain't yo mom. And I said"Uh huh," ask her"? Over the last 7 months plus I've always thought of you as my incarcerated mother. I just don't express my feelings to you as others do. But I really do appreciate the things you've done and the effort and care you put in me. You've been here for me more than half my family has, and you still continue to help me no matter what. I'm not really used to being around this environment and type of people. That's why I really don't know how to act or respond towards you. I guess I worry that all the people (staff) who work here look at us like criminals. I know a lot of them don't have that mentality, but the ones I've encountered over here (at the "A" Building) just seem to think of us that way. Mr. Dalton, Mrs. Renlin, Mrs. Arnold, Mrs. Howard, Kennedy, Black, etc. Well, most all of the teachers that I've had or come into contact wit helped me out. But the only people who I really like to communicate wit are you and your husband. Both of you are real good people. I hope the best for yall. My counselor, Ms. Scott, Long, occasionally and the nurse, Ms. Hartwell; those are all the people who I really trust and feel that if I needed to, I could tell them about my personal problems. But lately, I've been keeping to myself. But, luckily, Ms. Scott and your husband have stepped up to support me. And of course you like you have always done.

Mrs. Martin

Be yourself. You've got wonderful characteristics in you – act them out. You are just as special as any other teenager in or out of here ^{Happy Face Sticker}

F. Harris – Continued Journal Entry

So I've decided to start my journal back up and write to you about my problems and situations. I communicate better on paper than in words. So if you could work wit me by giving me constructive criticism and positive inputs, I'd appreciate it. As you can see, I haven't even really wrote about none of my real problems, but so far, it has took up 2-1/2 pages. Another thing I would like for you to do is, ask any questions about me that you have. I don't care, I'll answer them honest as possible. If you've ever wondered why I'm here or why I did what I did just ask me. It'll benefit the both of us. You, by understanding me better and knowing where I'm coming from. And me, by getting a little bit off my mind by writing it down. And anything you need me to do, just holler. Thanks a lot Ms. Martin. Tell Big Mart "Thanks a lot too" *H/97 Fred Harris – 966846 – 2/3/97*

Mrs. Martin

Fred – You have no idea what this journal entry means to me. You're really a special young man and to hear that I can help you makes my job worthwhile. You have come such a long way over the past several months, and I see you striving to grow even farther. I'm glad you feel comfortable talking (writing) to me – it's a wonderful way to express yourself – very healthy. I want you to be as open as you'd like to and deal with what you need to in here – it's <u>your</u> journal. Keep working on the SAT's – you can do it – prove them wrong. Whatever I can do – here I am. CSM

Ms. Scott – 2/2/97

For your next assignment, you've already described your love for Mom – but, how do you and your Mom and Dad communicate? Do you yell, scream, talk calm, ignore each other or talk to other people hoping they will communicate with your parents your feelings – Think of a specific time when communication worked well in your family.

Good Luck –

AS ^{Happy Face Sticker}

Stamps: of a Mouse, a Bull, a Yahoo!, a M/ Marvelous!

Fred Harris – 966846 – 2/2/97

A Ms. Scott. I decided to pass on the last assignment and write little bit about my aunt. I know I basically explained everything to you about her, but I just would feel a lot better if I'd write it down. When I can't talk directly to you, I just feel that writing is almost the same. I just get shitty when I don't get no answers or comments back to my questions or comments. (**Ms. Scott – "Do I not answer your questions?"**) It's cool though. I'm just glad you did give me this book and kinda give me the freedom to write and work at my own pace. I think things would've been a lot easier for me if I would've had this back in the day. Well, anyway, I just decided to write about my auntie's death to get it up off my chest.

My momma, Yvonne, got 3 sisters and 1 brother. My momma's the oldest. Ann, Karen, and Diedre are her sisters from oldest to youngest. Uncle Aaron is the youngest of all and her only brother. My aunt used to go wit this dude named Kevin. I don't know if that was his real name or not. Well, anyway, this was like her only love. They went together off and on for years. The bad thing about Kevin was, was that he was a drunk. He had been married a few times before, he had a couple kids, he didn't have a steady job. This dude wasn't even good looking. (I don't judge dudes or nuttin, but I couldn't see anything about him that my auntie would be interested in). This dude, Kevin, did my auntie all wrong. He borrowed money and never paid it back (large sums of money). He was going wit my auntie while he was married. But my auntie still loved this dude. My auntie always wanted a family, but she wasn't in the best of health. She smoked cigarettes, she was overweight and had high blood pressure. A couple doctors told her she was not in the condition to have children. However, my auntie paid them no mind; she instead searched for a doctor who gave her the

O.K. to have birth. During her doctor hunt, she as well hunted for a man. Kevin was sterile, plus he really wasn't the father family material anyway. **(Ms. Scott – "I agree.")**. So she did everything she could to find a handsome man and a good husband. Newspaper ads, dating services, friends, etc. She spent all kinds of money just hunting for men. She started becoming very depressed. She started smoking cigarettes like she was breast-fed off them.

That's when she depended on my mom the most. Both of our phone bills (Diedre's and ours) were skyrocketing. My mom would give her advice and tips on men and how to find a good one. They were already close, but they became even closer when she was going thru her period of depression. Then one day, the suggestion of adopting came up (from my mom). My auntie didn't like that idea. She wanted to actually give birth. That's when she came up with the idea of a sperm donor. Something fertilization, it's either vetro, invetro, intro, something. **(Ms. Scott – "Invitro.")** Anyway my mom didn't really agree to the idea, but she was going to support her in any decision she made. My auntie loved the idea. She could actually choose what kind of baby she wanted, Indian, Caucasian, Mexican, whatever. The choice was hers. So my auntie bought some sperm. It was a whole hell of a lot of money. She sacrificed so much stuff on her conquest for the perfect family, but I think that, that was the real reason for her death. She tried so hard it killed her. She paid hella scratch, she quit smoking, almost lost her job, and eventually lost her life. I am glad that she did at least achieve her dream of having kids. But it wasn't easy. Her first attempt was a total failure. She spent thousands of dollars for her first take of sperm. Unfortunately, she had a miscarriage. She was still determined though. She made another attempt though in her determination, and, finally it happened. She was pregnant. During her pregnancy (with the miscarriage) my auntie went through another state of deep depression. But my mom again got her through it and supported her to the point where she regained the courage to attempt again. During her last pregnancy, I don't think my aunt would've made it if it wasn't for my mother. She had been alone for a little while. Her and Kevin was on and off and she never really had a steady boyfriend. Just her and her cats. That was the real reason I think she wanted kids. Someone to love and someone to love her. My momma was the only one in the family that she was really close to. She felt all alone because the person she was close to (my momma) was so far away. The rest of the sisters and brother had they own lifestyles, and didn't bother in taking the time to conversate wit my auntie. So after 9 hard months of pregnancy, she had labor in the 2nd day of January in the 97th year with 2 twin boys, James Ryan and John Robert. She had to have a ceasarian section. My mom being the good woman she is, she scrounged up a few ends and bought a plane ticket to California so she could help my aunt get thru the childbirth. She stayed with my aunt for about 3 weeks (think 2 ½) longer than anybody else. My aunt Karen who stays in California didn't even stay as long as my mother. My moms changed the babies, fed the babies, burped the babies. Everything. Things were really starting to look on the up and up. She (Diedre) patched things up wit the rest of the family, had 2 beautiful twin boys, and she was from the looks of it out of her depressed state and over her cigarette addiction. But somehow she began getting sick again. All those things that the doctors warned her about, with her pregnancy came true. She went to the hospital and eventually died on January 26, 1997 in the morning. It's not a for sure cause for the death, but doctors state that an air bubble was in her arteries which got to her heart. That's when she checked out. The air bubble stopped her breathing pattern causing her to gasp for air which she had none of. So supposedly the air bubble is what caused her death. However, my aunties don't seem to think that that's the case at all. They believe it was the doctor's fault. That's why my aunties are filing a malpractice suit, and so far my uncle has custody of the twins, but he's going through the legal procedures to be their legal guardian, so he can withdraw social security off of my auntie. The reason I've been trippin is because I'm concerned about the twins. They don't know their mother. That's messed up man. **(Ms. Scott – "Yes, I agree.")**

I want to be a part of their lives. **(Ms. Scott – "That would be good!")** I be feelin like it's my obligation to help them. I know how it feels to be lonely. I just want to help them out. I want to be like their big brother or something. **(Ms. Scott – "Good choice.")** I'm old enough to be their dad, but I'd rather just be their big cousin. They live in North Carolina wit my Uncle, so I probably won't see them that much. But someday I hope that I could be a part of their lives.

Well my momma is trippin so I'm trippin. We like twins. We share each other's feelings and emotions. If I'm sad, she sad; if she upset, I'm upset. My sleeping pattern has been all twisted. I ain't been sleepin right lately. Come to find out neither has my momma, no wonder. I ain't been eating right. I don't know what it is, but whenever something happens to my mom, it happens to me. But even though all this shit is getting to me, I'm trying to maintain. I'm doing a pretty good job too. I done come this far, I can make it the rest of the way. So that's what I'm going to do.

I really appreciate you takin the extra time to help me get through this. I know how you busy most of the time, and I know how all these little Bebe kids be sweating. But I just wanted to say thanks for your help. *FH 97*

Ms. Scott – 2/3/97

That was a good choice to do this assignment instead of mine. I hope writing all of that helped you to feel at peace with your aunt's passing and the responsibility you feel for the twins.

Just remember the positive – Your Aunt achieved her dream and now all of you need to help James and John know their momma.

Is there any other topics you'd like to write about? Here's your opportunity to give input into your Treatment plan – so give me some ideas – O.K.

Great job – Fred as Always!

Ms. Scott ^{Happy Face Sticker}

Stamps: Excellent, Dynamite, Perfect

Ms. Scott – 2/3/97

Fred –

Is there any other topics you'd like to write about? Here's your opportunity to give input into your Treatment plan – so give me some ideas – O.K

Ms. Scott _{Happy Face Sticker}

Fred Harris – 2/5/97

I decided to discuss a topic referring to an incident that happened today. I want to discuss fighting, gang wars and hood wars. Due to Reddington rappin to me today, I figured I might as well discuss the brief summary, then go a little further and talk about gangs – fighting, hood wars, all that. So here's a little brief synopsis of the background of this situation.

Some of my buddies are in gangs and some are just from different hoods. A few of them are from both, (different gangs and hoods). Sometimes it's not necessarily gang related. For instance, Westside fueds wit Eastside: not necessarily the whole Westside just broke down groups (or hoods). Way back in Middle School, when I went to Westlane, the same dudes I be bumpin wit now were are rival Middle School. I went to Westlane and all of Reddington's cousins went to Northview. We used to fued back then because my boyz was G.D.'s and they was V.L.'s, plus we was all from like the West or the Eastside, and we hated the Northside. Both Westlane and Northview were both located on Northside. It's just that more G.D.'s went to Westlane than Northview. Plus that was when we all was younger so they swore they used to gang bang. So that kinda carried all the way to high school. In Middle School, they used to hate us because me and my dude, John, used to break boyz one, two, or three at a time. John was a grade younger than me though, and when I went to high school everybody used to be cool wit me cause I wasn't G.D. or V.L. I was just Westside, Freddy B, or from the Ville. My little dudes was still in 8th when I was a Freshman, they was still bumpin and getting in fights. Some I helped, some I didn't. But the next year when they came (8th graders), they came up in North Central disrespectin, talkin shit and gang bangin. So then that's when I started to get involved in buddie's affairs. Even though I had respect for all of them and they had respect for me. I just had that mentality if my boyz goin bump, then I'm goin bump.

So one time I was at the club and me, my boyz was up there clownin. All of a sudden, 3 Northside dudes came in there talking hella trash. Throwing up gang signs, spittin at us (not on us), doin all kinds of hellacious stuff. Anyway me and my dudes smashed them. (This was on a Saturday). That Monday is when we got our payback. Me and my boy, Ralph, walked in school. All these V.L.'s wit red rags on they hands and heads was calling my dude all kinds of bitches, hoes and you know the usual. I avoided the fight by walking off wit my dude, but I knew they were coming back, because they all ran upstairs, taking off they coats and bones (herringbones) and (rings). I told Ralph we better go rossi up (round up same thing) some boyz. I knew it was goin down. So we got Ralph's cousin and was about to get a couple more dudes. But before we could, they came rushing down the stairs surrounding us. It was at least 12 of them. They brought up the incidence about they boyz gettin jumped at Uptown (the nightclub). I simply told them we could handle this after school. They wasn't trying to hear that though. They tried to play it off smooth like they didn't wanna bump, like they wanted to talk it over. Anywayz, they got tired of talking and hit my dude, Ralph. Then the whole mob just jumped on him. He was too busy on the bottom gettin jumped (Ralph), so me and his cousin had to try to do the work. I prevailed because I was only fighting 1 to 3 dudes at a time. I ain't tryin to make it seem like I'm He- Man, it's just that I was the least bit of they concern. While they was busy pounding my dude, I was busy pounding them. Of course, I caught hella blows, but I handled mine.

Anyway, we got expelled and all that, so we plotted a revenge. We did too; it ended up in one of they boyz gettin stabbed 3 or 4 times in his chest, back and sides. He ended up going to the hospital. (I was involved in that fight). They was all so upset and plotted against us. One day they caught my boyz slippin and jumped. But, of course, we don't go out like that. (I was incarcerated at this point in time). The same night they (my dudes) decided this was the last straw, they called up they big brothers, and all they crazy cousins. They had oozis tech, handguns, pumps, gauges, all that. My boyz rolled thru they hood at about 8 or 9. Saw them rollin about 6 or 7 deep in a car. My dudes was 20 deep in 4 or 5 cars back to back. When they noticed it was my dudes, they put it in reverse and smashed backwards. But in reverse at high speed, it's hard to keep control, so before they could get to a corner and turn, my boyz just opened up the doors and started dumpin on they ass. They damn near blew the dudes car. Almost all the windows was gone. And that's when Reddington's cousin got shot. It was on the newz and everything. They was lookin for my boyz car and him. Reddington's cousin's name was Charles Williams. Tee-Tee was his nickname. He was paralyzed for at least 2 or 3 weeks. Ever since then, they wanted to kill us, all of us. Even me, although I wasn't there. I really ain't worried, because when I get out, I ain't goin to get caught up in all that bullshit. I'm gonna be too busy doin my own thing that I ain't goin have time to piss around with them little kids. The only reason I haven't really done anything yet or period is because for 1., I'm more mature, 2. I know I can whip him and for 3. I'm too close to going to the crib. So, I'm pretty sure I can maintain myself, but if he puts his hands on me, I can't promise anything. I really don't know what I'll do. When something like a punch or a blow happens, usually my reflexes or mind take over, like an instinct. But, like I said, picturing the crib will keep me cool, but I'd have to just be in the situation to know what'll happen.

When I first came here me and Reddington made a truce. Even though he didn't like the fact that I was involved wit the stabbing of one of his best friends, he still had to deal wit the fact that we had to be locked up together, and if we didn't make a truce we was gonna be bumpin everyday. So we made a truce and acted like we was cool. He never came to the wing so it was cool. But when he came back, he acted all shady. It was like we was cool, but behind my back he was sayin all kinds shit. Even when I was talking to him, he would say some little bullshit about my hood can't fuck wit his hood. I just told him he got me fucked up and went on about my business. Recently, though, rumors have been spreading about me upstairs. Stuff about me getting beat up or jumped and stuff. So I guess Reddington thought he'd look good if he'd throw in some stuff about me, about what happened on the outz. So he told about how his boyz jumped me, but he twisted it so much. So one day while we was in D-Hall, this dude was telling me all this shit that Reddington had said. So I decided to tell him the truth, the whole truth, nuttin but the truth. Well, I guess the dude told Reddington and when he mentioned the shooting of his cousin, Reddington started trippin. I guess the truth and those memories must've hurt. So then that's why when I went to school the next day, that's why he confronted me like that. So that's basically the story behind the madness. I'm not really worried about Reddington. But I ain't goin lie on tha streetz we both down for ourz. It's just that when I finally hit the streetz, I ain't trying to get back into that life style. See the first time I get jumped or my boyz get jumped or in a fight, it's gonna be on like Donkey Kong. And the thing about it is, its gonna happen just like before. My boyz get jumped, then his, then them, then us, until finally we getz to bucking and start putting bodies in bags. Or the other way around. The truth about the situation is even though I'm goin to try to non-affiliate myself with them, with the grudges we both hold against each other and this little bitch-made muthafucka about to set shit off in here and on the streetz, I'm afraid I'm going to find myself deep in this shit than I did before. I've tried to even attempt to talk to him, but he's too young and childish to understand. 66% sure, that I can maintain myself. But sometimes he know the right thing to say at the wrong time to say it. Since we on 2 different floors, so that makes it a lot better. So, I'm just going to keep cool. It's possible that I only have 5 weeks left. That's pretty much all I'm gonna focus on. Fuck what he (Reddington) talking about. If I really want to avoid or get away from Reddington in here or on the outz, I'll find a way. So know that you pretty much know the scenario, I'm just gonna go on ahead and finish this book by elaborating about gangs and hoods and hoods and gang fighting.

Now that I'm really thinking about it, I can't really explain to you about gangs. I'm not in one so I don't know all about it. But a lot of my buddies are so I do know a little bit about them. But first of all, most people who say they are gang members really aren't. Most people just hang around bigger dudes who claim. So they think its cool and want to bang too, but you ain't in a gang just cause yo buddy is. It don't work like that. You have to get initiated, then branded with a symbol of your gang to show your position or authority. Once you in, you in. Ain't no turning back. All these so called G.'s and V.L.'s today are phoney as hell. I haven't really seen real gang members before. It's all just wanna be's. The reason I really didn't want to get involved in gangs is because the people who run gangs and are leaders are praised and worshipped by all they little followers. They worship human people. In fact one is in jail. They refer to him as a King. King XXXXXX. That's messed up; one man can take over millions of lives by brainwashing them into believing he's their king. I ain't about to worship no human man saying he's my king. Gangs aren't nothing but menaces to the community and society. The only thing a gang does teach is respect and loyalty. The main aspect of hoods and gangs, both are based on respect. Since I really don't know too much about gangs, I'd rather just talk about hoods, and the wars and stuff they get in.

When you growing up yo hood is all you know, all you live for. Most hoods are gang- related. That's why all my boyz is G.'s (most of them). The younger kids look up to the O.G.'s. That's why so many younger kids are getting involved in gang activity. Where I'm from, it's strictly G.'s. But there is some that got inter-mixed gangs where there's V.L.'s and G.'s. So they don't really gang bang, they just all come together as a hood. In Nap, talking about yo hood is like talking about your moms. That's one of the most disrespectful things you could do to a person is to disrespect where they came from. It's basicall saying, Fuck you, where you came from and whoever you run wit. And like I told you earlier about my love for my niggaz, plus people take pride in they hoods. Every hood wants to be number one. That's why it be so much shoot-outs and fighting. Drugs are also one thing that is starting to get bad. A lot of bad neighborhoods is filled wit clucks. (cluckers are dope fiends). So it's real easy to make some scratch just walking down the street. That's how a lot of other stuff pops off because niggaz from other hoods be taking they clientele. But really the real reason why a lot of hood fights and gang wars pop off is usually because of just 1 or 2 people. I know people who jump other dudes or shoot them just so everybody think "Oh shit, don't mess wit them niggas, they crazy." I've seen it so many times, somebody will fight or shoot somebody just to represent or to show everybody his hood is the craziest. To me, I feel it really shouldn't be about different hoods and sets. People don't get along wit other people just because of their location. Some people won't move to certain part of town just because of it's gang origin. Truthfully, people will respect you more depending where you're from. For instance, I'm from the 'VILLE" (Haughville). And they have a pretty bad reputation (good to teens, but bad to adults) We (they) known for handling business when it's time. On the other hand, like where Reddington's from. 71V "The FAMILY." They're not really known to anybody since the Northside is like the wealthiest side of town, everybody thinks they just some rich stuck up pretty boyz trying to be hard. So their respect is very little. On the other hand the "VILLE" has a long, long history of murders, gangs, shootings, drug trafficking, etc. That's nothing to be proud of, but you can kinda see what I mean. Although I really ain't tryin to represent all that bullshit, I'm just trying to represent where 'ol Fred B came from.

When I start to look back about how all this hood stuff got set off, it was mainly because of me. When all those fights got set off when I went to North Central High School. All I did was make a few calls and got a few of my boyz and cousins. Next thing you know they called they boyz, who called they cousins, who called they brothers and so on. Before you know it, half the damn 'VILLE" hated the North Side. I wasn't trippin though; that's how I wanted it. When the 'VILLE" ran tight wit me, I got closer related to the hood. They showed me so much love. They watched my back when I couldn't or didn't. That's why I get upset when somebody disrespects. Also, as I said before, most of the 'VILLE" is G.'s When they heard the North Side was V.L.'s, that just gave them more of a reason to smash them.

A lot of other hoods have joined wit us to fight the North Side. This has got way out of proportion. Boyz is getting shot and killed over mere words. Sometimes it's not even about them, but like I said before, your hood is like yo family.

With me in this situation, I don't think there's a real way to get out of my involvement wit my 'VILLE' click. They brought me up and helped me out. We (G,'s and I) have rivaled so many other hoods. I mean warin, shoots outs, club fights whatever. People want to shoot me just because of my set. I know people who I used to want to shoot because they from different hoods. Now I'm stuck wit a problem on my mind. Knowing how Reddington's family and boyz are, I know that I might end up getting myself caught up in some bullshit. To be quite frank, I am a little nervous or concerned. Not because of the threats Reddington said, but because I know I might start fighting again or packing pistols. That might be cool to some and back in the day, it was cool to me too. But, I'm just afraid that I'm going to get involved in the same bullshit. Just because of a 15 year old child. That shit's scary. Like I said before 1 person can deeply influence some crazy situations. I don't actually fear the gang itself, it's what I'm going to do in response. I've been maintaining in here, but when fists and guns starts to poppin, I just don't know what 'ol Fred.B's goin do…. I don't really know myself.

<u>Fred Harris – 966846 – 2/5/97</u>

Was up Ms. Martin. I know you're a little confused about what happened today. So I'll try to explain it to you briefly. On the outs we know each other. We rarely ever see each other though. I just really get into it wit his family and brothers. See his brothers went to North Central High School wit me. When I was a freshman, we was all cool even though we was from rival hoods and most of my boyz was from rival gangs. But when I hit sophomore and Reddington and all those freshmen came in, they got to disrespecting and gang banging. My little dudes was in relations wit gangs and hated almost everybody in the school. So we started getting in fights wit them (outta school at like clubs and stuff). Anyway me and my dudes jumped his boyz at a club. They was mouthing off and disrespecting. Two days later, they jumped us, me and my dudes at school. That caused me to get expelled. So, of course, we retaliated causing one of his boyz to get stabbed. Then they jumped my boyz again. Finally my dudes did a drive-by on about 3 or 4 of his cousins in a car. One of them got paralyzed and couldn't walk for some weeks. His whole click vowed to get us back. On the last 2 battles (the jumping and the drive-by) I wasn't involved because I was in Juvenile. Even though I wasn't involved, they still got beef wit me (beef = problems or drama, dislike) just cause they my boyz. (The whole time we've been getting in these fights and battles and shoot-outs, Reddington was probably there only once. I'm not gonna lie. If I wasn't locked up during all that, I probably would've been wit them when they shot his cousin. I was present when they stabbed his dude. And a whole bunch of other fights.

Now when I first came here in July, Reddington was here, but he was in the P.V. wing. He never came to my wing, but while we was in there, we found out who we both were. He didn't like the fact that I helped to get his buddy stabbed. But we was both locked up and in the same place. So we decided to make a truce. So he left a little while later after I hit the wing.

So now that he's returned, we still been cool in the past, but recently my name and rumors about me have been floatin around upstairs. I guess he figured he'd look good if he'd tell everybody he used to help his cousins jump me. And then he spiced the story up by saying him and his brothers used to chase me home. They used to beat me up and chase me home everyday. I heard all of this from different students from A-2. Then yesterday during dining hall duty, J. Malcomb told me a few of those rumors. I didn't even get mad. I just said J. Malcomb sit down and I'll tell you the whole story the truth. So I told him just what I told you. So I guess Malcomb told him. And I'm presuming that he twisted the story a little bit. I don't think he did. I just think Reddington can't handle the truth. I guess it brought back painful memories.

So when I went to Ms. Renlin's class today, Reddington said, "A Fred, do you got something on yo mind. If you do." Then I just looked at him and said "man stop talking to me." I told Ms. Renlin I'd ignore him. While I was talking to Ms. Renlin about using the computer, he was talking about how my boyz shot his cousin. I didn't say nuthin at all to provoke him. I guess he got all worked up talking about it, and caused him to get in a frenzy. So that's the story, The bad thing about it is I'm concerned that I'll make the wrong decision and get in a fight wit him. See, it's different wit him. When people talk crazy to me, it don't really effect me. But when it's technically like an arch rival or hood rival, my blood gets to boilin. They're not mere words no more. They're fighting words. I know I'm the bigger man, and the most mature in these situations. I'm not worried about the threats or words he be saying. I just hope he don't put his hands on me. I overheard him saying that on his nation, he was gonna split me. (his gang nation G.'s or V.L.'s). I just hope he doesn't because I'm afraid it'll be a fight instead of a battery. My counselor told me to ignore him, but I need more than that. I know this is a tough cookie to crumble because there is no real solution to this problem other than ignoring or avoiding him, but I need more solutions than this. Help me out Ms. Martin. *FH 97*

FH – 2/9/97

P.S. Give me a real challenge Ms. Scott. You must be trying to tease me. 10.8 pages in a journal. "Damn I'm Good."

FH –97

P.S.S. This isn't my best, but I'm just ready to start my next book so I kinda rushed outta this one. Sorry if it's not meeting the expectations of my old ones. I kinda rushed into it (out of it).

FH 97 – 2/9/97

P.S.S.S. I was just curious about something. I really shouldn't ask you, but I don't care. On Friday, you was real messed up (crying and stuff). I was just a lil concerned about what had happened to you. I know it's real personal, so I understand if you don't want to tell me.

Fred Harris – 2/10/97 – Monday

Was up Mrs. Martin? I thought I'd just take a few minutes to write you a few lines to let you know what's been goin on wit me lately. Today when Ms. Scott came to see me, she told me Reddington wrote some stuff in his journal about me. I guess his counselor, Ms. Gibson, was real worried about both of us. So she told Ms. Scott. Ms. Scott then showed her the letter I showed you. That's when they both came to the conclusion that we need to both sit down and talk through this. So, I'm not sure exactly when, but sometime soon we should be having a conference or meeting to talk through all this stuff that's been going on. I haven't had any real problems wit him lately. The last confrontation was in yo class. Now all he do is try to mug or smile at me. But I ain't even thinking about that little boy. So hopefully, wit this talk we'll stop all the disrespect in here, and hopefully won't start a whole damn neighborhood riot. Nothing else really new has happened. Just my auntie from California came to visit me this weekend. My mom and my aunt seem to have both handled real well. Ms. Scott really helped me out. She got a special visit approved verbally in like a day and a half. Usually there's a lot of paperwork involved. But Ms. Scott emphasized the fact of me needing the visit. I was very happy to see my mom and auntie both handling the situation good. The only thing I'm worried about now is this Wednesday's Treatment Team. 99.9% I'm pretty sure I'll get a SAT, and hopefully if everything work out, I'll be eligible to leave a month after that, but it's not a for sure thing. I just pray that court on the 4th won't interfere. Only God knows though. I'm just taking it one day at a time. *FH 97*

Mrs. Martin

You've done so well and come so far – Keep going – don't worry about the 4th until it's here. We'll make the most of the <u>now.</u> I'm glad the counselors talked. I was worried too – there's no need for nonsense! Wednesday should be fine – you can do it! I'm glad you're writing again!

Ms. Scott – 2/10/97

Fred –

Congratulations on finishing one journal – You are the first student I have ever had accomplish this honor. (Hence, the Certificate!)

For your first assignment:

Please write about Anger Management Group – The Act Like a Man box and The Act Like a Woman box. Society's expectations and your expectations – do you meet or exceed these expectations?

Ms. Scott ^{Happy Face Sticker}

Have a good evening – Thanks, for the talk today!

<u>Fred Harris – 2/11/97</u>

I haven't been to anger management in a while. From what I remember though, there was a list that was showing the opinion of how society viewed women and men. It's gonna be kinda hard. – check out

<u>F. Harris – 10:15 p.m. – Thursday – 2/14/97</u>

Mamma Martin! I'm running out of patience. Of course, as you know, today was one of them days. My mother sent a program of my auntie's funeral in the mail. I haven't been trippin about it. But as I began to read it, then saw her picture on front of the program, it started hitting me. I couldn't talk or nothing. It didn't really hit me until I got in the count line. I couldn't hold it. I got outta the line, walked over to Ms. Scott, who was sittin on the lockers; then I just started crying. I was resisting to let it out. I don't know why though. I don't care what everybody thinks. I guess I was just trying to impress myself. But me holding in all my tears will only frustrate me in the long run. Man, Ms. Martin, don't take this the wrong way, but I think I love you. Not like a woman, wife, or girlfriend. Just for you, my teacher, and my support system. I'm starting to love Ms. Scott too, but, you've been here since day one. As you heard, me and Ms. Scott weren't the best of friends. However, recently some of the things that she has done lately for me, like what she did today. I don't think I would've made it without her, or you, or Big Mart. I love Big Mart too. He's like my pops. He's the only man in here whose ever gave me a hug and asked was I O.K.? He really tries to help, not only me, but a lot of other kids too. I know that he'll always help me if I need it. That's why I love the both of you and will miss you both dearly whenever I leave. I'm not trying to make you feel uncomfortable by saying, I Love You and Mart. I'm just writing my feelings and what's on my mind. I wanted to talk to you so bad, but you know how I get when problems occur. All choked up. That's why I've decided to stay on task and continue to write entries to you and my counselor. You don't know how good it made me feel to hear you and Ms. Scott both tell me how special I was and how you both cared. Also, you taking the time to see me period was a help. Man, Mamma Martin some of the stuff I wrote and told you, along with some of the feelings I've shared wit you won't be shared with anyone else. Or may not ever happen again. You take it upon yourself to get involved when you see that you could be of help. Never ever think you're imposing in a situation of mine. You're always welcome to join in or observe or listen to whatever happens to me. I really didn't want you to leave when you did, but, my head was not up to par. I'm not thinking straight. With the thought of like 29 days left or going back to court in 20 days, my auntie's death, babies, moms and pops, Man, it's starting to get too deep for a 17 year old brother to handle. However, with you and Big Mart and Ms. Scott helping me out, I'm sure I'll last 29 days. Hey, you got me through the G.E.D. Test in like a day and a half; so, I know you'll help me make it the last 29 days. I really appreciate everything you've done for me. I'll never forget you or your husband, my parents of N.C.J.F. Thanks for being there for me in any type of weather.

Sincerely,

Fred Harris – 966846 – H97

Mrs. Martin

This was heart felt. What wonderful words you use and put together. I'm sorry that I left earlier than you'd wanted me to, but, I know sometimes "counselor time" is hard to come by. It means a lot to me as well knowing how you think of me. You've come so far. We'll get through any storm.

2/15/97

I'm bailin on this assignment. It was cool but I decided to go wit plan B again. I basically wrote you everything about her, I guess. I basically did what I thought and said my mom would do. I'd be cool and hold in all my feelings, then when I went to the funeral, I'd just have a nervous breakdown. Even though I really didn't over react. I still think that my mom handled this better than I did. You would think my mom would take it real bad, considering, Diedre was her youngest sister. She kept in touch wit her more than any of her other siblings. They both shared each other's feelings, emotions, and secrets. Most importantly, my moms supported Diedre through everything including her childbirth wit the twins. She (my mom) even stayed 17 daysafter the twins birth to help my aunt recuperate. That was real important because Aunt Diedre was real sick and unhealthy. My aunt who lived in California didn't stay long as my mother. My moms nerves are real bad, plus she usually worries a lot and blows things out of proportion with all the stress and pressure of me going through court and being in here. Any extra problems could cause my mother to snap. Same situation wit me. I'm already upset about being here. But I accepted later on down the line. Then I got extra time for something that I thought I gotta way wit. Plus, I'm still going to court for some more stuff. I'm taking it bad because I'm looking at the overall picture. Not just the fact that my auntie died, but much more. My moms reaction to this, the twins, my court appearances, past deaths, etc. When one problem hits (you know how I go to my dead-mouth mode). I usually don't say nuttin when I'm in that mode. I just go into deep, deep thought. I talk to myself, reason wit myself, evaluate and weigh things in my head. That's why I don't talk. I'm too busy to talk so I just don't. When I first heard the bad newz, I was upset. I was sad about my aunties' death, but I looked at the overall big picture as well. The twins and my moms well being on the situation. So I was sad, but I was a little upset about the bigger picture. Once I saw how my aunt and mom took the death, I felt relieved knowing that my moms and aunt took my Aunt's passing very well. My moms had a few good hard cries, but she finally came to peace wit herself and accepted my auntie's passing. When I saw that my mom had accepted it, and took it good, I did the same wit me. I pretty much left it alone until (here's where it all fits in wit Thursday), Thursday, when I actually read the program, and saw the picture of my aunt. I just couldn't hold it in. I wanted to cry right there in the office, but I guess I just didn't want to cry in front of you and Wells. I wasn't ashamed or embarrassed, but as you can see, I'm better at writing and expressing my feelings through paper than through tears and emotions. See I'm so used to be seen as a thug and gangsta. **(Ms. Scott – "I like this <u>title</u>.")** Thugs and gangstas ain't nuttin to be proud of, and I'm not boasting about being an ex-one. It's just that other people look for me to be a little more stronger or dependable in situations like this. A lot of people like my buddies in my hood, or I grew up wit, when they get killed or shot, I'm usually the one who'd get revenge or retaliate. All my other homies usually cry or get all worked up. I just stay cool and plot my revenge or chill and pay my respects. Since I done been here though, I've changed and been through so much that I ain't got no other choice other than crying or clicking or breaking down and giving up. On the outs, I was pretty much carefree. I had no feelings or remorse towards no one. I didn't listen to my parents or the law. When someone died, I would be hurt, but it was here and gone like that. I had trip for a couple seconds, then go on about my business. You know how I was when I first came here. I didn't listen, bar, or fear none. But when all the trials and tribulations would happen, I'd just overlook it and hold it in. That's why whenever I get mad, I just dead-mouth and think things through wit myself. But wit all this pressure and court and death, I can get choked up every now and then. I know you wanted to know what I was thinking. It's hard to say. Too many things were going on in my mind. Plus, I was steady listening to you and Ms. Martin, so I was thinking, listening, and projecting. What I mean by projecting is seeing what's to come for the future. What I was thinking was not pretty. If you remember in some of my last writings, I told you at times I use certain things like problems and deaths, to give me the adrenaline or hypeness to do something stupid I was thinking when people was talking crazy to me, and when people disrespected me. When I thought of that, it made me want to just break somebody off proper. I was also thinking about the twins. How would they end up. Who will raise them? How will they know and find out about their mom? All kinds of stuff about the twins. Like I said before, I want to get in touch wit them and be a part of their life. I was thinking about my moms and auntie. A lot of stuff was going through my mind. The main thing though was splittin somebody. I'm not playin, Ms. Scott. I couldn't stop shakin and thinking about it [while I was standing] in line. I wanted to split somebody so bad. I started feeling like I couldn't keep carrying the burden. I felt like throwing it all away. I'm tired of being here; I'm tired of seeing all these playbabies day after day. I'm tired of suffering for all these hoes. So I had made it up in my mind that I was going to SEG for battery or fighting. That's why I started crying. I couldn't do nuttin. I felt powerless. I ain't just trying to say this, but if you and Ms. Martin wasn't there, I'm not sure what I would've did. When I saw how much you and Ms. Martin was trying to work and help me, I couldn't help but to listen and calm down. You sat on the dirty ass floor for an extra 15, 20, 25 minutes just so I wouldn't click. Then you still saw Henderson and whoever else. Plus, I don't know why, but Ms. Martin was there (basically for support) late to let me know that she cared about me and didn't want to see me click. When yaw was saying all that stuff why I shouldn't go off and telling me what I've done and achieved, plus how you told and showed (showed me by stayin late and trying to cheer me up and talk to me) me how much faith you both had in me, I had to tell myself that I couldn't let yaw down. A lot of people look at me as the mature one, or the one wit the most common sense. I also had to think of that. I'd hate to build up so much trust and respect, then lose it because I can't keep myself under control. It took me a minute to realize it, but wit yaw's help, I got the picture. Sometimes that's all I need is a talk or someone to let me wake up and smell the coffee. That's why I try to talk and help you (even though I can't do too much behind gates and in orange) out any way I can. Just like you do the same for me. I really appreciate it again for the millionth time. If I could help you in any way, just let me know. For now, I'm just trying to be the best student

I can be and finish and complete all of your and my assignments to the best of my ability. I'm doing a lot better and did a lot better after your talk. I was almost completely over by Friday night. At this point in time, I choose not to think about it. So I haven't really been worried. But now I'm a little concerned wit my court appearance in Hamilton County on the 4th. My folks told me that they're trying to get me for burglary. So we might end up spending another 3 to 6 months together. I really don't think that's what they'll do. But you never know. Only God can judge me now. *FH 97 – 2/16/97*

Ms. Scott – 2/17/97

Fred –

Great job on the essay and the talk! If you feel the need to write about your aunt – then do so – but, please try to do your assignment too!

Go on and laugh, but I think you are doing a great job on everything. Relax, about court, together – you and your uncool counselor will face your current situation. Remember, you have done such a wonderful job – don't forget, how far your progress has taken you.

AS Happy Face Sticker

(Stamp – Tiger – Excellent!)

(Stamp – Star with A+)

Ms. Scott – 2/17/97

Please write about "What made me decide to change?"

<u>Fred Harris – 2/17/97</u>

Change. What made 'ole Fred B change? It breaks down into many reasons, but I'm gonna sum it up in 2 topics. The 2 reasons are for my parents and family, and the second is for myself and my future.

First – My folks is my number one priority and number one in my life. Over the years, I've made one of my goals to make my parents proud of me. Back in my earlier days in here, I used to disappoint my parents all the time. I'd hate telling my parents, "A yaw, I got another UNSAT." My parents have done so much for me, and I always hate to let them down even if I am in the wrong or upset. Every time I get locked up, they visit as many times possible. Regardless of time, place, or whatever, you see I get a visit damn near every week. Especially through all this it's been so much going on during my incarceration. They've put so much work, faith and effort into me. Even when I want to be mad, I can't. I always remember what my folks have done for me. They know and I know that I've got much more potential than a lot of other kids. **(Ms. Scott – "I agree – you have tons!")** I'm always stressing to myself how I need to change. I'm representing the Harris' in the D.O.C. What kind of example or reputation is that on my parents or family especially when the paper exploited my name all up in the papers. My family was disgraced. Ashamed. And I was feeling the same way about myself. Having an ex-convicted felon in the family isn't something you want everybody to know about. Even when I approach people or go to a job interview, I don't feel too comfortable explaining certain felonies to the interviewer. That could get me fired before I get hired. My moms went through so much stuff to have me and raise me. I hate disappointin her and my father all the time. I just made it one of my goals to try to change or alter my behavior so I can at least attempt to repay my gratitude. So one of the main reasons for my change is to make my parents proud, to stop disgracing the family name and to turn my shit around so all my 'lil cousins and nephewz can look at me as their cool and hip cousin or uncle who got his life together. Believe it or not some of my cousins and aunts and uncles don't want their kids to hang around me because they think I might get into some trouble. I'm tired of being looked at as the rebel or outlaw in the family.

(**Ms. Scott – "2-Pac."**) Sometimes I even get compared to other siblings or relatives (behaviorwise). My behavior is usually compared to a goody-2-shoes in the family. (**Ms. Scott – "What?"**) I usually get my face stuck in the mud because I'm always hearing about their (relatives or siblings) straight A's, or honor roll, or scholarship. I don't like to be downcasted by the family or my folks, or by giving everyone the impression that my parents aren't good ones or didn't do a good job raising me. (**Ms. Scott – "People know you. Own your behavior."**) That pisses me off. But talking about it only sounds good. <u>Doing it looks and feels good</u>. (**Ms. Scott – "Glad to hear it!"**)

<u>My second reason isn't really a basic reason</u>. It's a lot of things together: myself, my future and God. <u>These 3 pretty much tie into other</u>. When I change (I haven't made my full change yet, so I can't say I've fully changed. I still have a few of those bad habits that I did when I first came here.) (**Ms. Scott – "What are those habits?"**) I don't want to half ass or front or fake. I want to fully change. I also want to do it for me. In my first part, I mentioned my parents. They're just influential. The choice is my decision. Sometimes I get upset because I find myself teeter-tottering back-in-forth from old Fred to new Fred. I hate that, it makes me feel as if I'm fake. Like for an example, one day I be good and avoid all trouble and fights. The next day I talk shit and aggrevate people. Then I realize (whether I'm in a good or bad mode), "a Fred just ignore him you about to go home." See I can't be doing that. If I'm arguing and talking shit, I shouldn't argue and talk shit unless I'm ready to do the shit I'm talking about. Ain't no "aw I'm too close to going home." I shouldn't say the shit unless I'm going to do it. I also get a little upset when people be like "aw you gonna let that ride, hell naw you got hoe'd." Words don't fade me, and I ain't no show off type of dude. It just pisses me off because I'm so confused on what I got, and what I can do. I can't do shit wit my attitude or behavior. (This is starting to lead into my future.) My auntie always says if you goin do somethin, do it. Don't half ass, don't

YVONNE STEVENS WALTON HARRIS

bullshit, don't fake it. Be real and stay real. (**Ms. Scott – "I agree with Auntie."**) I hate frontin or fakin or doing something I don't want to. Change is what I want to do, but I get misled or indulged by my bad habits, and sometimes make wrong decisions. (**Ms. Scott – "We all <u>do</u>."**) Most of my problems or charges was from bad influences. I never was really a bad, bad kid. I'm tired of not givin a fuck. I'm tired of being locked up for some stupid shit that I've done did (my fault for the bad grammar). Anyway, when I did do a lot of my crazy ordeals, most of it was for show, peer pressure or to impress somebody. After a while, I just got used to it and started doing it on a regular basis. After another minute, it became a habit. It was like smoking. I couldn't break the addiction. I used to sit and look at stuff I stole or robbed or jacked, and the big picture was it was nothing but trouble in the long run. I used to steal stuff I didn't even want. Just do it because I was so used to it. I'd always think to myself, "What the hell am I doing?" I wanted to stop, but I couldn't. I wanted and still want to change because this life style don't amount to shit.

<u>Future</u>: My future is still bright and shining and still popping wit options. The way I live now my only future will be the D.O.C.'s best laundry and dining hall worker. I ain't trying to go there. I got a lot of things that I could do too. I got common sense (from my father. He didn't go to college or nuttin like that. In fact he got his diploma when he was in his 30's. My dad lives on common sense. He's not too bright in the books, but he's still up-to-date wit his common sense and reading the newspaper.) I catch on to things real quick I know when people trying to slow head me or give me clues or hints to do or not to do something. I also got brains (a little). I ain't no damn wizard or genie, but I did do pretty decent on my schoolwork and my G.E.D. I ain't super intelligent or nuttin, I'm just capable of doing good. (**Ms. Scott – "I <u>agree</u> – you are very bright!"**) (Brains is something my momz got hell of lot of. I get all my bright book smartz from her. She helps me wit my speech, grammar and posture. She helped to intellectually enhance my brain power.) My mom is a very good person who's real smart. She done helped me get myself ready for the future.

Last, but not least, street smartz is another thing that I've got a lot of. I know where to go and not to go, or if something like a gang fight or a drive-by, something like that's about to happen, I know when to take my ass elsewhere. Put it like this: none of that stuff matters up above. I can survive on my own. I might have to get to doing something illegal. But I know what my boundaries are (I got my streetz smartz on my own. It's just something everybody learns over the years runnin the streetz.) My street smartz is what I'm really going to have to need for the future when shit starts to getting rough and looks like I can't make it. Wit those street smartz, I'll be able to adapt to any type of environment or neighborhood. (I'm kinda sugar coatin it a little, but it's the truth.) All of these things broaden my options on my life. If I keep doing the silly stuff I did when I was out, I'll never amount to anything in life. I'll end up dead or shot. Like I said before, I never really was a bad, bad kid. Just a little mischievous. I had plans and a future. I never really planned to get into all this trouble. After a while, I didn't really care. Now I'm trying to change all that, my behavior, attitude, mentality. All of them is getting me nowhere but here. So to prevent myself from ending up in a place like this again, I need to change and prepare and focus on the future. You never know next time, I could be 6 ft. deep. **(Ms. Scott – "Good Point.")**

To rap it up, I'm goin to go on ahead and end this on the spiritual tip. My final reason would have to be God and Jesus my Lord and Savior. Every once in a while when I'm doing or have done something I have no business doing, from time to time, I take a minute to converse wit God. I usually ask him the same questions. Why do I act like this, why did you create me if I'd end up like this? Or why can't I change? I want to change for all the reasons above. But Hell is one place I never want to go. Not only do I want to change so I'll have a good earthly future, but I also want to reap God's blessings and go to heaven. Since I'm in my in-between period, I find myself struggling to obey God's rules. **(Ms. Scott – "This is really normal – people struggle everyday between good and evil!")** I try to prevent myself from certain things, but I get tempted so easily because I haven't fully made the change yet! I know the better you are, the easier things go for you. God helps those people out. I'm tired of being the one getting banked. Change is the only way to stop it. You know each one of our days is numbered. Even the world's. It's not too much longer before the world ends. The way my family is dying on me, I might not have that much time left to go either. You never know what tomorrow brings (or the future). That's why the sooner the better, the later the worse. Why wait when it might be too late? Don't mess around your whole life, then when you're on your sick bed pray for God to help and change you. So I'd have to say that by reading God's word, I get the motivation I need to at least try to change. Because God and Jesus both have done a lot for me, plus they offer the gift of life. I hold the choice whether to change and live for the Lord or be against him.

Well, I pretty much summed it up. Except for 2 more reasons. 1 is being here in this place 8 months to any teen is too much. After 8 months, I'm starting to get strung out and depressed. This place has made a major influence. It has made me never want to get locked up again. I think that's a good enough reason to want to change. (**Ms. Scott – "Let's see being Sunkist orange, pumpkin, etc. – These are other reasons!"**)

My second, last but not least, is the last one. Freddy "B" couldn't have come a long way without supportive people like you, Ms. Martin and Sgt. Martin. (**Ms. Scott – "Ah – That's <u>nice.</u>"**) There's many others, but I wouldn't of had the motivation to want to try to change. You all help me realize, to stop the play baby bullshit. I ain't a kid anymore. Them UNSAT's and extra months hurt me a lot. But it also helped me want to stop messing around, change my ways, so I can get the hell out of Dodge. But even though I did get them UNSAT's, you still hung in there wit me, so I could tough it out the next 4 weeks. Same thing wit Mr. and Mrs. Martin. They've been there the whole way as well. So my change is a product (partially) of all you all's help and motivation. Buts it's also to show my appreciation by not getting involved in the same bull stuff and getting locked up again. So there it is. CHANGE

By Freddy B – 966846 – 2/19/97

P.S. I still haven't forgot about the hip-hop dictionary; if you have anything in particular, tell me. *H 97*

Ms. Scott – 2/19/97

Fred –

Wonderful, terrific, splendid and all that positive stuff – I can understand some of your confusion. Change is hard, plain and simple – So for everybody that has attempted change – sometimes you may feel frustrated or like you are swimming up a stream – You have to hang for dear life – because in reality you will end up with major pay-off – no worrying when the cops come around – no more ugly ass uniforms – no more looking over your shoulder – Yes – being a good citizen is occasionally slow for some people – but life is an adventure – it's what you make of this precious gift!

Fred, you have so much talent, support, brains, charm and good looks – it's a shame to waste it –

Understand too, <u>We</u> all feel confused about certain issues – So you are experiencing L I F E as we know it

So, we've talked about now. Write about – <u>Your Future Plans –</u> Where do we go from here! Give me some idea of where you think you will be in 2 or 5 years –

Good Luck

AS <small>Happy Face Sticker</small>

Fred Harris – 2/19/97

Ms. Scott, I don't know why you had to pick this of all assignments. You probably have a better view of my future than I do. I'm trippin, you know I be askin you for clues and tips to my career future. I'm going to try to do this, but it might not be no good.

A you told me to play around wit this assignment, but I don't even really have nothing to work wit, but I guess I'll just babble a bit about whatever. O.K. in about 5 years, I see myself still writing in this journal because I don't know what I'm gonna do until I do it. **(Ms. Scott – "Wow – Do you see me still reading them?")** I don't even really have a clue. You have a better outlook on my future than I do. People tell me certain things I'm good at or qualities that I possess. I haven't really tried to direct them anywhere though. I'm still confused. Once I hear one thing I'm interested in, I hear another. It's always something that attracts me to a career, but, then I begin to research the career, there's always something about it that turns me off. Like you said, there'll be many jobs, many offers and applications done before I get a stable job that will meet my expectations. Since I really don't know or have a clue, I'll do it just to do it, by writing about 3 industries that I've begun or began to explore. My choices are: 1. A computer operated industry, 2. A skill trade (goes along wit it) in a specified career (like tool and die, auto mechanics, etc.) **(Ms. Scott – "Cool.")** 3. or a military type of career (to get me on my feet). Not for good, but just as a place of experience or something for good reference in the future. I'll briefly explain my reasoning to choosing these 3 careers. **(Ms. Scott – "Good Ideas.")**

1. My first choice (a computer operated industry) of computers is number 1 due to the fast growing need for computer trained people. This might be where I'm headed for the future, because I like working wit computers, and I already have a little experience at computers. I'm also real interested in computers because they are fun to work wit and are becoming the necessity of businesses, companies and households. With this becoming such an essential product to society, any computer training at all will be very helpful for your career options. Almost everything today has been updated and modified with computer digital technology. I'm not exactly sure what I want to do in the computer industry, but computers' horizons are so broad the choices are unlimited. **(Ms. Scott – "True.")**

Another area or profession that I've been looking into is specified careers, like auto- mechanics, plumbing, construction, etc. My mother has suggested tool and die to me many a time. That's where you make the actual little bitty parts that make a big thing like a car or bus work. **(Ms. Scott – "Good explanation.")** They make the parts that actually enables it to work. Specified career industries are very good because your pay is a lot more. Since you're a specialist in your career, you're also more than likely to get more business than a company or business who works on more than 1 specific field. Depending on what you're specialized in, your clientele and loot depend on your specialization. You should get an all year round career. You know nobody wants their heaters fixed in the summer, but in the winter, you'll have so much business you can't even fix your own. So I've been looking into some all year round specialized careers. Hopefully, I'll find something of interest. When I was out, I did a little construction work when I was out. That's basically a bi-seasonal or whatever you want to call it. **(Ms. Scott – Wow – big word!")** I didn't really like it that well because I only did it in the summertime because it was too cold in the winter. Construction just ain't about houses, it can be a lot more. But in the winter, it's not as important. Maybe, I'll be able to find a specialized job where it's importance will be an all year round need.

Finally, the military has been something that I've been deeply considering. Not just for a career, but for discipline. I think the military or any type of it's services is just what I need to straighten my act out completely. I've had family members go into the service bad as hell. I mean I'm talking bad. Getting locked up every week, going to the county at a very early age. More than once. When he got into the service, he got into God, found a wife, got discipline, got paid, gotta family, tight crib, car, etc. Plus, he got to get his education. The government even funded him to get it. You know if he was getting locked up like I said, he was, you know, he really didn't have an opportunity to get his education. He was clothed, fed, and living for free. At the same time though, he was saving up all his money from him signing up, and (after his job) saving up his money for working on base. I guess that's why he just got a house built. (This is the one whose taking care of my cousins). He's doing real good. He has 2 kids and (2 nephews). Nice car, everything. He not only got Discipline, he got God. I know he's gonna do good with the kids and everything else he has. I just think this career would be perfect for me. It's more than a career, it doesn't just offer job skills and things like that, you can learn survival skills, help your country, get in shape, etc. I really think it's a good idea because I need help and that will give me mad discipline. **(Ms. Scott – "Sounds like pro's/con's. Good way to make a choice." Happy Face Sticker**

That's all I'm pretty much going to cover. This is probably my worst assignment yet. **(Ms. Scott – "Knock it off.")** Yet, I really didn't want to do it at all, but I gave you the benefit of the doubt. I just said forget it. I'll fill up a few pages to make it look fat. It took me about 5 days just to write this bullshit. Please give me an assignment I can actually work wit. *FH 97* *Happy Face Sticker*

P.S. I'm glad you got the magazine. But what's up wit the test you gotta take? I hope you didn't forget it. If you did, your test will pretty much be shit like this assignment I'm writing. *H 97* Put it in here if you got it. *Freddy "B" – 966846*

Fred Harris – 2/23/97 – Sunday

Was up Ms. Martin? I usually write you when something bad is going on. Not today. I wanted to tell you how good everything was going and to explain or clear things up. First of all, I'm doing great. All the staff have been doing nuttin but complementing me. This past Thursday, I was voted into the priviledged dorm and in Lt. Holme's support group. I still don't want to move, but they're moving in where I am. They're closing down N.E. and combining N.E. and S.E. (+ filtering out all the play babies) and putting them into 1 dorm,

N.W. Until they move dorms, I'm staying put. We also have the authority to vote and who enters and gets kicked out. We've made proposals, like T.V.'s in the priviledged day room, more priviledges period. We also are the people who the community are supposed to come to when they're in trouble. I wasn't too excited at first. I didn't want to do it for the simple fact I didn't want to let anybody down. I know how every now and then I throw my little hissy fits. I don't want to be on such a high pedestal, then take a nose dive on my face. But after today, I completely think differently about it. After today, me and the rest of the support team went to SEG (Me, Bingham, Lambert, McMann, Toler, Boyle, Henderson, Durham, Thomas). Lamb was trippin in SET, telling everybody he was gonna tear it up. He flipped his bed and every thing. He had to get tranquiled when he went off. Not today but previously, he demanded to talk to Lt. Holmes. So she got us 9 and we went to visit him and talk him out of making a grave mistake. We sat and talked wit him for about 45 minutes. With our help, he changed his mind and is going to strive at getting back in the priviledged dorm. So he should be getting out. I felt kinda good because it was a little animosity between us, and after today I feel that we buried the hatchet. Also right when I came back, I had to mediate a dispute between Sgt. Corey and Watson. I talked to both of them respectfully and positively. I hooked up a deal wit Sgt. Corey. I told her I would process wit Watson. I already did by myself. But I told her I'd do it wit the group. He also is going to apologize to her and the community in a positive manner and ask them do they accept (as if he was on S.A.S.). Then I kinda gotta shadow him and make sure he doesn't do anything silly. Being that he goes to treatment team this week, he has to be on a 100% best behavior. If it wasn't for me, he would get an UNSAT for sure. But wit my help, she's going to try to process wit me and him so we can get things straightened out. He's been agitating people a little by throwing the fact that he's going home tomorrow in their face. That's why I'm going to have him apologize to everyone in the community. I'm sure he'll be all right, but I hope his SAT review will be the same. At first I just wanted to worry about myself, but like you, if you weren't a teacher, I'd never have my G.E.D. or it's the same to say, if I didn't help Watson, where would he be? You never know. I just hope my success continues like this. In case I do have to come back, I might have to be in here til I'm 18. I'm 17 + 6 and the charge I got is probably worth 6 months, so it's a possibility. So overall, even though this could be my last week, I'm going to do all I can to leave on a good note and help everybody out anyway possible.

Now that I cleared up my weekend, I wanted to tell you what was/ and or is going down wit me, Lowry, Upshaw, Hanley and etc. At this point in time, I'm not directly involved in it, and Hanley and Upshaw don't really have any problems wit me. I simply stated that I wouldn't let my boy, Lowry get jumped. I know I probably will never see him again, and I owe nobody nothing in here. It's basically like this though. If someone was to get mad at you in class and try to hurt you, Boy I'd smash they faces to the ground and beat them to a pulp. Same thing. I got love for you as a mamma, but I got love for Lowry and Thomas like brothers, cousins, family, whatever. I don't exactly love them, but I do care strong enough for that, that I wouldn't let them get jumped. I know you're probably thinking like you know I've been through this and getting over it. But this isn't exactly something I try to do or avoid. It's like a reaction. That's why I got into it wit Reddington's family so much on the outz. I never had no beef wit them. I just fought wit my dudes because I got love like that (Not real love, Homie love) (like you and your best boy) for my dudes. It's basically a reaction. I really don't think I can stop it. I've seen it happen many a times before where I joined in wit no thought, remorse, or recollection. I'd be very mad at myself if I'd disappoint you or hurt you. I hope I can control myself and make the right choice. But odds are my instinct will get the best of me. I know I've been through all this stuff before, but I'm not worried about anything like that when something pops off. Like I said, I'm only going to get involved unless there is more than 1 party involved. I know he's a big boy. He could handle all 3 if he wanted to, but I usually let my matter get before my mind. I hope I'm able to be strong enough to do the right thing. *FH 97*

<u>Fred – 966846 – FH 97</u>

P.S. I know you goin be mad at my stubbornness. But I'm going to try to avoid this from even happening.

Mrs. Martin

I wouldn't get mad at you for being you. I'm glad that you've got good things to write about – I like to hear about them – also – I like to hear the change in you too wanting to help someone. It is a nice feeling to make a difference to someone – even if they're someone you don't know well or even particularly care for. I am aware of the situation that is brewing and I appreciate the peacemaking you're doing – but please don't get caught up in it.

Ms. Scott – 2/26/97

Fred –

Understand your point about the topic – also about the test! So here goes!

For your assignment …. Is, what is one thing you would <u>never</u> change about yourself and how can you use it to build your future?

AS Happy Face Sticker

<u>Fred Harris – 2/26/97</u>

There's a lot more than one thing that I wouldn't change. So to sum it up into 1 category, I'd have to say that the one thing that I wouldn't change would have to be my life itself. I know that I've had many problems and hard times, but overall my life is one thing that I'll never get to have but once. It's the most important thing I have. From what I've been through my 17½ years and what's been going on recently, I've seen that my life is very special and precious and although I'm in a sticky situation right now, I can tell that I'm headed for a pretty decent future. It may start off rocky and bumpy and look like I won't be successful, but I know that the things I've been through and continue to go through will only help to make me stronger. So the next time I will be able to avoid or overcome the situation. I find my life and my previous life style unique. Not too many people have done what I've done, or seen what I've seen. Not too many people have the mentality I had. I don't really know how to explain it. I came from a bad neighborhood, but was raised in a middle-class area. I have both sides of streetz (good and bad). I have both sides of brains (well all 3 streetz, common and book). I've fought, stole, robbed, shot, but at the same time, I've cried, given, loved, cared, and sorrowed. I've had good times, bad time, it goes both wayz. I got so much knowledge, wisdom, and understanding about the streetz, people, the world itself, it's crazy. The thing is I have a hell of a lot more to learn. That's cool though because I pick up on things easy and can adapt to most environments. I couldn't think of changing my life, it's so very special and unique. I've been a bad and a good guy. **(Ms. Scott – "Ah – That's very nice.")** It's so many reasons why I don't want my life to change. Everyday of my life is a challenge. I like the edge, I like to live dangerously, and I occasionally like a challenge. Right now getting up outta here is my primary goal and challenge. Since I've been here, I've been settin goals and tryin to overcome challenges. SAT's, going to the crib, completin my program, etc. all those are goals. Maintainin, not going to SEG, or getting in no fights are challenges. I know how to weigh things out and process things in my head. Sometimes I get worked up, but, usually I know when to chill or turn it off. I'm socially and intellectually endowed. Happy Face Sticker I can socialize or communicate wit anyone: the president to the ice cream man. **(Ms. Scott – "Very subtle test.")** I know how to relate. I'm not too big, not too little, not too tall, not too short, not too black, not too brown. I'm just in the right place, where I wanna be. I'm cool to talk to, easy to get along wit. In general, I got some good traits Happy Face Sticker and characteristics. Like I said before, although, I'm in a sticky situation now, I see my plans for the future almost endless. And from the experience of fraud, stealing cars, shoot-outs, hood wars, robbing, etc, plus the 1 year plus in total time of me being incarcerated, those will all be some good reminders to tell me what I should and who I should get involved in/and wit. My parents another major, major thing I couldn't change ever and never will. Will always support me and help me through each and every one of my endeavors. I'd probably be dead witout them. They'll always be something I couldn't do witout. I have a lot of things to look forward to. By me continuing to strive and struggle to reach my goals, will only make me stronger and build me up. I don't have that much longer to go to the End of the Road. I know I can make it. *H 97*

Freddy "B" – 966846 – 3/6/97

Ms. Scott – 3/6/97

Freddy B –

That was a good job – not bad for a throw together job! I agree with everything you said!

<u>F. Harris – Wednesday – 2/19/97</u>

Good Morning. I'm real sleepy today. I worked Dining Hall the whole day and was wore out and tired when I finally got finished. I had to wait a couple of more hours before bed. Then when that rolled around, the same problem happened wit me like it did Buckner. People kept me up. talking, jamming, playin, etc. Anything to keep me and a couple of other people up all night. But the talking and playing haven't been bothering me as much as all this stuff on my mind. I haven't really been thinking about my auntie too much. My main concern that's been on my mind now is court! Every single time I'm about to depart to the crib, something always holds me back. November 20th, I made my releasement SAT. I was going to leave on the 22nd, but no, I had to go to court. I was extremely pissed when I found out I wasn't going to be home for Thanksgiving the second year in a row. Due to being incarcerated, I stayed like an extra 2 weeks waiting for court. December 4th (Now it's March 4th. I hope it ain't a repracussion of December 4th) was when I got recommitted back to here. Before I came back I had to go to court the 6th in Hamilton. So, that's what I did. I was supposed to go back January 7th, but, they rescheduled it to March 4th. They want me to come for trial as well as testify against someone. They're supposed to be combining these all in one. So on the 4th at 11:00 a.m. and 1:30 p.m. I have to go to both the trial and the testimony. The reason I'm getting worried is because I talked to my Dad this last Saturday. He was telling me what could happen, and what has changed. Hamilton wanted to charge me wit auto theft, but that was the same auto theft I got recommitted for in NAP. I'm not sure if they changed my charge because of that or not, but now they're trying to get me for burglary. They claim someone broke into the house to get the keys, then stole the vehicle. My dad said, they're not really trying to waive me, but they have brought up the idea of committing until I'm 18 years of age. I'm not sure if that's here or where. But that's not saying the judge could change his mind and waive me. It's looking 50-50. The people who snitched on me aren't anywhere to be found. Also, this is only my first offense in that county. However, burglary is a high-ranked felony. If I get convicted of any more felonies, I have no other choice but to get waived. I talked to Hickner (Chris) (when he was here because he's from Hamilton), and he basically said the same thing. He did say if I got convicted of it, that I would get stuck as if I was an adult. My mind is getting fried dealing wit all this. Most people would trip, or go off the deep-end. But me, even if I did get more time, I wouldn't really care. I know I've done some hellacious things in my life. These 8 months are a down payment of my dues. If I get more time, GOD has felt that I haven't paid the full price of my wrongs. I know that I'll probably get more time, or something I'm not trying to do (like probation or house-arrest, etc). But I know that whenever I get out, whether it be 3 weeks, 3 months, or 6 months, I know that I've paid my dues in full and GOD's happy wit that. I won't have any feeling of guilt or nothing. Each and everyday of my incarceration is like a check to all the victims (and GOD) repaying and apologizing to all of them for my behavior. So it's not really the fact of more time, it's just that I get so excited and hyped up about going home or thinking my struggle is finally over. Then something always smacks me in the face and says uh-uh 3 more months. Not that 8 months is a whole lot of time or nottin (to me, it is). But after doing 8 months, I feel that 3 months ain't nuttin. Or 6 months is just a hop, skip, and a jump. However it ends up good or bad, my struggle is almost over. I'm almost to the end of the tunnel. So all I can do is pray and hang in there. You know I've been here so long that (this might sound strange), I'm kinda going to miss this place. Ever since I've been here I knew I wasn't going anywhere anytime soon. But, I've been here so long that I'm going to kinda miss it. Not necessarily the actual facility itself. But the people and memories I've had in here. I've done a lot of bad and a lot of good. I've also done a lot of change. I'm always gonna remember those things; the fights, the trips to SEGS, the time I took my test (G.E.D.), when I cried or exploded. All of those things happened here. I can't forget that stuff. Especially the people, you, Sgt. Martin, Ms. Scott. Thomas, Jordan, etc. I'll never forget none of you, and I'll never forget what they've done for me. I'm so used to getting up and seeing you everyday; helping you, writing "The Phrase That Pays" everyday. Plus, the time I talk to Ms. Scott and find out something bad or good. These will all be here to. I'm trippin because I've never felt like this before in my life. Especially toward correctional officers or staff or nuttin like that. Now I don't really want to cut-out wit-out ya. I don't know, maybe, I'm crazy. I don't know. It's weird. I never thought I'd change like this. My attitude and mentality was so different at first. Now before I leave, it's so different again. I don't know how to explain it. It's hard to do. I want to leave, but I don't want to say good-bye. I don't know; why don't you tell me what you think of the situation? I'm all confused.

H 97

Fred – 966846

Mrs. Martin

It's O.K. to be confused especially, about something like this big of a change in yourself. You've grown so much and I think you'realizing that, and that you can do some things that you've never done before. Also, that you are so helpful and reliable and needed around here. It's O.K. to miss people, especially people who've impacted your life – that's my goal in life is to make a difference in someone's life. Missing this place – you won't other that it's a very safe atmosphere for you. I'm worried about you leaving and going back to the same family and neighborhood that you came from while you were getting in trouble. That's the part of the program that doesn't work when you leave for court on the 4th. Do you know if you'll be back until you're released from here? Will you be released first or do you know. I won't be ready for that – what will my room be like? A mess! And who will journal and learn so much while I watch? What can we work on for the time you are left here? What are you going to do when you're <u>finally</u> out? Have a good one!

<u>Fred Harris – 2/28/97</u>

Was up Mama Martin. I wanna apologize to you for my actions yesterday. You know the last thing I'll ever do is disrespect you. I was being cool at first. I didn't say nuttin. Then Burgess and Buckner jumped in. I'm minding my own business, playing on the computer. Frost got to rappin to me, I was cool telling him to keep my name out his mouth. Then other people started jumping in meddaling sayin I'm scared or tryin to protect him. That made me upset plus dude (Frost) was cussing at me calling me Fuxxin Liars this and Fuxxin liars that, and you excused it. Well you probably addressed it at a later time, but for the time being, you had excused it. Then on top of that I was the one getting yelled at and told to be quiet. That made me super hot. I tried to tell you it was only going to get things hyped up if you talked about it. I didn't want to curse or disrespect, but I was tired of hearin they mouth. Then the cherry on top of the cake that made me mad, was when I went out in the hallway (taking the incentive of tryin to be positive) you didn't even talk to me. It was like you purposely did it (I know you didn't but that's how I felt). To me, I felt like you were sayin, "I'm glad you're out, so stay out." I know that wasn't your thought or intentions, but that's how I took it. You remember the last time wit my auntie here at the A-Building. Even though I wasn't talking, I still wanted you here. Listen. When

I'm angry or upset, I get argumentative and loud. I was angry and upset. The time wit my auntie, I was (excuse my French) shitty, sad and depressed. That's when I don't be talkin. You seen how verbal I was. I'm sure I would've said somethin. And regardless of talking or no talking, I'll always listen to you no matter what. Besides I love you too much to get mad at you. I was just trippin. I wasn't mad, shitty or angry. I was just trippin, that's all. Also, this may possible be my last day. Court's this Tuesday, so they might pick me up on Monday. That's what I'm expecting to happen. I couldn't leave for a week or 2 or leave period with a grudge at you. So I want to apologize again. I'm sorry Mrs. Martin for disturbing your class and using any profane or inappropriate language that may have offended you. I hope you accept. *FH 97*

P.S. I got some pictures of the twins, so if you can remind me, I'll bring them in after lunch.

FH

Mrs. Martin

I am so glad that you told me all of that – it feels better doesn't it? I appreciate you telling me the difference between the 2 emotions. I'm not even sure of what to say having the thought that this might be the last day you are here.

I need to tell you that you have done a great job as a student, friend, and a teacher. I have learned a lot from you and have enjoyed every minute we've had since July. I wish you the best of luck at court and hope it goes the best way for you. I hope you will make good choices while you're out there – please remember all you've learned. M.

Fred Harris – 3/6/96 – Thursday

Was up Momz? I missed you over my 1 to 1 ½ vacation in Hamilton. I thought I was gonna be gone longer than that. Oh well, I ain't complainin. I'm glad I wasn't stuck in there any longer than I had to be. That place makes me go crazy. Anywayz I pretty much told you about everything that happened, and how I feel. I'm really just writin you to talk to you. Sometimes I be wantin you to be my counselor so I could see you in the evenings and talk your ear off (don't tell Ms. Scott that though). To me Ms. Scott is more of a teenage type of person. To tell the truth, she cares a lot more about her life than ours. I mean ain't nuttin wrong wit that, but working at a place like this you know you're gonna have to devote a little more time wit the kids. Don't get me wrong, she's been a great help to me recently, and she has spent a little extra time than usual. But at times, I feel that she do it just to do it. I still greatly appreciate everything she has done for me past and present. It's just I can see thru people like they transparent. I can tell when somebody's sincere or fake, or half and half. That's why I say she act like a teen because she gets sidetracked wit her personal life easily. Anyway, I want to seriously work on my future plans. If I ever run into some money, you know I'm gonna hook you up. You've done so much for me. You'll probably have to buy or give me another book because I'm gonna be writin you often. I'm really tryin to get my stuff together. I'm through wit all this bull-shxt. I'm startin to get real upset from being in here, but I know God wouldn't give me too much that I couldn't handle. I know if God and you, Big Mart, Ms. Scott, etc. believe in me enough to do it, I know I can. I got faith in myself too. I'm kinda bored sittin here not going to school, so I'll probably write you a lot more this week.

Mrs. Martin

Write anytime – it keeps your head clear of things – no problem – I've got lots of notebooks! Happy Face Sticker

Ms. Scott – 3/6/97

You can write about how you <u>feel</u> about your recommit.

Fred Harris – 3/8/97

How I Feel About Being Recommitted

If you really want to know my feeling about me being recommitted, you better prepare yourself. **FUCKED UP!!!** Is how I feel. I'm getting to the point where I'm bout to be like Fuck all this shit! I'm tired of being good! I'm tired of fronting! I'm tired of gettin disrespected! I'm tired of the playbabies, the group punishment, the crooked ass staff, and these backstabbers smiling in my face, but steady tryin to take my place! Yeah, I know I gotta be good. Yeah, I know that this is my last commit or court date. Yeah, I know I'm smarter, better, and brighter than all that. Yeah, yeah, yeah, same shit, different day. And now I gotta put up wit 3 more months of the shit. A nigga can only take and do so much. Pretty soon I'm gonna snap and jump in a boyz bones. Ain't none of the positive shinin bright enough to filter out the negative. Same people, same faces, same places, same playbabies, same shit day after day after day. Even our privileges and rewards don't compensate us for the shit we go through; orange, brown, sweats, draws (not boxers). I don't know; I'm just plain sick wid it. I be feelin like I'm trapped. Like I'm in a dead-end for life. I be feeling like I can't breathe sometimes. SATS, UNSATS, dining hall, school, laundry, late night popcorn, commissary, visits, who gives a fuck. Not me recently. You see, I couldn't (and didn't) even talk to my mother or father (or you) yesterday. I be feelin like don't nobody understand me, or can't nobody feel me. Not you, not my folks, not Ms. Martin, **NOBODY!** Sometimes I think even God don't understand me. I know he does, but I try to make myself (convince I mean) believe that God don't understand. Knowin he's omniscient, omnipresent and omnipotent, that's when I usually be dead-mouth. I, myself, try to understand myself and understand my reasonings and ways. I don't always dead- mouth it because of that. You know I process and evaluate certain situations and problems in my head. I've been in deep, deep thought. Not only about my recommit or my 3 months. I've been processing and thinking about hella stuff. The past, present, future, careers, my friends, family, my living arrangements, what I've done, why I did it, all kinds of stuff. The stuff I just mentioned isn't even a 1/10 of all the other major or complex things workin thru my mind. Nobody understands me. I'm tryin to understand myself. No one can help me at this point in time. I'm the only one who can reason wit myself. I have to do all of this on my own. The shit I'm dealin wit now is too complex to even attempt to discuss. I'm gonna be actin and talking a lot more different towards you, staff, students, etc. Whoever. I'm not really gonna be talking that much, and after this assignment, my future ones will vary along wit my thinking and attitude. Some will be long and detailed; others will be short and sweet. No more tryin to fill up all the pages, or breakin records. Fuck all that dumb shit. I will do all the assignments to the best of my ability, but if I don't like it or choose not to do it, expect to see some bullshit or a paragraph of some slapped together babbling. No more trying to impress people, no more bitin my tongue, no more frontin or kissin ass. Straight real. You be real wit me, I'll be real wit you. If you actin fake or phoney, or I think you are, I'm just goin let you know off the barrelhead. What I mean is if you just rappin to me about some 'ol bullshit, tryin to be sorry for me just cause it's yo job, you can save it. I ain't sayin you did and I ain't saying you do, but if you do, or I think you do, I'm just gonna go on head and bounce. Fuck feeling sorry for me, Fuck sympathizin wit me. Just be real. I'm a criminal. I'm doin my time for it. I get what I deserve. Just cause I feel the way I do now, shit don't feel sorry for me, because on the outz, I didn't give a fuck about none of the people I did that shit. So in return, I don't want people to sympathize or pity me. All the shit I done did, I should have life. So a year or 11 months ain't shit. If I got a attitude, let me know. If I smell like shit, let me know. But whatever you do or say be real wit it. If I'm mad, don't cheer me up, just talk and reason wit me. If I'm sad, don't make me feel good, just try to understand. I know you won't because no one can, and while I'm in here, no one will. Don't try so hard to be my counselor, tryin to have the right answer or remedy to all my problems. Don't try so hard to explain stuff to me scientifically or psychiatically. Just be Angela Scott rappin to Fred Harris; not a staff to a student, not a counselor to a patient; just Angela Scott to Fred Harris. No fake or phoney shit. One on one, me and you, just spithin about the real, what's on my mind and my feelings and emotions. We talk about that now, but we both kinda sugar coat shit. Let me know what you really thinking, what's really on yo mind. Not what you think might offend me or something you said or used wit someone else. Whatever you feel or think, come wit it. Even if I'm a muthafuckin bitch, be real wit it. Let me know by telling me straight up as Angela Scott, not like Ms. Scott, guidance counselor of North Central Juvenile Facility. Straight up on the real; sometimes you try too hard at being a good counselor. Not sayin you ain't. It's just don't try at it, just do it. Naturally, be a good counselor. Don't use the same method or approach wit the same students. You gotta know about 'em. I ain't sayin you ain't a good counselor or I dislike you or nuttin because you've been one of my best friends and helped me get thru a lot of shit. But I'm getting older and things like jobs and the future are startin to flash before my eyes. Sugar coatin shit's only tryin to blindfold the truth. By me getting older and becoming a man, I need to know and hear the real shit. It's really almost check out time this time. So I need to have a good perspective on future things. In realitie's eyes, not a sugar coated department of corrections guidance counselor, who's not tryin to hurt my feelings or hid the truth from me. Like I said, I ain't goin hid nuttin from you or lie. I ain't got no reason to. Tellin you the truth or whatever will only benefit the both of us. But like I said before, I ain't bout to keep goin for all these people in here tryin to play me false. You along wit the staff ain't goin have no problem wit me because I know what to do, and I know how to control myself. But I ain't goin keep overlookin shit. I've been lettin too much shit slide, that's how the bigger shit comes about. They figure they can do whatever (like disrespect me or push me or talk shit) so they start to doin it on a regular basis. It ain't gonna be too many more of dem dayz. I ain't promising or threatnin no shit like that. I'm just spittin the real. I know you probably trippin about this whole assignment, and my attitude. If somethins botherin you about it, or you don't understand some stuff I said, just holla at me. Shit, I'm goin be here for a minute.

FH 97

Freddy Harris — 966846

Ms. Scott – 3/10/97

Fred –

When you feel like writing. Write, O.K.

AS Happy Face Sticker

<u>Fred Harris – 3/10/97</u>

A thanks for that little talk today. I wasn't quite sure how you was gonna take it; whether you thought I was disrespecting you or if you thought I didn't like you or whatever. To tell the truth, (this wasn't my intentions from the jump. I just thought of it after the talk we had today) you really proved or showed me somethin today. With your response, comments, and understanding to our discussion we had today. I felt that you passed the test. It (the journal entry) was the real, the truth, and nothing but the truth. I really didn't care what you thought of it because it was on my mind and needed to be expressed. But, with the talk we had today and your understanding of all of it, showed me a lot more about you than I wrote. No bull-shit! You read by yo'self, then read it wit me. Anything you didn't understand, you questioned me about it. You asked me how I saw you and why (how I saw you in the journal, like when you asked me about you being fake or phoney). You usually 95% of the time

131

do come at me straight up. I was basically referring to the sugar coatin. Anywayz, I'm getting sidetracked. Our discussion and that last entry was like a test. You basically passed it. You gave me my space in the journal and personally, you didn't take the entry as an insult, or disrespect. You held no grudges or tried to use it against me. I don't know? I just really didn't know how you'd react. But after our talk, I gained my trust in you more, my respect towards you and your understanding towards me increased. I just don't know how I can explain how I felt when we talked, and what I feel now about you. Of course, you won't understand or feel me, and granted most of the problems that I am dealin wit, you really can't help me. But I do want you to continue to work wit me, but under my conditions. I know you the counselor and all, but like I said I need to work on **MY** problems. But I do want you to help me along the way. I think you kinda took my assignment the wrong way. I wasn't meaning it as you're a no good counselor and you couldn't helpd no one. Naw, no shit like that. I was basically sayin if you (and whoever else staff, student, teacher, etc.) gotz to actin all fake and phoney, or if you got to dickin me around, I said I'm goin straight bounce. You cool, you know what I'm sayin, ain't nuttin wrong wit you. You cool as fuck. But I think you thought that, that whole assignment was me tryin to knock you. That wasn't my intention at all. It was more like a prophecy or warning to tell you of things to come; my attitude and behavior, my feelings towards others, my plans in here, etc. You took it the wrong way, straight up. I could feel that you perceived some of my statements and comments as offensive or that you was no good. But peep, it ain't nuttin like that. In fact since you basically let me write my own, I done made a plan, and I do want you to help me through it. Here's my plan. I'm goin work wit you (and Ms. Martin) on 3 of my problems wit myself. I figure 3 months, 1 for each problem. After this team, I go back in 4/9/97, then 5/7/97, 6/4. In between those 3 months I'm goin to work on 1 problem each month. I'm goin write the basic problem I have wit each individual problem. Then you can ask me whatever or throw in suggestions or whatever. If you have an assignment that goes wit my problem, go on ahead and write it in. You know I have many problems other than my 3, but I just chose and decided I wanted yaw to work wit me on these 3. Actually, I only have 2. I'm going to get some advice from Ms. Martin on what my second one should be. First, Respect. Everything about it. I know you remember the first one I did on respect. I'm basically broadening it. Why I feel I need it? Do I have it now? From others, For others and for myself? A lot more than that, you could help find out what I do and don't respect and/or why I do or don't. Second, this is where I'm gonna get some input from you, Ms. Martin and possibly my folks (parents). I was thinking about my temper or attitude, but that'll change a lot when I get outta here. So, I'm open for suggestions. Last is my future. You have 2 months to help find careers and get booklets and pampthlets on college. I chose this for my last one, so I'll have a whole month of thinking about my career options, friends, plans, etc. Ms. Martin will be helping me too. If you want, you could help me work on the career field, and she could get the school stuff; or vice versa. I really don't care just as long as you both helping me. Like I said before, you misinterpreted the assignment or took it the wrong way, but you said if I ever need to talk, come and get you and I need to let you know what's up or what I'm plannin on doin. So, if you got a minute, I wanna rap to you today and tell you was up (in school here, whatever). *FH*

Freddy B – 3/11/97

Ms. Scott – 3/11/97

Fred –

Nice talking to you – I'm glad to see someone taking a part in their Treatment plan! Here's the questions we talked about:

1) What does respect mean to you?
2) Identify the person you Respect the most and least.
3) How do you show Respect?
4) How do you feel when you're disrespected?

5) How would you like Respect shown to you?

6) Develop a role play for a Respectful situation.

7) Demonstrate Respect.

8) What are the benefits or consequences from Respect?

9) Draw your interpretation of Respect.

10) Observce Respect being given/displayed and write about it.

11) Develop expectations of being Respected.

12) Write an essay on how to handle it if Respect or Disrespect is being received.

13) Name 10 songs with Respect in the title.

AS Happy Face Sticker

<u>Fred Harris – 3/11/97</u>

1. I've already wrote a 4 page thing over respect. To briefly sum it up, respect is basically being courteous, thankful, and polite to kids, adults, and elders, regardless of race, sex, or age. Showing your appreciation and manners are part of respect too. Knowing when to curse or be quiet or just following by the rules. All of these are involved wit Respect. Respect basically is to be polite, courteous and somewhat humble in the presence of another person, or place, or thing. ^{Happy Face Sticker} You have to equally show respect to everyone.

2. Jesus Christ is who I respect the most. He did so much shit for everybody. He paid the price wit His life, for everyone else's sins. I respect him the most because He loved us when we didn't know or love him. ^{Happy Face Sticker}

   There's a lot of people who I don't respect, but until they disrespect me, I won't disrespect them. Prejudice people, Adolf Hitler, David Karesh, KKK'S, Sadaam Huesain, etc.

(Ms. Scott – "I doubt people with brains respect any of these "people" listed."), people who don't have respect for themselves, people who kill, steal, rape, etc. for no reason or purpose at all. (I know you're like "well you stole for no reason.") Well to be straight wit you, Hell yeah, I did, and I didn't give a fuck who they was. My respect was a little low in myself, but I spit about it a little later thru this.) It's a lot of low down, dirty muthafuckas in this world. People will do anything to survive or stay on top. I don't know I gotz love for few niggaz and hate for the rest. I don't know shitz scandalous.

3. I show respect by treating everyone equal. The things I said about respect in Question 1 apply for me on how I show my respect. Another way I show respect is by doin what I have to do or tryin to make what this place calls an awareness. Payin my dues and showin my gratitude. If its to people who done helped me out or to people who done passed, I'm goin show them my respect.

4. My feelings towards being disrespected vary. If its someone who is high in authority, rank, prestige, or whatever talks to me like a damn dog. I'd probably take it hard figurin somebody wit so much power and clout think I'm this or that. I'm probably goin take it like its real. That's why I kinda be (well used to get) shitty when muthafuckas used to say that chester bullshit. So much of that get you to thinking and actin precautious that you actually try to avoid situations where they could say you was cheating or molestin whatever (This is past tense though). I used to be hard on myself. I was depressed, shitty, all kinds of people, things, and shit. I was shitty at myself too. **(Ms. Scott – "It's very easy for everyone to get down on themselves.")** That's why when people said shit to me like that I took it hard because my self-esteem wasn't that high. I felt like a fuck up and a asshole. Plus people used to me, so I had to be

all kinds of bitches and hoes and shitz because I wouldn't bump. Muthafuckas talking shit behind my back, all kinds of shit. I wanted to split 'em, but I couldn't jeopardize my cases and sentences. So I'd let 'em hoe me, because I wasn't trying to get caught up. So I let it get to the point where I started thinking, feeling and actin like a hoe. But I did know I was still deep down inside down for whatever. But I let 'em play mind games wit me. I let 'em take over my mind by talking me down and me believing it. Saduced. That's the word. Anyway that had me trippin a 'lil bit. Not really about that chester shit, it's a lot more than that.

Anyway if it's by someone (like Philly) who you know don't even have respect for theirself, my reaction is a lot different. I kinda find it humorous. A muthafucka who try to knock somebody else to make theyself feel good aint nuttin but a phoney ass hoe. Straight up. To tell the truth, it make me feel good a little bit. Evidently, they must be hatin me for some strange reason to come out the blue and disrespect. **(Ms. Scott – "Good point.")** I must have something they want and don't got. So my reaction is totally different depending on the person and situation.

5. Basically I want respect shown to me how I described it in Questions #3 and #1 equally. If I treat you like a hoe, you have the right to refer to me the same as I refer to you. So it ain't no black, white, male, female thing. Just straight equal.

    Questions #6, #7, #9. I ain't doin cause I don't really understand and if I did, I still wouldn't do them.

    Question #10. I already wrote about it.

8. BENEFITS

    a. less trouble
    b. less fights
    c. less arguments
    d. you get respect in return
    e. people will help and support you
    f. Seen in a positive way
    g. you'll be looked at as a good supporter
    h. In life or in a career, you'll be looked at wit hella prestige. **(Ms. Scott – "O.K. – I support – kinda dumb, huh!")**

CONSEQUENCES

    a. People will try to take advantage of it
    b. Some people may not want it
    c. Get depressed or stressed out from trying to deal with everyone's bullshit

11. EXPECTATIONS

    a. No racial slurs or disrespect at anytime around me
    b. No profanity or abusive verbal language around me
    c. Never mind I don't really know how to define them

(Ms. Scott – "The first 2 really <u>GOOD!</u>")

12. How to Handle Questions if received

    a) Respect. Of course if respect is given, it needs to be returned. Make sure you keep a respectful relationship going and growing. Try not to say or do anything that someone else might find disrespectful. In the long run, you'll lose their respect or probably yours as well because a respectful relationship is the best thing to start wit. So handle it like a prize, because if you got it, you earned it, but don't do anything to lose it. **(Ms. Scott – "Prize – I like the way you described it – Respect can be a true <u>prize</u>.")**

b) Disrespect is a little tricky to handle. If you try to take it and be cool, people will take advantage. If you come back at them, it's likely you'll get in an argument, fight, etc. And if you try to hold it in, it'll just eat away at your insides. Plus holding it in will depress you and build up so much tension and pressure that you'll probably mess around and snap on somebody.

The best way I see to handle it is by when you first start to getting in to it wit somebody, you should let 'em know off the barrelhead, how you feel (well, first the problem) about the situation, let 'em know why you think it wrong or whatever, then, ask him why ? wishes to do that to you. Explain how you never disrespected them and if you did, you had no intentions. Then apologize. If ? keeps up, just avoid them as much as possible. In yo head, keep remindin yo'self how you ain't goin get on his level and hoe out by disrespectin ? the ones lookin like an asshole.

13. I can't think of none? **(Ms. Scott – "Fred – I added this one for fun – I couldn't think of 10 – so I thought you could help me!")**

<u>F. Harris – Friday – 3/7/97</u>

A Momma. It's about 9:45 (late night). I'm just sittin here in the laundry thinkin. I got a lot of stuff on my mind, but I don't think I can write that long. If you haven't noticed from what I wrote yesterday, my interest in Ms. Scott is at a considerably large decline. Day by day, I get more and more frustrated wit her. I can tell she don't really truly care. Of course on the clock she could be the most caring and compassionate person. But when she hits the gates, it's like, oh well. I hate phoney fake xxxxxxxxxxxxx (excuse me, I'm a lil upset). That's why I care for you so much. I know what you spittin to me and doin for me is sincere, and you do it from the heart. You just naturally nice and sweet and understanding. You really want to help people and you're genuine and sincere in your attempts. Ms. Scott tries too hard to; it's not natural. She does what she can do to make you feel a little better (like to overlook it by jokin around) not by actually helpin you. You help out and try to cheer me up. Every time Ms. Scott tries to explain herself towards me or my problems, she usually get a little long-winded and makes the whole explanation into a scientific psychiatric explanation. You just automatically got that vibe where you can work wit people's problems and relate to them no matter. You didn't have to get a diploma sayin you can scientifically describe people's problems (you may have, I don't know). It's just you don't try to relate and understand, you just naturally do. I feel Ms. Scott is tryin too hard. She needs to lose all that psychiatric bull-sxxx and come to me like a real person to person. You look behind the oranges and D.O.C.'s She kinda reflects on what and why your'e in here for. Whenever I talk to you, you don't care or ask (I usually tell you). You just focus on what's bothering me. Ms. Scott is basically always tryin to scientifically approach problems instead of talking it out real and truthfully. She tries to explain your problem in her words, often relate wit something in your past or present that may not have anything to do wit the situation at all. I don't know, maybe I just relate wit you. Today, when I saw Ms. Scott in her office, she let me call my momz (this brings up another issue I want to talk about). I couldn't (and chose not to) even talk to my momz. My mother made me very upset. She thought Ms. Scott had called her alone. So my mom tried to sneak in a couple of quick questions (thinking I wasn't there). She asked about my extra time, and how I was doin (the basics). Then she brought up the issue about my medicine. You know how I feel about that issue. She asked her about the counseling, how to get it on the outz, all that. It made me so mad I wanted to scream and holler. Plus wit the extra piece of my growing animosity towards Ms. Scott on my mind during this, it really boiled my skin. I expressed to you before how I felt about takin medicine. I don't like it at all. When I confronted my mother wit the situation over the phone (at a very subtle, indirect approach), she tried to play it off actin like she didn't know what she did. Then tried to get out of it by givin my pops the phone. Although I had no beef (drama) wit him, he did what the other (each other) usually does. Sided wit the other spouse. That made me more angrier. I wanted to throw the phone against the wall and run outta Ms. Scott's office. I concluded the phone call and our session. At times I feel like don't nobody understand me. Not even my parents. No one. Nobody in this world. Each one of my feelings and emotions needs to be handled differently and wit different understanding. You know when I'm in my dead-mouth mode compared to my get upset curse and rave walk out the classroom mode. You know to understand me in each separate feelin; you have to approach me in a different understanding and perspective. There's only so much people know, and there's only so much I want people to know about me. I want you to know. That's why I be telling you stuff, but there's some stuff I don't even know or understand about myself. I know and understand, but I don't comprehend. Like I know the answer, but I don't compute or understand how I got it. Right now, I want to help myself anyway possible and do everything I can to better myself. But, at the same time, I push people away and have the attitude of F.T.W. (Fxxx The World) I just don't be knowin. You don't understand how bad I need to talk to you. You should realize it now being this is my 3rd page. I know you got stuff to do and all that, but at times I be wantin to talk to you and you only. I can't even talk to myself because I don't even make sense at times. Why do I do and say the things I do. Why do I picture and think the things I do. It's hard to explain. Maybe I can explain it better face to face. I don't, it really makes no difference. I just like talking to you. People joke around wit me (like Big Mart and Ms. Scott) talking bout me and you have grown a mother/son bond. Or, I'm the lost son of yours, or I miss you and you miss me. That's cute. That's how I really feel at times. You treat me like a son. That's why I relate to you so well. Along wit the fact that you be real wit me and in return, I be real wit you. Even if it's Fxxx me; if you bein real I accept that. That's why I always listen and talk to you. You just straight up naturally real. You be sincere in what you do. So don't never feel like you imposing or medalin. I'll always listen to you or what you gotta say. Just keep it real wit me, and I'll keep it real wit you. You see I do 2-1/2 to 3 pages of my feelings and everything else I try to do for you and myself should show how I really do care. I hope you know and understand that I do love you and love all the stuff you do for me. Although my actions don't express it in person. I relay messages best through paper, plus my attitude isn't always gonna be loving after 8-1/2 to 9 months of incarceration. Everything I say and do for you is real. My real feelings and emotions. How I'm thinking and feelin at this very point in time is in these 3 pages of this entry. All real. All true. No bullshxx. I gotz more on my mind and lotz more to say, but a man's hands can only take so much. Plus it seems that at 1:45 min have dwindled away so quickly. So I must conclude this hoping that you can somehow attempt to help and advise me especially thru times like this. My mind and soul is beginning to get restless, and I'm not sure how much more of this I can take. *Fred – 966846 – H97*

Mrs. Martin

I'll_always_ be real with you – it would be a waste of both of our time if I wasn't. I do appreciate what you do in my room as well – helping keep kids quiet, collecting books, paper, pencils, etc – I get side-tracked a lot with students and you help refocus me – I'm learning to. About mom – don't shut her out – she wants what's best for you; that's her job! We can talk more about that later.

F. Harris – Saturday – 3/8/97

Day Trey. Maintainin. I'm really startin to lose it though I had a visit today. It started off cool, but after the first half hour, things started getting rough. I asked my mom about her addressing Ms. Scott about my meds on the outz. She tried to act like she didn't know what I was talking about. That made me upset. Then she kept playin and jokin around tryin to make me feel good and cheer me up. It only made me more upset because I was in a serious mood and everything I said or did, my momz made a joke. Finally after a while, I just told them straight up, "if you ain't bein real don't even talk to me" (I know this is my folks and all. I was just very upset). I want yaw to help me by understanding. Not just sayin the same-o same-o whenever I get in trouble. I told them I loved them both wit all my heart. I'd kill damn near anybody for them. But, I basically told them to continue to support me like they do, but with the simple adjustment of 100% space. My folks usually try to persuade me into their ideas. Right now, I can't be getting distracted wit all this other stuff. I'm working wit myself on important issues that will help me for the future, the present, etc. I still would like your help and support, but I might not be as open wit my problems as before. For the simple fact that in a couple of years, my parents might not even be around. If they babying me or getting me through stuff witout me helping myself, I'm gonna be dependent on everyone else's help. I'm kinda tough loving myself. I'm tryin to prepare myself but takin this all on, I know I shouldn't and that it's not a good idea, but it goes a lot deeper than that. I try to take my problems head on instead of always askin for help. Help's cool every now and then, but I'm startin to get reliant on it. I'm still basically in a mind puzzle. Even after overlooking what I've wrote so far get me confused. I need to talk wit you seriously. School will probably limit our time, but if you could squeeze in a little time to rap to me I'd appreciate it. Big Mart told me you'd be here tomorrow, but he's not for sure. He said he would talk to me tonight, but wit these 2-10-40's and a signal 8 in less than 10 to 20 minutes, I know he'll be very busy. Plus I think A-2 is goin on Lock Down.

So, he'll probably be processin. I understand though. After damn near 9 months, I know how things work. It's just we in trouble too because of A-2 and wit C/O like Ms. Lockhart; she likely to start a riot. I'll be cool though. I'm in the Laundry room washin clothes and writing. *H97 – Fred Harris – 966846*

Mrs. Martin

I will be able to be over after school today if you still want to talk; it's very hard during class. I'm going to be looking for some info for you too about other topics we've discussed. Nothing will change on my part of the support chain – you come to me about what you want and feel comfortable with. You are right, you are getting older and will need to begin making decisions, but getting direction and input can't hurt – you're learning (we all always are). Hang in – you will make it!

10:45 p.m. – Wednesday – 3/12/97

Help! I just damn near went to SEG. Luckily there wasn't enough room, and luckily the C/O's and God both were keeping an eye on me. Guess what it was basically about? Respect. That's why I chose this as my main thing to work on first. If I don't, I will be in SEG numerously throughout my time, Not to get too detailed or nuttin (because I want to briefly talk to you about it anyway), I'll tell it in short. I was doin my usual late night commissary. Two students were eating their commissary back there wit me. I asked Student Pratt numerous amount of times to leave; he acknowledged me, but didn't do it. Finally, I softly tapped him and told him to leave, a little harder the second time, but still respectful in my approach. Finally, I gave him a stern nudge, he stated he was "goin to hit me in my mouth if I touched him again. In my persistence I kicked off my shoes, when he didn't leave. I had to go on ahead and escort him out. A little aggressive, but nuttin to hurt him. When I was escorting him, he got to kickin and punchin, swingin, whatever. So then I got aggressive and took him to the restroom. By this time, he was wild. I told him to stop disrespectin me, and to leave me alone. Instead of listening, he turned and tried to get aggressive back. So, I simply threw him against the wall a few times. Then Wells stopped it. Pratt went totally AWOL, I mean beserk! He ripped his shirt off, lounged towards me, wrestled wit Wells. All that over a damn laundry room. Anyway we were both gonna go to SEG. Me for putting my hands on him, and Pratt for going haywire. Instead, we had to talk it over, and Pratt wasn't exactly tryin to work things out. I on the other was totally calm and reasonable. But if one went the other did too. So we eventually made up and separated dorms. I have no remore (or had at the time) for goin to SEG, getting a future UNSAT, Battery, fightin, etc. I didn't and don't care. I'm not exactly sure why. I even gotta SAT wit some positive comments. You see I didn't even bar walking outta line in team line. I don't know, I was shxxxy because of this Friday I was supposed to leave. Now I got 3 mo' months left. It made me mad to think I was goin home this Friday, but now I ain't. I don't really have a distinct clue, but respect was the main factor.

Mrs. Martin

I would like you to go through the steps of this and retrace what were good choices and what were bad choices that you could do different in another entry.

We need to work on the <u>why!</u> I would like you to also explore and explain to me what that was all about. Yesterday in line you were definitely in bad sort. I haven't see you that stubborn or defiant since you first got here. We'll address this, "I don't care" attitude. Write about it.

F. Harris – Continued Journal Entry – Wednesday – 3/12/97

Another thing is, I'm very over protective of the laundry room and the clothes themselves. When you're incarcerated, you really don't have too much you can call yo' own. There's not too much you can take pride in havin. But the laundry room is something I take pride in and put a lot of work into. People don't understand that. They think I'm just kissin axx or frontin out. I can say that's my laundry room or area, or my job. Like my real house on the outz, I must defend it and keep it cool. Pratt disrespected me, me in my laundry room, and my laundry. I don't know really, I guess I'm just over reactin. Uh, I don't know? What do you think? *H*

Mrs. Martin

You aren't over-reacting – you are taking pride in your work and that is normal. I think everyone should have special details that are their own, so everyone could develop that sense of pride. We need to work on how to approach others when they're invading that space.

F. Harris – 3/16/97

Was up Ms. Martin. I know you're probably wondering why I've been actin so strange the last 1 or 1-1/2 days. Well you remember I told you I ain't goin be putting up wit that fake sxxx. So now I ain't as hesitant to bite my tongue. I told you I ain't really tryin to front or kiss axx anymore. I do front a little bit around you because if I didn't I would probably get kicked out more than your students. When I be sayin I'm goin split boyz if they disrespect you, I ain't really playin. I'm not just goin split 'em out the blue, but I do know who be disrespectin and who don't. So I got those in my mind. I ain't goin forget. No, I ain't threatenin or nuttin like that. But that's why you've seen a lil change in my actions and behavior.

Now my impatient stubbornness is just me being sick wit being in here. Like last Wednesday, I really didn't care or bother if they gave me a SAT or an UNSAT. I wasn't going home like I was supposed to, so who cares. These people be (95% of them) dickin me all around. Fxxk 'em. I ain't bout to sweat these people. Why should I? I ain't got or getting out no time sooner. So that's why Wednesday I was trippin, and it kinda went in to messin up my whole week. Especially Wednesday. I'm just basically impatient due to the fact that I got 80 something days left. A whole year. Hell naw. A whole entire year in this ----! I ain't trippin though, this is what I needed to get my stuff together. But I am startin to get restless. More and more each day I get homesick. 80? Days ain't nuttin. But after damn near 280? Days, sxxt starts to get to you. I've loosened up and relaxed a whole lot since I came back, but I still got hella lot of work that needs to be done like my "I don't care attitude" as you call it isn't exactly that way. It's more like a "I can't take this sxxt no mo. Straight up. People don't care about me, so why should I care about them. You know what I'm sayin. I am working on Respect and this is 1 reacon why I chose it. First so I could knock it out the way and be cool for the future. But as you can see, I'm still struggling. So let me know what you think. Straight up. *Fred Harris – 966846 – 3/97*

Mrs. Martin

Respect is an excellent first choice. It does all make sense, but it can't be O.K. – this is where you are getting a real lesson in self-control and discipline. It's hard, but I know you can do it!! No – people in here aren't going to be the most caring – that's why <u>self</u> respect needs to be worked on too. Along life's path, you will run into a few people who will care – they will be <u>treasures</u> – this (NCJF) more than likely won't be that time, but you'll sure be able to learn from the people you meet. Time is time – Life – learning is important.

3/19/97

Was up Ms. Martin? I really ain't got much to say today. Just the same ol' I'm sick of being here, and I wanna stick my foot knee deep in somebody's axx. I know that ain't what I wanna do, but I can almost promise you, I'm gonna mess around and hem me up a boy. I ain't going lie either. I'll damn near go to the back at anytime and bump wit somebody and won't really trip over the consequences. Plus all I need is 3 SATS and my 3 to 6 allows me to get 4 SATS. I have been thinking about using that 1 whole month to act a straight complete total asshole and break down any boy who talks sxxx. I ain't sayin I'm goin do it, but I ain't sayin I ain't. 75% says I won't, but, like I said before, if I mess up once, I tend to throw it all down the drain. That's how I got caught up wit all dem cases in all dem different counties. Once I had ran away from the crib and violated my suspended, I said, "Fxxx it" and did what I wanted when I wanted, how I wanted. Now I'm paying my dues. I felt like my 8+ months was my check back to God, but I guess he wanted interest, 3 mo months. I still ain't trippin really.

Mrs. Martin

> 75% and <u>all</u> of my hope and faith that you won't
> do it. Why? It just doesn't make sense.

F. Harris – Continued Journal Entry – 3/19/97

It's just all these hoes in this place pissin me off. So many niggaz wanna be grown, and can't act right alone. They gotta be babysat. I'm tired of all these kiddie bxxxhes, and these kiddie staff. Kids like Alexander intimidate some of them. They be afaid to do they job.

Sometimes I be afraid I'm goin do they job for them by putting a boy on his s-back. I ain't really worried about the SAT or UNSAT either.

It's basically the fact that I done built so much and doin something stupid will just tear it all down.

Mrs. Martin

You should be worried about your SAT – if you don't get it you stay.

F. Harris – Continued Journal Entry – 3/19/97

Damn near all the staff, C/O's, teachers, etc. trust and respect me. I can do, or get away wit certain stuff other people can't, because I earned it. Like in the real world start off the bottom and work yo way up. I'm already damn near at the top. I got pull wit all the staff. And all the Sgts. are cool wit me. I worked hard to get all that pull, respect, and clout. It costs some trips to SEG, some UNSATS, and some snatch-ups. But I didn't trip although it took awhile I did make it. Now, I ain't constantly gotta be watched like a hawk, or getting picked at like a punk. I done been through and came through. I don't know though. Every dog has his day. If niggaz keep rappin, I'm goin have mine. I ain't trying to take it there, but I ain't goin have no control of what's goin happen. I really don't know how to explain it. I just hope it don't never happen. *Freddy Harris – 966846 – 3/97*

Mrs. Martin

Me too! Why would you want to blow what you've worked for 8 months – chance to have privileges and not be watched over every minute. Seems to me not to make much sense – actually, I don't understand (and can't) – feeling of if I make a mistake – I'll just blow it completely. Trial and error is what life is about and I'll be honest, what you're thinking will happen, to me, sounds like an excuse and a way to cop out if the time comes. Straight up Right?

Anger, frustration, sadness and pure volatile explosion waiting to happen is you – it's also your test – I know you have it in you to pass – but I don't think you know.

Wednesday – 3/19/97

A Ms. Martin. Basically everything you said was true. All that stuff is what's goin on inside me. And yes, I can control it and yes I can hold it in. But it's not that. Sometimes I want to let it out. If I couldn't control it, I'd be in SEG everyday. It's just be those times when I gotz sxxx on my mind, and I want to be left alone or not bothered. Then all of a sudden, if it's not a staff, it's a student hasselin me or giving me a hard time. That's what I be tryin to stress. People don't understand me. I mean it's cool.

Mrs. Martin

No one can understand you or how you feel because it's you . That's life. I need to ask why to see if you can explain things to me or to see if you know. You need to do what is necessary for you. I am trying to help direct your decisions to benefit you now and later.

F. Harris – Continued Journal Entry – Wednesday – 3/19/97

I know ain't too many people goin relate. But I mean that's why I don't understand why or how you ask me why? It's a very good legitimate question, but it's like asking why do you enjoy having sex, if you've never had it (not saying you or nobody). Unless you've had sex, you can't tell no one not to have it or it's wrong. Same thing, if you've or no one else has never been locked up for 9 months, how can you tell me you don't understand why I shouldn't smash somebody. Of course it's obvious, for the extra time and shxx, but you don't even think about none of that wit everything else goin on around you. Plus, like I said, I be havin problems and pressures on my mind especially from trying to uphold my high expectations of what everyboy has in me. I be getting frustrated from trying not to let everybody down by goin to SEG or getting in trouble. Now, hopefully, I can especially maintain wit Reddington on the Wing. (I'll tell you why he came down tomorrow.) You know what we done been thru on the outz and in here. Now it ain't A-1 or A-2, it's A-1 and I will bump wit him if he gets to rappin. Hopefully, I pray it don't. I was talking to him today and we was all cool, but that could be a lot different a week from now. So I hope don't nuttin pop off wit that.

F. Harris – Saturday – 3/22/97 – 4:30

Whats up? Today is Saturday, and I'm sittin in the laundry room bored as hell. Ain't nuttin really to do. We watchin "Independence Day," but I'v already seen it about 5 times, so I ain't even interested in it no mo. Plus, I'm sleepy as hell and want to go to sleep, but the T.V. chairs are full. So I decided to write what's been going on, and what's on my mind.

Yesterday, me and Ms. Scott had a little talk about my meds. We made a deal that I didn't have to take them unless I got a major, for fighting, battery, or threatening and intimidation. L.O.P. and S.A.S. don't matter. You don't need meds to avoid those, plus anybody can get on either one, with or without meds. So we have come to an agreement that I no longer have to take them. She said that she didn't feel it was safe because I'm forcing myself not to take it. So for the past few days, I haven't been taking my meds. Then today, Sgt. Corey told me (and damn near forced me too). She's been seeing me act up a little more lately. A lot less tolerable and more playful. I don't see it. But she basically made me take it by blackmailing me. She was stressing about how good I was doing and not to throw away all that I have. So I decided to take it. When I did, it just hit me. I couldn't even take it. I was so drowsy. I haven't taken it in so long, I can't even handle it. I'm not even trying to get back in the program. When I talked to my folks, they had mixed emotions.

Mrs. Martin

I sure do, and I'm <u>very</u> concerned about it. I'm afraid you're going to fall apart – after all this play – by losing control.

F. Harris – Continued Journal Entry – 3/22/97

I had to emphasize the seriousness of the recent incident that just happened. A couple of the pills he took were my kind of meds. Plus the laundry room NW1 side was brought up as being one of the places where they had sniffed them at. Although my name wasn't exactly involved, two things were brought up where they could bring up my name: meds and the laundry room – two pieces of evidence. When I explained it to my parents, they kind of just went along with it. They didn't agree or disagree, they just accepted. Plus, today Nowell went to SEG again for that pill stuff. Now it's a 99% chance he's going to 13. I don't do that stuff, and I haven't or will do it. But, I'm being as safe as possible. Regardless if I do it or not, the new rules and regulations are so much bull sxxx. I don't want to go through the trouble. So far, I've been doing good, but I must admit, I have been slipping a little. Nothing to get me an UNSAT though. I'm still contemplating on what I should do. Most likely I'm going to discontinue my meds, but your advice would be most helpful. *Fred Harris – 966846*

Mrs. Martin

I am concerned about the reason you are stopping your meds. I have to disagree with the decision you have made for your health and behavior reasons. I have seen a drastic change in you in the last week or so. I'm worried – to be very honest with you. Let's talk.

F. Harris – Monday – 3/24/97 – 10:00

A momma, momma. I'm so very, very glad you came to see me today. I was in a troubled situation too. It's like you have telekinesis or something. When I seen you I thought I was dreaming because you were one of the people I so desperately needed to talk to. When you around, things seem to brighten up and happen differently.

Mrs. Martin

I'm glad I could be there. I just had to check out how you were. I had a strange feeling.

F. Harris – Continued Journal Entry – 3/24/97

You see that incident with Pickett was resolved without me even talking to him or nothing. In fact you just cleared my mind of all thinking and got me to thinking about deeper and more important stuff. A lot of stuff was on my mind when I was talking to you and a lot of stuff is on my mind now, but I pretty much told you everything. So that just leaves me to the part where I write what I need to work on and problems on my mind. However, like I said before, 2-1/2 months ain't going to cut it. There's no way in God's green earth that that is possible. However, I'm at least going to give it a try.

Mrs. Martin

Good.

F. Harris – Continued Journal Entry – 3/24/97

So here's a compact list of what I need to work on. Things I need to work on (in here and the outz)

1. My attitude
2. My use of profanity
3. Minding my own business
4. Respecting others
5. Respecting myself
6. My temper
7. My determination
8. Acting my age
9. Taking things one by one
10. Getting easily misled
11. Think before I act
12. Read more
13. Spend my time more wisely
14. As well as my money
15. Listen before I act or speak
16. Don't talk shit unless I'm going to do it
17. Don't talk shit unless I can back it up
18. Helping others out
19. Not being so shady or greedy
20. Stop hanging around fake people
21. Trusting in myself
22. Doing all I can for my folks and family
23. Stop affiliating with gang and activity
24. Stop talking back
25. Change my thinking
26. Change my ways

27. Getting closer to God again
28. Showing my respects and paying my debts
29. My impatience
30. My stubbornness
31. My female authority problem

Mrs. Martin

I agree with the list – some are more important than others though. I'd like you to number the top 5 or so you really need help on – write what you think your problem is – how it affects you and how you think you should be (or want to be.)

Now – about what's going on with you. Your whole demeanor and attitude have changed dramatically (LOTS!) I'm not sure I liked some of it that you handed me today. You seem to be having difficulty with me running my classroom, and that's a problem for me. If you see things I could change – let me know, but you need to understand that I am in charge – I'm the teacher. I appreciate every single thing you do for me and my classroom, but you seem to be starting to abuse your privilege. You also seem very angry – I'm concerned about that. Is it about me, someone else, situation, or in general? I'd like to know because you look and seem so sad. This afternoon you were angry – I'd like to be made aware if there's anything I have done or can do. Otherwise, when you're having a mood – I leave you alone.

This will be a long weekend. I hope it goes smoothly for you. Remember to use your journals as much as you can. Happy Easter! I wish I could send an Easter Bunny to see you guys this weekend!! Happy Face Sticker

F. Harris – Saturday – 3/29/97 – 12:20 p.m.

Top 5 Plus 1

1. Getting closer with God
2. My temper
3. My attitude
4. Change my thinking and ways
5. Stop talking back or giving input
6. My stubbornness and impatience

Was up Momma Martin? I read this; it made me so upset. You told me everything that was wrong with me and a little more. I'm upset about the situation because you were right about the whole ordeal. I am actin different, talking different, thinking different, all that. The thing about it is you are, were right about it's probably because of my meds. But I don't want to accept that though. I'm trying to fight my reasonings and thinking; trying to say that isn't right. But deep down inside, I know it is. That's why (well, one reason) I was trippin a little bit. I don't wanna think that's the reason. But I know it is. Also, just seeing the weather and thinking 'bout the crib is getting to me. When I got here, it was summer. It's damn near that time again. When I was walking into school, my momz, my boyz, my girl (well, my significant female); all that was on my mind. Like I said, I'm goin be in here for every damn holiday. I'm sick wit it. I like you telling me the truth, but it hurts sometimes when its something you don't wanna hear. Plus the stuff in the classroom where you think I'm trying to run it. I'm simply trying to help or defend you. At times I usually get mad because you take it the way as if I'm trying to run you, your class, or whatever. So when I do something out of good intentions at times you take it the wrong way. So it makes me mad

155

because I work so hard and do all I can to help and make you happy. When you start to telling me all this bad shit, it makes me mad and disappointed in myself. I know it's just the truth, and you don't do it to hurt me. It's just I don't like to hear shit like that sometimes. Hold up, let me rephrase that. I do like to hear shit like that; it's just the fact I ain't used to it. My folks and family tried to hide and disguise stuff from me. That's why I had to venture out and explore things on my own. I don't know, this whole place is starting to get to me. That's why I act so different so often. I ain't goin lie; I know I act sometimes, whether it's aggravating, annoying, stuck-up, etc. Sometimes I just gotta vent out my feelings and frustrations. Like before in the past, I used to occasionally refuse my meds because I felt I had to voice my feelings whether soft, violent, aggressive, etc. I knew my meds couldn't allow that. I'm not saying that's why I don't take 'em, know but in the past I did do that a couple of times. Like the time I went to SEG for tearing up the Day Room when I couldn't finish my G.E.D. the first time. I had to vent out my anger sometimes. I just need to do that. I think that's one of the most aggravating points about this place. It's good that it teaches you to handle and deal wit your problems. But some people can take so much. I'm just hoping I can handle it. My futures on my mind too. I had a visit not too long ago, and the whole visit we were talking 'bout my future. The thing about it is I ain't nowhere close to being ready. I got baby plans to maintain myself, but the thought of me going to school or having a full-time job or leaving my folks, I ain't even got to that point yet. I don't know once I build a plan or get a good view for the future, it seems like somethin happens to mess it all up. I don't know, every 'lil thing pisses me off. Not trying to be funny or disrespectful, but I be feeling like I be having periods or something. I just be having attitudes or throwing fits for no reason. Just me being sick wit this place. When will it stop? *H – 3/29/97*

Mrs. Martin

I'm sorry that truth/constructive criticism hurt –
I have a hard time with it too. It's always for the

best, and I'm glad you are able to see that part of it. I didn't mean to make you angry. I understand that you try to help me, and I <u>really</u> appreciate – what I want you to avoid is getting angry and getting yourself into trouble by creating more of a situation. If we can continue that way, no problem. I am concerned about you and your mission in this type of situation.

I know it's hard to accept the med. situation, but it's definitely affecting you and your performance – you also seemed much happier or able to tolerate more. Is that correct? I know you're tired, worn-out and sick, but let's make the most of the rest of the time you've got. Did you see anyone/visit this weekend? *H*.

F. Harris – Wednesday – 4/2/97

Was up? Man, today I'm so shitty. Coleman hoe ass put me on S.A.S. for some bullshit. We were in the dining hall, and I asked him if I could get some more pants when I got downstairs. He started talking shit. Then I said I'll mess around and catch a sexual overt. So then he started talking shit again. So I said, "Fuck it. I ain't even goin rap to you." Then this hoe ass dude put me on S.A.S. I was about to cuss his ass out, but I chilled. The whole rest of breakfast I as chillin, thinking about what happened just then. I wasn't goin trip though. Coleman been fucking wit me this whole week. But I been letting it slide. So when we went back downstairs, I figured I'd talk to him. It was almost time for court and meds had to be done. So I figured (when I was thinking earlier in dining hall) I'd take my meds, plus talk to him about my S.A.S. at the same time. When I tried to, he rushed me stating that he had no time because meds weren't through. I was so shitty. I even tried to talk and reason wit the nurse about it. But Coleman was still being a hoe. So I said (to another officer) could I go to time-out. But now Coleman had to be a hoe again. "We don't have time and we're not writing paperwork, Boy!" I just wanted to tag him off in his shit. I knew what that'd do. Then I figured to just kick a trash can or hit a barrel or something. I really, really, really wanted to. To tell the truth, I don't know why I didn't. I can't explain what stopped me. But I sucked in my anger and frustration and let go. But I'm still hot about the whole situation. For one, Reddington had got on there early for not accepting like me. But he talked to him and got off. Then when I try to rap to him, he ain't got time. Next he played me like a hoe; he refused to talk to me, then to let me go to time-out. The fact is he did it intentionally. That's some of the same shit, I clicked for in the past. Muthafuckas don't wanna hear me or play me like I'm some pissy 'lil peon. I'll fuck around and let 'em know. That was one of the reasons I went to SEG for when I missed my first G.E.D. test. Another reason is because this is my second S.A.S. for this 4 weeks. Plus Coleman has been actin real shady towards me lately. So I'm thinking I'm goin get an UNSAT. Coleman gave me an UNSAT before in the past for some bullshit. I ain't about to get an UNSAT again for no reason. If I do or think I am getting an UNSAT, I'm goin get one for a reason. Last is because of my meds. I took my meds this morning, and I'm feelin a difference already. It makes me mad cause I don't wanna take that shit. I don't feel like fuckin around wit these people in here. I'm fuckin sick wit all this fuckin bullshit. Sometimes I wanna damn near tear some of those bitches tryin to hold me back. I'm startin to want to shit wrong (wit or witout my meds). Everybody tryin to help me and talk to me and shit and I guess you could say it's workin, but, I'm really startin to get tired of this shit. These punk bitches don't wanna see me. They want me to click. I'm tryin to be cool. I ain't 'bout to trip over no muthafuckin S.A.S. But I will trip over these bitch-made stuff (not all, just the bitches) tryin to play me false and act like I'm a little hoe to pick on. I'm telling you it ain't about to be too many of dem dayz. SAT or UNSAT, fuck it. A year and a month ain't too much further to go. Just July. That's what some of these hoe ass bitches doin any-way. Fuck it you know what I'm sayin. I damn near live here anyway. And I did tell you I got one UNSAT to spare. I go to team next week.

But I don't really care. I'm just goin sit back and chill for damn near a week. If I find out I'm gettin an UNSAT I don't even know. And about my meds, I don't know if I'm takin anymore after today. I'm still contemplating!? *H*

Mrs. Martin

> I'm not even sure how to respond to you or if you want me to. I've not heard you this angry since you've been here. And your language is horrible – so hateful and vulgar. I also am hearing some paranoia about Sgt. Coleman – don't let him catch you up – show him you got more in you and you can deal with what he hands you. About your meds – they will affect you immediately and continue to level out your thinking, etc. You know that you felt better and were able to control yourself more while you were taking them – would you consider taking them just to get through your time here? Tell me what you think. How has Ms. Scott been able to help you? How can I help you. I feel like I'm really letting you down because I just don't know what to do for you. Tell me if there is anything. Otherwise I leave you alone.

F. Harris – 4/2/97 – 12:20 – Continued Journal Entry

A Ms. Martin. I'm sorry if anything I wrote down offended you. It wasn't meant to do that. You always tell me if I have something I wanna get off my chest, write it down. Then when I do, you question me. I know I ain't never talked to you like that before or wrote down so much hate and profanity. But, it's best if I write it down so you can read it rather than blow up on somebody or staff. This place is getting to me, and I'm tired of all these busters tryin to bother me.

I really would like your help, maybe if you play another movie, I could talk to you then. I kinda wanna be left alone, but I really kinda wanna talk. Ms. Scott gave me some half-way decent newz. Well, my minimum is June 4th, but Ms. Scott's going to see if I can get out on a parole board. It's gonna be the first week of May. Mr. Mayfield said he's going to support her 100%. So, I guess startin today they're going to dig in and research in my files to come up wit a legitimate argument to let me out in May at my Parole Board. I brought up the fact that my charges were supposedly concurrent, so that should be a legitimate argument. Even though I most likely ain't goin get out, it's at least a shot. Hopefully, Mayfield and Ms. Scott won't be the only 2 supportin each other. So I just pray to God that He looks out for me. He makes the impossible possible. I also pray that I get my SAT, so no disrespect towards you. I'm trying to help myself. I still feel the same way. But I feel a little better, and I did take my noon meds. I guess I'm going to start back. But, I'm still unsure though. So again don't take none of this personal. I didn't leave because of you. I left cause of all those trifling ass 'lil heathens makin noise, disrespectin and not listenin. You told me to not meddle in yo business. So before I got pissed off, I left. I just had to be alone. I still kinda do but I'd rather rap to you for a minute so I can let you know whats up.

Mrs. Martin

O.K. I accept that. I worry too much, <u>but</u>... it's only because I want you to do well, and I know you've been trying for so long. You didn't offend me – I've heard all the words and phrases – it's not new to me, but, it usually is new to "you guys" when you talk, think and write without it. I try to give you a chance to write without it to show you that you can. When you feel it's necessary – use it – language is language and journals are for expressing. I am very proud of you today for excusing yourself from class when you needed it. I do still want to try to explain about the room/

support deal. I like to have your support with the other students – I only want to avoid you getting too worked up to help me. See how this is – please don't distance yourself from these students – they need peer reinforcement and guidance. You should get some time with Sgt. M. tonight – I asked for it – have a good night!

F. Harris – Monday – 4/3/97 – 9:25

Was up Ms. Martin. I'm a little worried and upset about a 'lil incident that happened tonight. First of all right after you left, I got into it wit Franklin. He came at me as if I was a dope fiend. I was walkin towards the laundry room unsupervised. So Franklin runs and tells staff, "You know what happened last time wit those pills in the laundry room wit them." He said it as if I was involved in that ordeal. So I kinda got mad and told him about himself. Then Mayfield and Ms. Scott talked to me and calmed me down. I was really hyped. I was just upset. So that was the end of that. Ms. Scott said she wasn't goin let him talk to me like that. So she said she'd handle it. Anyway, about 20 minutes later I decided to take a piss. (urination) While I was back there, Keene and Farling were in the Southwest laundry room knuckling up. I ain't goin lie, I was in the wrong for not stopping it. I just didn't wanna get involved. So after a few seconds, I went on about my business. Next thing you know BOOM BOOM, clank, clank, thud. I don't really know what happened. But Butler, Martin, Ms. Pearce, and Wells. So to make a long story short, I had to stop Keene from going to SEG. So I told Martin and Butler they were horseplayin and to me it looked like it was because they both were holdin each other but aggressively pushin and tryin to swing. Anyway, after I told them they decided to let him go. Then all he got was L.O.P. But the other guy, Farling, was on there too. When they questioned him he denied it continuously. When they brought me back there, and I told he got to rappin to me. I just felt like splittin him. I didn't wanna disrespect Butler or Martin. So I kept my mouth shut. Ms. Gardner seen I was upset so she called Ms. Scott. We cooled out again, but I knew when he get out of SEG it's goin be some drama. And to tell the truth, I ain't even goin think. Once he get to rappin, I'm just goin tag him, Wham! Just like that. I'm not sure if I can contain myself. Another thing that made me mad was that after all that, Keene and Farling went to SEG anyway. And Martin and Butler came to me asking me why I lie? See, ma, Butler and Martin gotta trust in each other like that. So I felt like I violated. Even though in my eyes I didn't lie, it seems like I did to them though. So now I feel like they don't trust me. But I'm goin talk to Martin and see what's up. But to let you know for sure I know I usually maintain and control myself. But I'm just goin have to let myself get off mission for a minute. Before I do some right, I have to do some wrong (It's a saying). Anyway, it's just life. You see me write and tell you I'm goin do it or snap. So you have to figure maybe just maybe that it's goin to happen. I told you to trust me, and that's what I want you to do. That'll increase my faith and trust in you. But we all human, so expect a few mistakes. What Big Mart done said about me? *H*

F. Harris – Sunday – 4/6/97 – 9:00

Was up momma? Man today was horrible. Well not the whole day, just showers. You know how I feel about my laundry, and you know how hard I work on it. Well during showers Lt. Howard came and got about 38 rolls for upstairs. I had about enough laundry to clothe the facility. That wasn't the point though. It's the fact I put in hard work on the laundry. So after about 20 minutes, Lt. Howard called us for about 20 more shirts. I got mad because I'm tired of doing all the work. So me and C/O Bilbrey got into a verbal power struggle over some t-shirts. I was debating the fact Howard was only getting 10-15 shirts or how many over I chose. He was debating he was given an order he had to do it. I didn't really think of it that way. I just was protecting my goods. So it came down to where he grabbed me and told me to come with him, but I snatched away and told him he had me twisted. So he asked me a couple times to step out and talk to him, but I refused. Finally, Wells came and helped me out. We briefly talked so I chilled. I decided to stop passing clothes out and wash them. When I walked back to the laundry room, he had wrote me a major. Boy, I was 'bout to tear this up. So I hollered at Butler and Wells, told them I was goin to SEG and walked off. But of course they stopped me to talk to me. So I promised I'd chill. Wells said he's make sure I wouldn't get the major. But Bilbrey talked to me first and tried to find out why I tripped. But I was too salty to talk. All I said was if I get an UNSAT major or no major, I'm going to tear this up. So we talked for a couple more minutes. He had still decided to write the major. He had just wondered why I acted like that. Anyway Wells asked me what happened, and I told him. Right before I finished the story, Bilbrey came out so Wells told me to leave so he could convince Bilbrey to throw away the major. I left and about 5 or 10 minutes later, my major was in the trash. I was still mad though. And even though my major was dropped, I still felt guilty. So during court I calmed down and thought about the situation. I realized I made a mistake because he was just doin what he was told. So after court I apologized. I still feel bad. I didn't get a major or a punishment. Plus I totally disrespected him, and he looked like a fool. I told him that my apology wasn't good enough. I know that that doesn't justify my actions. I'm glad because team is this week and 2 S.A.S.'s is already bad enough. I don't need anymore paperwork. But I know I did something wrong, and I do feel a little guilty. I kinda regret it. I mean I don't regret what I did, I just regret who I did it to. If you have time, I wouldn't mind talking about it with you. I need your advice and opinion.

Mrs. Martin

No problem – let's talk or – you earned your SAT! Good Job and well done – you've come through a really tough time and a big decision. I'm real proud of you – I see the "old Fred" in you again – keeping _me_ on mission and keeping busy. You've been smiling to which I like to see – it will be so much easier to get to the end if you're not so angry and worked up.

As far as the laundry room goes – different staff do things differently, and I know that's hard to get used to, <u>but</u> we wll have to work together for the good of the whole facility. Sometimes that means doing things for others – that's a <u>good</u> thing not a bad one!

I think you need to make the decision about the meds on the outs. You've now experienced it both ways while you're in a controlled situation. Write about how you think you would be/act/feel on the outs taking/not taking. Think real hard and be <u>honest</u> – deeply honest. Look back to the marked page – how many of those issues are directly affected by how you feel at the time – are they affected by meds or not? And how? Or why not?

Now the issue about getting closer with God. Tell me about it. What does that mean to you? What things do you want to learn/know/read/hear? Are your family members Christians? Do you go to church here? At home?

Fill me in on some of this – how are you? ^{Happy Face Sticker} Thanks for all of the help and refocusing!

Stamp with 2 zebras that says: There's nobody quite like you.

Ms. Scott – 4/8/97

How do you think your siblings will react to the changed you?

Fred Harris – 4/10/97

To tell the truth, their reaction really wouldn't differ. They'd still treat me like their bad ass little brother. After a while, I guess they'd treat me different. They're so used to me being bad and getting in trouble that when I start being good, they'd have to grow into that too. Regardless of any reason, they're going to give me my respect for doing a year in the D.O.C. I think they might look at me a little different, like try to label me. An example if something come up missing or gone, I might be accused. So I'd have to really show my change and prove myself. But I feel their reaction will be the same until I actually prove my change. They will commend me on getting my G.E.D. and doing a whole year. *FH*

P.S. Oh, my sister, Lois, will expect to see me fail. She'll try to knock me or put me down any chance she can. *H*

F. Harris – 4/12/97

Was up Ms. Martin. I was glad to see you happy today. You made me happy and clown right along wit you. I like it when you're in your moods like that. It makes me feel more comfortable around you. You know how you got your business outlook, and regular outlook. I felt like I didn't have to be so serious and professional since you weren't. So I hope you continue to feel good and keep yo good attitude.

Mrs. Martin

Always feel comfortable to be you – have fun!

<u>F. Harris – 4/12/97 – Continued Journal Entry</u>

Anywayz about my medz. I'm still convinced that I'm going to try without them, on the outz like I said before. Freedom is almost my number one value now. You don't really appreciate Freedom until being by yo'self, doing and eating when you want, etc. become luxuries. Regardless of medz or not, I'm going to be so determined not to get in trouble. I won't need medz. I know, I have tried both with and witout. And to be honest, I feel I do need them (in here). I admit I failed the "witout the medz in here test." And I held up my part of the bargain. I take it again. I wasn't being as successful as I wanted, and although I didn't like the idea, I did it anyway. So now, I have to give the medz on the outz a chance. You should trust me. I did this time. I can do it again. Now to answer your question.

Mrs. Martin

I'm proud of you that you kept <u>your deal.</u>

<u>F. Harris – 4/12/97 – Continued Journal Entry</u>

1. If I took my medz on the outz, I would be more relaxed, calm, alert and aware to things around me. But the side effects every now and then make me lazy, tired, drowsy, and I tend to lose my appetite. If I get a job requiring physical work and strength, I'm not sure how I'd make it. But my overall, I'd be less of an aggressive, frustrated or violent person. I'd probably be real good in school too because the medz help me to concentrate.

Mrs. Martin

I see all of these as positive effects.

F. Harris – 4/12/97 – Continued Journal Entry

If I didn't take my medz:

I'd probably be a lot more frustrated. Being in here so long I'd mess around and try to take all my anger out on whoever steps in my way. I'd be a lot more bouty (apt to fight), less tolerable. I might find myself getting into a few arguments, but nuttin serious.

Mrs. Martin

These are very dangerous effects to mess with. I think how rough it could be.

(1) Act – Like I said before, chilled and relaxed. Not as much physical energy, but my awareness and alertness would be keen. I'd probably sit around all day and play video games unless I was in school I'd probably never wanna go because I'd be too tired.

(2) Feel fine. Other than knowing I'd have to take medz on the outz, I'd probably be a little more secretive or a little ashamed. But I've learned to handle responsibility, so I'd know what I need and what I don't need. So even though I may feel bad about it, I think I'll be able to make the right decision.

Mrs. Martin

I personally don't think it is anyone else's business but yours that you take meds – no one would need to know.

F. Harris – 4/12/97 – Continued Journal Entry

(1) Act – Like I said, a little more bouty, probably argue. This is just what I'm thinking. You never know what could really happen. I could blow up a building, or I could be the sweetest thing on earth. I just don't know. I've been locked up so long, freedom is going to be a new experience to me so if I don't, I'd just have to give it a shot.

(2) Feel – I don't know; depends whether I feel I need it or don't. If I feel I do, I'll procrastinate and make excuses why I don't need it or shouldn't take it. I'll do that until I need it for sure where it's a must. If I feel I don't, I won't.

As I look back at that page, I agree wit you totally. But that's still from the standpoint of in here. I took it when I realized I needed it. I feel I can do the same on the outz. Medz was part of it, but my freedom is and will be a part of it too. I ain't going to lie though, I might see myself needing them in the future. But when this happens, thatz when I'll start again. So that's how the med issue is goin be.

Mrs. Martin

Well, I'm glad you've made a decision about it, thought it through and planned.

F. Harris – 4/12/97 – Continued Journal Entry

Now about my relationship wit God. I feel it's good in all, but I just want to get into the word more and practice it's sayings. I was raised in church, but strayed away as I got older. All my family are Christians, excluding maybe 2, but I've been real close to God at one point in time. And I saw how good things were goin for me. I was so peaceful and cool. I didn't need no damn medz. I was in peace wit

God. I want to build that back up. I know and understand a little about him. There's still much more I want to learn and hear. I just be too lazy. I hate to read. I want people to read it and tell me about it. I need someone to break it down to me. Interpret it. I go to pastorial counseling in here and occasionally Bible Study and church. On the outz, I stopped going completely. I need to try to get that bond back wit God. However, there's not much you can do about that. I have to do that alone. *H.*

Mrs. Martin

I can always encourage you! I think it's very important that you take an active role in this par‐ticular issue of yours.

You are going to have to do some of the work – this one is on you. I have magazines, books, etc. if you're interested – I'll be glad to bring to you – All you have to do is ask – I'll check in – peri‐odically on it. ^{Happy Face Sticker}

Temper is the next issue – let's start with that one next. (marked page) Think about where it comes from? How it affects you and others, what do you do? Changes?

Ms. Scott – 4/14/97

You know Fred, since you've been here you've covered lots of emotions/feelings – everything from Anger to Grief to Silliness and everything between. I want to ask you about power/control.

– Do you feel more powerful than before, if so why?

– Who controls or owns your life? Is it different than before?

– How did you start to believe in yourself?

Fred Harris – 4/15/97

1. Do I feel more powerful than before?

I don't exactly understand what you mean. Physically, mentally, spiritually? In here, or the outz? What? Either way I do. In every aspect. Even though I ain't that much bigger or smaller in size. I know how to use and control my weight. I also know when I'm outsized or powered. But I do think I have got a little bigger.

As for my Spiritual power. It has increased too. A lot. I just be too lazy to read the Bible. I go to Bible Study every now and then too. On the outz, I didn't go to church at all. I believed in God and all and loved him, but I was never ready to change, or even try to make a change. So I do think that I've become a little more spiritually powerful. I never really put forth any effort. I wanted God to do all the work.

Mental. Pheww. Boy my shit's mental. I'm damn near a walkin, talking, poetical, lyrical, rhythmic, super slang, lingo, master mind. I'm a damn dictionary of wisdom and knowledge. (**Ms. Scott – "I agree."**) An intellectual, sophisticated street spokesman. I've learned so much. Like so many times I said before, all I knew was me and my crew. That's was all it was, no one else. If it was, they was goin get dealt wit. Even when we lost, I was always victorious. When I came up in here, it was South Bend, Evansville, Ft. Wayne, etc. All of 'em was damn near just like my set. Even 'lil niggaz from sets in NAP that I thought wasn't about shit, proved me wrong. So it opened my eyez and mind. I know for a fact that I'm powerful mentally. Back in the day, I always had to put my hands on somebody or get loud and wild to handle my business. I don't have to do that anymore (although I ain't completely stopped.) I know how to get my point across and let a person know how I feel witout cusin 'em out. (**Ms. Scott – "Good, See anger management and maturity = a powerful Freddy B."**)

As for me being my in power and control over my life. Hell yeah! Ain't no way to say it. Going back to that, I felt obligated, to fight, rob, thieve, etc. Somethin wit my guyz. There's been many situations where I could've avoided a fight or a shoot-out or something like that, but I felt like I had no other choice, but to whatever my boyz did. Not because I was jockin them, not because I was scared, or a hoe. Nuttin like that. It was just the love we got fo each other. Just like a gang when you see yo nigga or gang member in trouble. You gotz to help him out. Same thing wit us. We was gang, but we wasn't joined by the 6 or the 5, or by red and blue, or by fightin each other to get initiated. We was joined and bonded by our homie love, gangsta love, thug love, and our heart. We had to have the heart to help each other out, and be there whenever we need each other. I was as close to them as I was wit my folks (almost). I'd do anything for my folks, so that shows you that I'd damn near do anything for my niggaz. I ain't goin lie, now that I think back, my niggaz did have me going like a toy robot. I'd let 'em get me hyped up and all that. But then it wasn't control in my eyez, it was just my love fo my niggaz then. Another thing is that I used to try too hard to live like Freddy B. I wasn't tryin to impress nobody else, I used to do it for myself. What I mean, back in the day I used to do shit for the glory, and fame. As I got older, it stayed wit me. I did it (all the shit I did) because I had a passion for it. (**Ms. Scott – "Think of what you can do with all that passion now!"**) I'd sit and think in my head, hell naw, they can't talk shit to Fred B like that. Not because I was worried about what everybody else thought. I builded my reputation and status all my life. So when you have that you ain't goin wanna lose it, because you earned it. In the 'ol school, I was a little mischievous, but I did some stuff just for the recognition. After a while, it became a habit. Then it became a hobby. Then it became a passion. Me, who I was.

So after I built that up, I didn't do for everybody else. I did it because that was who I was. I was Freddy B, and I didn't take no bullshit, or go fo the okie doke. **(Ms. Scott – "? I'm not sure I understand! ?")** That was just me, what I was used to, what I lived and learned. But as time passed, I found myself doing shit just cause I was Fred B. Not cause I wanted to. It got me stuck because I wanted to change, but I had did so much to get to where I got. Now that I'm really serious about changing, I'm ready to stop tryin to live like "B." I've even been thinking about droppin my alias. Just so I could start off fresh. I got more than Freddy B. I gotta couple of names (but that's beside the point). People still goin be wantin people to see Fred B be Fred B, or whatever else. But since I've learned so much and observed so much, I know what I need to do to maintain my control and power. I've gained incredible control and power over my life. I know and see where I made mistakes at in the past. So I think I have got more control and power over myself and life.

2. Who owns my life?

    I own my life. I have control of my life. I've always had control and power, but I'd let people influence me to right and wrong. Even if they (my friends) had control over me or my life, I gave them the power to do it. They didn't put a gun to my head. I did what I did. Why I wanted. So it's changed in a way, but it's the same in a way too.

3. How did I start to believe in myself?

    I really didn't have no other choice. I had to believe in myself. I'm wit me 24 hours a day. I can be supported by everyone else the rest of the time I'm here, especially when I was thinking so hard, and problem solving things so complex. I couldn't talk or tell no one else about it. I also was (and still am) trying to figure myself out. **(Ms. Scott – "Everybody struggles with who they are!")** How I think, why and what I do certain things for? Or why this or that happened to me? I had to start working things out wit myself. If I didn't, I'd probably do the same shit I've been doin because I never would've understood or figured out why I did what I did. So, since I really decided to make a change for real this tine, I figured I'd work on wayz and things to do to avoid getting in the same situations. Before when I said I was goin make a change, I was never serious. I was just talking. But since I've been through some shit, and thought things through, I understand I gotta do this shit for myself. So in order for me to get through this, I gotta believe and help myself. But if I didn't (believe in myself and start depending on myself), I'd be so strung-out and in trouble it be ridiculous, so ridiculous. *FH*

Straight-up Ms. Scott, we gotta find some better choices, options, or assignments. And I didn't like your big, big assignments. For my project, we gotta think about something. *FH*

Freddy B – 966846 – 4/17/97

Ms. Scott – 4/17/97

Nice job, even though it wasn't the best topic(s). O.K. Fred, I have no idea what we can work on – We will try to think of a project tonight!

I know I tell you a lot how wonderful you are – but I need to tell you that I really care about you and your progress. Fred you are such a different person, than when you entered the D.O.C. Listen, Fred, I know it's hard, but keep your head up and keep focused!

I read your poem to my Mom and she was really impressed – See I told you – It was fab!

Straight up Fred – We have to think of something for you!

Ms. Scott – 4/17/97

I know you are going to hate me for this, but I am curious of your "before" life. Was drugs a part of it? Is there one particular event you remember that changed your life?

AS ^{Happy Face Sticker}

Fred Harris – 4/19/97

Well, I really ain't got no assignment. But to let you know, there's some stuff about me you don't know or that I might have twisted the story. I ain't goin just rush into it. I'll tell you things about me slowly and gradually. I'm still a mystery to you and everyone else, believe me. Some are secrets, some are things I lied to you about. (**Ms. Scott – "Unbelievable?"**) Some are just things that make and have made me the way I am. I'm goin tell you a little, but not everything. I gotz to have my own 'lil privacy.

Anywayz this ain't really shit, but I twisted the truth a little. Back when I first came and they was askin me all those questions. One of 'em was about weed and drinkin. I said I only smoked and drunk once. Boy, I was lyin my ass off. When I was on the outz, I was an off and on smoker. I ain't smoked no crazy shit like dope or rocs or pills, none of that 'ol bullshit. I smoked straight herb, weed, chronic, mary jane, indo, green, donk, bluntz, phillies, doza, dodie, do-do, killer, marijuana, reifer bud, etc. You know what I'm sayin. Anywayz, I probably first started smoking when I was 13 or 14 years old. My older hog, turned me on to it. I basically looked up to him. He was about 17-19. He lived so care-free. He was the weed man. He smoked it, grew it, ate it, knew it, lived it, all that. He was even smart as hell.

174

Even smarter when he was high. He had women, money and always greened out high than a mothafucka. He had always pressured me, but I never did it. I don't know why I decided to that night. But, we was in his car, and back then joints was in (bluntz is in now). So he had a fat ass joint, right. And you know I told you how I'm known for being down. Well, my younger hog was around us too. I couldn't back down. That's some of my reputation I built up (I ain't proud of it now, but it was something I thought I had to do). Anyway, when I smoked it, I damn near choked. But all of the smoke I inhaled and maintained. It straight busted my face. I was so toasted. I was cheesin the whole night. From that point, I started kickin wit him, and he was telling me all the rules and ropes of weed. He also busted my shit for free. He even gave me a plant, so I could grow my own, but it died. **(Ms. Scott – "So Fred doesn't have a green thumb.")** After a while, we lost our contact, and I stopped smoking weed. I would only smoke when I was at a party or celebration. Along wit weed came drank. "Drank and clank made a nigga thank." I wasn't really a dranker. I just drank so I could get to back Cloud 19. Sometimes (most of the time) I didn't even know what I was drinkin. I was just partayin (party'n, chillin, clownin, depending how used) wit my nig-gaz. I never was addicted or hooked. **(Ms. Scott – "How do you know?")** It was really just on an occasion, when my nigga had some, or if somebody was tryin to fleece some for a player price. When I got older and partying and goin to the club got old. It wasn't shit else to do but to smoke weed. I was never at school, or never had a job long enough. So to make the day pass or have a half-way decent day, I'd blaze a sack every now and then. Then I started working at McCyds. It was this white dude that worked there that was a straight fiend. He smoked anything. I sold him some weed a couple of times, and we blazed up a blunt a few times. Everyday after work, I damn near smoked, because my nigga from across the street always had a fat ass sac. Anywayz here's the crazy shit. One day the white dude at my job gave me a player price on an oz. of green. I calls my buddy before I leave work to let him know we was goin to have a smoke out. He tells me he got 1-1/2 oz. or 2 oz and some drank. Shit. So I was like fuck it. I goes to the crib and my guy was walkin down the street. I meetz him half way. We went to an abandoned house and got to cutting up Swishers. We had over 10 bluntz and weed still in the bag. We got everything arranged and organized before we started. I forgot to mention this was in the time period of November 1995 thru February 96. So it was snow outside. Anyway we blazes up blunt after, after blunt, after blunt. We had some 'ol nasty M.D. 20/20, but it didn't matter. I was just tryin to get fucked up. So after about 4 or 5 bluntz, my partner gave up, while I'm still takin. I was so fucked up. I didn't know what I was doin. My nigga was stedy splittin swishers but wasn't smoking 'em. After about 7 or 8, he joined in again and smoked about 2 mo. After that I was gone. Spliffed out. I don't really know how much more I smoked or drank. We had a decent ass rotation. Blunt, drank, Newport Cigarettes increased you high. I don't know how or why, but they do. So finally, I got tired of burnin my fingers and coughin. So I got my last sip of the drank, and got me a to go roach. Awe I forgot to tell you, I ate about 3 roaches. I don't know if you know what a roach is or not. It's the end of, very end of the blunt, or joint. It's so little you gotta smoke it wit yo fingernails. Eatin roaches fucks you all the way up. So I walked back to my crib wit my nigga. My dad was gone, so I finished my last blunt, went in the crib, turned on some music and chilled. All of a sudden, the music started getting slower. I thought my tape was messed up. I checked it, but it was fine. I turnz it on again. It's still slow. My vision got hazey. I was blackin out, I started sweatin, my mouth and throat was dry and choked. My heart was beatin fast one minute, then normal, but I could feel every beat. I started trippin, like if I had smoked dope or something. **(Ms. Scott – "You did smoke dope! Interesting way to handle this situation.")** I got so bad that I took off my clothes, ran outside in my draws and prayed to God askin him not to kill. I was burnin up hot and couldn't breathe. I was so fucked up, I really thought I was goin die. My buddy was laughin at me and freakin at the same time. He was laughin because he knew nuttin was wrong wit me, but he was freakin because I was really actin strange. **(Ms. Scott – "You're right – I'm laughing a little.")** Anyway, I got to the point where I decided to call my mom. But she was on her way home wit my pops. My buddy kept threatenin to leave if I called, but she wasn't there so it didn't matter. I didn't want him to leave because I thought I was really goin die when he left. After I did all my crazy 'lil shit, I said fuck it and called 911. My buddy straight vamped. I wasn't goin die, I was just goin pass out. But I was too shook up to realize that. So after about 8 minutes, I couldn't take it, I ran outside wit no shoes and socks. I was goin next door, but as I was headed to it, the Fire Truck hit the corner. I ran back and they followed me. When we both went in, they strapped me to all this equipment. I didn't understand a word they said. As they was doin, police came and my parents did too. The cop wanted to know where the rest of the weed was. And my folks wanted to know what was goin on? I really don't know what happened after that. I just remember layin on my back on a stretcher headed for the hospital. I got there in about 5 to 10 minutes. And stayed about 3 hours. Come to fine out, after an X-ray of my lungs, I had burned a hole in my lungs. (Ms. Scott – "Aw, sounds painful.") It was from all those roaches. I was way over my being high limit too. I took a few pills and water and found out my weed could've been laced. It means, wrapped in, sprinkled, mixed, combined. Like my weed could've been laced wit dope. Not sayin it was though. But, it's possible. My parents were cool because I told them that, that was my first time ever. That's why I reacted that way. They had no other choice but to believe me. They had never known of me doin anything involving drugs. So I used to my advantage, saying that I was trippin so bad about it, because that was my first time. After that I ain't goin lie, I smoked about 3 or 4 mo times, and I damn near reacted the same way each and every time. I had went through it before so I knew how to react. But I didn't even really care til about the 4th time, and I hung it up. My lungs retired. I didn't smoke cigarettes on a regular basis. I just smoked them after a blunt. And I only drunk when I was celebratin or just plain tryin to get split. I don't do none of 'em no mo'. But when I get out I know everybody goin try to bust my face. To tell the truth, I probably will smoke one more time. As for alcohol, hell naw. Liquor is nasty as hell. I don't know how people can drink it. When I drunk I was so high I couldn't even taste it. So I know drinkin ain't goin be no problem. Weed ain't either, it's just I know I'm probably goin be tempted, because I get the urge in here every now and then. I ain't no fiend or addict. If I did smoke weed, I would a couple times and no more. I ain't tryin to fuck around. To tell the truth, I think you should try it. Not sayin now. You could try 10 years from now. Just as long as you try. You hear all the talk about it. It wouldn't hurt one time. (I sound like a pusher don't I?) (**Ms. Scott – "Yes."**) A matter of fact they're safer than cigarettes. You ain't gotta listen or believe me. I ain't really tryin to influence you either. Experience is better than he say, she say. Believe me.

H

Freddy B – 966846 – 4/21/97

Ms. Scott – 4/21/97

Fred –

O my God – The story was good and interesting – Now I don't mean to sound like an old person, but is it really O.K. with you to look like a complete fool in front of everybody just to chill?

I do agree. Experience is better than people's word, and I need to know did the hole in your lung heal?

O.K., Fred, earlier in this assignment, you said you lied about some stuff – was it only about drugs or was it about other things too? I guess all people lie to a certain extent – no one is 100% honest. So would you be willing to let me in on some of the things you've lied about – not all necessarily have to have been lies to me, just anyone? I know it is important to keep some mystery alive in the Myth of Freddy B – so only tell what you feel comfortable telling. O.K.?

Talk to you later,

Take care – I am proud of you!

Ms. Scott

<u>F. Harris – 4/18/97</u>

Was up Mrs. Martin? Yesterday I talked to Ms. Scott, and she said they don't do concurrent sentences. I was so hot. First of all, she usually sees me last every Thursday. The last two Thursdays she's been dickin me. She's only seen me about 15 to 20 minutes each time. She seen Delong yesterday. He was all worked up and cryin cause he can't go home. So for some reason, I mean I know she had him before, but she goes and gets him. He already gotta counselor, Ms. Gibson. I only got 1 counselor and she be actin so shady towards me. I understand that 'lil Delong was hurt and sad, but, damn, Ms. Gibson can handle that. If Ms. Scott goin do all that she might as well just take him back. She damn near see him as much or even more than me. I know it kinda sound like I'm jealous, but I ain't. I'm just upset she keep dickin me. What if I'm cryin or hurt or need to talk to her. You know what I'm sayin? I ain't got 2 couonselors. Well, I kinda do. You! That's why I always be doin stuff wit you because you don't bis me around like she do. You always be there for me. You always have, and I know you always will (at least while I'm here).

Mrs. Martin

Whenever you need me!

<u>F. Harris – 4/18/97 – Continued Journal Entry</u>

Anyway, the real purpose of me writing was to tell you that I most likely won't be leavin in May no more. I guess they gotta call back from Henry, and he said they don't do them (concurrent sentences). Ms. Scott said she would double check wit Henry the next board, because she thinks Ms. Boyd mightv'e got things twisted. Plus she was goin spit a 'lil game to him about me tryin to butter him up. Most likely it still won't work, but who knows. It made me mad because now it seems that I ain't got no chance at all. So it went from like 20 somethin dayz to like 48+ a wake up. Who knowz though. I'm goin keep prayin 'bout it. *H*

Mrs. Martin

> Hang tough my boy – what <u>needs</u> to happen will happen – of course that doesn't mean that you'll like it – things happen for a reason. I believe that. We can then choose what we are going to do with it – move it in a positive way or let it drag us down more than life, things, and people already do! I'm really sorry that you're disappointed and the law wasn't what people thought. I also hope you don't get your hopes up on someone's "game playing" skills. Be true to yourself and continue to work on your issues to better ready yourself for release. Thanks for all of the help lately! Have a <u>good</u> weekend. Happy Face Sticker CM!

<u>F. Harris – 4/21/97</u>

Was up Ms. Martin? How was yo weekend? Mine was shakey. I damn near missed my visit, because me and Hooten almost got into a fight. I got a minor, it was only for loss of rec, because I was dunkin. I cussed out about 2 or 3 officers and a rec. staff (C/O Healey, C/O

Wilbur and Coach Sutton). Wit or witout my meds I've been so so shixxy lately. Even today Hooten and my 'lil guy, Mike Massey was about to bump, and I know they was goin try to jump him, which got me involved. Plus, I got so called traffikin, so I'm on a S.A.S. time-out thing. People's been sayin they've seen me act more arrogant or aggressive. Like I told you, these boyz is pissin me off. I'm runnin outta tolerance, and patience. I'm not even really worried about the consequences either. If it wasn't for that visit on Saturday, I was goin split Hooten, Mike Massey's 'lil ass. Meds ain't got nuttin to do wit it either. If I want to split somebody, medz or no medz ain't goin matter. I try to realize the big picture of my 40+ days count, but that just makes me more hype. I'm ready now, not 40+ dayz. I don't even know or think I can maintain. I mean I can, but if this ol' bullsxit don't stop, I'm goin snap on a boy. Straight up. It'z always a confrontation or problem every single day. I'm doin all I can, but I know my tolerance is wearing thin. I hate that I feel like this, but I can't be cool and peachy creame. I'm even worried that I'm goin get an UNSAT. I haven't worried about that in a while. Not sayin I am, but, if I keep it up, I know I will for sure. Writing in my 2 journals is very good, but it's not the real yaw. I need to think of people, ways, and things to do to keep me calm. Laundry ain't doin the whole job. I need some help and suggestions. *Freddy H.*

Mrs. Martin

I'm glad you had the visit to keep you focused – there's <u>always</u> something to look forward to that you'll miss – remember that. No one expects you to be cool all the time, and you've figured out that coping skills are what you need. Probably a good idea would be to identify a staff on each shift that you can go to when you get to your limit. Also you need to come up with some ideas of things to do when you get to that point:

- time outs

- journaling

- I think also – rec time you could use to get out some of the extra energy and built up stress by really getting into a game of basketball or football – something active, physical and mind escaping.

Take care; keep working on it, and I will too! CM

4/23/97

Was up Ms. Martin? You know I'm mad right. You left me hangin, plus you didn't even tell me you weren't going to be here. Now I'm in Ms. Kennedy's class watching "Top Gun." I hate that movie. We gotta watch it the whole period. I don't know what we goin do after lunch. Right now I'm playin chess, but that's so boring. I feel like goin to sleep, but I can't. I'll get in trouble. I really ain't got nuttin to write about. I just wanted to let you know, I'm mad, you straight played me false. That ain't even cool Ms. Martin. I'm goin remember that. Ain't nuttin really happened. Oh yeah, I forgot I got put on S.A.S. for talking in the T.V. chairs. Coleman put me on. Me and Bernie was playin cards in the T.V. chairs, and we was talking a 'lil bit. It's cool though; I got off before 4-12 and worked Dining Hall. I got a little worried about my behavior. So I talked to Sgt. Corey, and I told her to put me in her special lines for line movements and dining hall. So far, it's worked pretty good. I ain't even really been on there a whole day. But I know it's going to be the best of my benefit. And after talking to Coleman today, he doesn't seem too upset wit me about that S.A.S. So now I got an S.A.S. and a minor for Loss of Recreation. Other than that I should be cool. I just gotta maintain. Forty-4 + a wake up. *H.*

<u>4/24/97</u>

Man, Ms. Martin, was up man. You b.s'n. When I need to talk to you, you gone. I need to talk to you more than ever, right now. I'm jugglin options in my head concerning SEG. Today I almost lost it, and chose SEG over something petty at that. It wasn't the fact over the consequences, it's why and what it happened for. Today, I got put on S.A.S., me and Bernie (again) was arguing. C/O Fitzgerald was talking to us about arguing. So Bernie was playin around as usual telling Fitzgerald I wasn't acceptin and to put me on S.A.S. I said, "Whatever, Fitzgerald would never put me on S.A.S. That's my guy." So Fitzgerald to prove a point and make an example goin put me on S.A.S. If he was goin put me on there, he shouldv'e put Bernie. Plus he shouldn't be tryin to make an example outta me. If he goin put me on, he goin put me on. So at first, I thought he was playin. He got to talking to me 'bout some ol' bullshit sayin I ain't goin make him look like a fool in front everybody. I kept tryin to explain to him that, that wasn't my intentions. I was sayin we was real cool, so he wouldn't do it. So he kept on rappin that ol' bullshit walkin me back to S.A.S. So when we got there, I told him for the last time to stop playin wit me. He said I ain't playin, then he grabbed my arm. I snatched away and told him I wasn't playin wit him. That's when Coleman jumped in. He was telling me don't snatch away from an officer, and I'm going to sit down and all this other bullshit. So I chilled and sat down. I was still so shitty and still am. Venable walked out; I explained what happened to him. All he says is, "Talk to your counselor. Whatever." Then Fitzgerald comes over there meddlin again, rappin that ol' bull-shit. Then I don't know what happened. I just went off. "Fuck that." Venable grabbed my shoulder, but I got to rantin and ravin down the hall. V.A. (Venable) and Fitzgerald both followed me back tryin to talk to me. I was so shitty. I was ready to knock Fitzgerald's old ass out. I threw off my shirt and my headphones and ran towards time-out. V.A. kept yellin, "It ain't worth it" and shit like that. Coleman came back there after he heard the commotion. My fists was balled. I was cryin and breathin hard. I wanted to either bust a window or somebody's shit. While V.A. and Fitzgerald are talking, Coleman intervened and asked to talk to me personally. They didn't wanna leave because I was still 'bout to explode. Fitzgerald was still talking that ying-yang after Coleman asked them twice to leave. Talkin 'bout if you're angry take it out on me. Coleman told them to leave again, so they left. Coleman wasn't even shitty wit me. He even congratulated me on maintainin my temper. Then he was telling me that SEG ain't worth, I'll still be on S.A.S. and all this other stuff. He told me not to let it get me down and mess up my whole day. I didn't really say nuttin, but it was stop movement, so he told me to throw cold water on my face and go back to the dayroom. So that's all that happened. I'm a lil' pissed over the S.A.S., but it's all that bullshit Fitzgerald was stressing, and the reason he put me on there. I don't even wanna get off S.A.S. I wanna stay on there. I'm ready to be like "Fuck it all." I wasn't even goin take my meds, but like I said I put my promise and trust in Sgt. Corey's hands to help me out. At first, it took Healey and to radio the nurse and tell her I refused get up and tell her I refused. That made me mad because they did that just so the Superintendant could hear it. Like I give a Fuck. When I'm shitty, "Fuck the world," so I don't know shy they tried to threaten me wit that. Anywayz the nurse came out there and talked to me for a minute. I still refused though. She got Sgt. Corey over there to start rappin and pickin wit me. Finally, I decided to get up and take them. So I took it, but it don't matter. Sgt. Corey told me to stop poutin cause I'd get a vote at lunch. But I don't even wanna vote. I don't want shit. Just for people to leave me the Fuck alone. I'm real, real, real shitty because you're not here today, and you won't be tomorrow. A lot of stuff can happen in 5 days. I'm tryin to keep myself cool. Thinkin 'bout the crib, my 43 and wake-up count down. That's all fine and dandy, but I know if I get upset wit somebody, that I'm just goin mess around and smash a boy. I wanna talk to you. I really don't wanna talk to nobody else about my problems. Ms. Renlin tried to talk to me. I know she real nice and sweet, but I only feel comfortable talking to you. Even Ms. Scott, I might tell her, but not as in depth, or not wit as much feeling. To tell the truth, every time I talk to her, we basically just bullshit around, or talk about other people and other stuff. You really the only one I talk, talk to about my problems. I don't even talk to my momz and pops like that. I just usually tell them or explain things to them. I don't really get in depth. If I was out, I'd tell my momma everything, but now I'm in, so it's stuff she really don't know. Every now and then though, I try to show her or let her understand. So I gotta cope by myself for now. Ms. Scott is supposedly seeing me tonight, but the last 2 Thursdayz, we only rapped for about 10 to 15 minutes. I'm 'bout to be through wit her completely if she keeps bullshittin me. She ain't even goin be here for my next team; she's barely goin be here for my parole board. I can damn near promise 99.9% that ain't shit goin happen on the 6th. I might mess around and get an UNSAT. Things have been fallen apart. One day be so good. The next be a nightmare. I just pray that I don't have this much trouble 5/6 to 6/4. Shitz getting so hectic. I'm goin crazy in this place. I seem to be getting into trouble, conflicts and drama everyday. Medz or no medz. I don't know what it is. When you read this, I'll either be cool, more shitty, or in SEG. Most likely I won't go to SEG. I usually avoid that. But I could get into a lot more mischief, which I pray that don't happen, but I'm goin try to be cool. I feel a lot, I mean a whole lot better after writin in this. Shit 4 pgs and about an one hour of writing. I know you see how much work and effort I'm puttin in myself tryin to be cool and good and get out. I just hope everybody else knows or seez it too. *H*

4/24/97

A Ms. Martin. It's about 2:15, and I'm still in Ms. Renlin's class. During lunch, I had a chance to get a vote. I chose not to though. I don't know why I'm so damn stubborn. I plan to stay on S.A.S. for 15 dayz. I know I won't follow through wit it, but I'm goin try. I feel like I'm giving up. I know it sounds petty over S.A.S. It's not really even over that. I'm tired of getting dicked around like a hoe. I wanna do something so bad, but if I do this, I don't think I will trip as much. I even feel like I wanna get an UNSAT so I can have a reason to tear this place up. That's how I feel, but I don't wanna do it. So I think I'm usin this to get me an UNSAT purposely so I can vent all my anger, frustration, and animosity from today and the past. Ms. Renlin kept talking to me, and I finally told her the external problem. Me bein on S.A.S., but I didn't tell her how I feel, and the part about me 'bout to go off. I think I'm 'bout to go back to just dead-mouthin it. Talkin gets me in trouble. But if I bottle it up, I'm goin explode. I know this is really no big deal and nuttin to get worked up over. It's just 10-1/2 months of this shit. It ain't the first, and it ain't the last. I don't know what I'm going do. *H.*

Ms. Scott – 4/21/97

Fred – O.K. Fred, earlier in this assignment you said you lied about some stuff – Was it only about drugs or was it about other things too? I guess all people lie to a certain extent – no one is 100% honest. So would you be willing to let me in on some of the things you've lied about – not all necessarily have to have been lies to me, just anyone? I know it is important to keep some mystery alive in the Myth of Freddy B – so only tell what you feel comfortable telling, O.K.?

Talk to you later,

Take care – I am proud of you!

Ms. Scott

Fred Harris – 4/25/97

Well you wanted to know so much about me, so here's a 'lil bit about my female thing. I ain't goin be able to tell the whole story in depth because I'm goin forget some parts and pieces of it. Plus, I don't really know where to start. But first of all, my viewpoint of females changed quick as a younsta. When I saw how easy it was just to say something to a girl to get her to turn it out, or how many neighbor-hoods turn outz it was in the hood, you'd understand what I was sayin. As I gotz a 'lil older, hoez was all bout getting a nigga to trick off his scratch. So those were just a few things that I just observed. As for my personal experiences, it was one instance that really changed me and futurely changed my name. Like I said Freddy B is just one of my many names. The B stands for something, and each individual letter does too. F.R.E.D.D.Y. B. all stands for something. Freddy B and F.R.E.D.D.Y. B. have nothing to do wit each other either. But they both apply to me. Anywayz, this story's got a lot of insight on me. And you might understand where I'm comin from about the female tip. This is goin to be long, because I'm goin try to tell you this whole situation. I might miss parts, so if I do I'll try to put 'lil footnotes by a place it applies to or somethin. Anyway, here it go.

Well, at about 6th to 7th grade, I had pretty much had a good percep-tion and experience of sex. I was real young, so it wasn't really noth-ing. When I did have sex or relations wit a female, it wasn't really because I liked her or wanted her. It was for brownie points wit my niggaz, just experience, or just to do it. When I was younger, all the ladies thought I was cute, but never would really holla at me, either because I was chubby, or because I was 'lil bad ass Freddy who every-body was cool wit. I didn't never trip though. I'd ask a girl to holla, and they'd be like, yeah he's cute, but we just real cool. I remember when hoez used to talk to me about dudez they liked when the girl that was telling me, I wanted to holla at. Well I got a 'lil older, thinned out, gotta 'lil gear, and hoez paid attention a 'lil more. I wasn't as cool as I was wit 'em no mo. I was getting a 'lil more attention. I started havin a 'lil bit of endz too. Anywayz, I'd say after I got expelled my 8th grade year, I think, that's when I started tearin it up. I started doin my thang getting scratch on my own, clothes, all that, gold, shoes, gear, fresh fades. Boy, I was getting back. When 9th grade rolled around, boy I was rappin to all kinda chicks. See N. C. (North Central High School) in Nap, the high school, is the high school to 3 middle schools: Eastwood, Westlane and Northview. When all the new chics rapped about me, then all the old brauds wanted to holla then. I didn't really trip though. Girlz wanted to rap me. I didn't have to pass messages, or slip in smooth game. Ladiez did what I was doin to me. But of course, I didn't stay at N.C. for long. I got expelled again. Back in business again. Doin whatever it takes to get paid. That only lasted for about one week though. I had to stay wit my auntie off and of, because I enrolled in a public school, I.P.S., my first one, Washington. Boy when I.P.S. girlz see a township boy, cute or ugly, it'z on. I swear, so many girlz asked me, what's yo name, what grade you in, etc. Most of 'em was older, so when they found out I was a Freshman, they didn't bother, but to say cutie every now and then. But it was still some Juniorz and Sophomorez that wanted to holla. But I was new, so I had to chill for a minute and peep out the scenery. After I got settled down for a minute, my nigga getz kicked out of N.C. too, so he comes to Washington too. We ended up clownin in that school. Runnin from the principles, security, all that. Well anywayz all that trouble endin me either in I.S.S. (in school suspension) or out of school. One time I was in I.S.S., and finally peeped out the girl I wanted. She was in I.S.S. too. I loved a girl wit heart, and had a 'lil bit of thug in her like myself. Anywayz, she was tall, about my height, slender, she had a maroon tint in her hair, wit the prettiest hazel eyez you'd ever see on a fudge flavored female. She was beautiful in a thugz eyez. The way she carried herself, talked, looked, moved, everything. I was peepin her, but I guess she had peeped me before, way before I.S.S. We couldn't talk, so we communicated through her buddy passin letters across the room. I found out her name (Tasha Pullins), age, (17), grade, (11), address and phone number. Come to find out, she only stayed 2-1/2 houses away from my auntie. (The ½ is because she stayed in a double). I could tell that I wanted her, and I was goin to get her and do whatever to get her and keep her. I didn't call her the first night for 2 reasons: 1 was I didn't wanna make it seem like I was sweatin her, 2 is because I was goin to see how she reacted. If she didn't say nuttin, she really didn't bother. If she questioned me, then she must've been really interested. So she did question me, so I figured I'd really give it a try. This was kinda like the first time I gotta girl I wanted, instead of someone who wanted me or a 'lil hood rat. So, I was goin get her. I was convinced.

I started ringin her, we had some deep ass conversations. She was even on house arrest during all this. Come to find out, she done did damn near as much dirt as I done did, been locked more, more fights, all that. I was like damn, I never rapped to a township girl like this, not even a hood rat or a neighborhood turn-out. I knew we was goin just goin to click like that. After school every now and then, I'd sit and rap to her for a minute before she had to go in. She had a gang of brothers, but we really didn't have no beef. She had been goin wit Cooper off and on for about 4 years. Come to find out though, she used to go wit this dude named Cooper (who was from that hood.) (He was like 18 or 19 at that time). He had got her pregnant a couple of times. She had ran away and did some crazy shit, which led to some of the reason why she had got into so much trouble. She had been in a gang of fights (hands up) wit him, her brothers, mother, everybody. She even wanted to fight one time for fun. I didn't but that ain't the point. After a minute of contemplating, I had to figure out if we was goin to hook up or what? We had got so close the only thing was she was on House Arrest and culdn't have no company. But it didn't matter though, I wanted her, so I had a chance to get her, so I took it. When we started goin together, all kinds of shit started poppin off. I was hearing rumors that she was a Highland Hood Horror. That's the name of the street she stayed on. That she still went with Cooper. That she had all kinds of diseases and she'd burn me. Even a few niggaz in school told me they hit or had the chance to. One night I even damn near got jumped by some of the niggaz that lived in tha hood (It ain't my hood.) (I think it was some niggaz that went to Washington that was Cooper's 'lil peons.) Anywayz, Tasha was a mind playin, manipulative seductress. She convinced me that all them niggaz was just player hatin, and that they was jealous they couldn't have her. So I paid it no attention. Shortly after all that she got to talking 'bout me and her havin a baby. How pretty it be. That we (me and her) wouldn't get in trouble no more, or break up if we had a 'lil baby. At first I was like hell naw, but she got to rappin to me and rappin to me. So I considered it. Once I did that, she made a whole 'lil layout. She already had the plan for the baby (if it was a girl or a boy). So one day, she told me wasn't nobody goin be at her crib, so I could come over after school. Shit, I didn't mind. So I went over her house after school, and we did what we had to do. But she manipulated me to have sex wit her witout a condom. She knew I didn't have one, and she knew, she didn't either. But we both got caught up in the heat of the moment. And like I said, we did what we did. Next thing you know, she rappin 'bout she pregnant. It wasn't even that long after we had sex that I found out. Another rumor had spreaded that she was already pregnant by Cooper. I still didn't pay no attention though. That's when I really fell head over heels for her. Just thinkin or knowing she'd be my baby momma. We had all kinds of plans. We even was goin get tattooes of each other's name on our arm, and the baby's name on the other. Between me and you, that's what's on my arm or what was on there before I tatted something else over it. I had changed the plan that I was goin to do it wit a razor so it will always be on there forever in my blood. I did minez on my left, wit a razor. Tasha was too long. So I put T.A.S.H.. After that it wasn't too long before I got expelled again. That's when shit started getting crazy. All kinds of niggaz was telling me that she was tryin to get on. During school! People was telling me, she had been over they house and all that. I still didn't trip because most of the time I was on the phone wit her. She'd skip class and call and most of the time right after school too until one day her momz had found out she was pregnant. So Tasha ran away. Didn't go to school or nuttin. You know she was on House Arrest, so her momz and the police was lookin for her. She'd call me every now and then, but she would never tell me where she was, or what was goin on. Everybody was telling me she was wit Cooper. So I questioned her about it, but she denied it, and still wouldn't tell me what was goin on. At that point, she damn near had me ready to go right wit her. I guess you could say at that point, I loved her, and was in love wit her. I didn't want nuttin to happen to her. I was even tryin to get a job, so I could build up some scratch. She's the one who got me to do it (getta job). All my methods, back then was strictly illegal, but she convinced me again. I didn't have a job, but I was lookin for one. Well, after a while, Tasha got locked up, but didn't stay in juvenile nuttin but about 3 to 5 dayz. When she got out, she was hot as hell (horny) (which no mention made me think what she was doin when she was on the run). So she said everything was cool wit her, and her momz and that she'd be gone again that week, and she wanted me to come over. She also told me, that Cooper wanted to kill her, because she was pregnant by me. She told me she seen him while she was on the run. They was goin scrap, but didn't. I was trippin because I had seen and heard about Cooper. From what I peeped and heard, he wasn't shit. Well anyway her momz left late a school day and Tiffany didn't go to school because she was sick (yeah right). Since I had got expelled and damn near jumped, I didn't stay over there that much. So I went to my auntie's house a 'lil early and waited til school let out. Her buddies was goin keep an eye on the house. When the school bus came, Tasha was at the porch waitin. So we goez in, and conversate for a minute. Tasha tells everybody the game plan if her momma come. Her 2 buddiez was goin distract her momma at the door. While I sneaks out the back. So we rapped for a minute wit her buddies, then we went upstairs. While we was upstairs, her buddies downstairs, went halfway down the street talking to some nigga in tha hood. So wasn't nobody in the crib, but me, her and her dog. We didn't know they was gone. Anywayz we was sittin upstairs in the bed chillin. I decided to put my pants and shit on. But before I could, I paused because I heard footsteps. After I paused, I didn't hear it anymore, so I didn't trip. Then all of a sudden, the door started creakin open. And that's when it happened. It was Cooper! He was drunk or something comin in Tasha's room lookin through shit, throwin it around, all that. So, I'm like, a nigga what the fuck you – ….. But she told me to be quiet, she'd handle it. So they sittin there rappin for a minute. He disrespectin and all that. Next thing you know after they exchanged bitches and hoez and all that, they got to fightin. She was on the bed, and he charged her He didn't really swing, they was wrestling. I'm like fuck that, I ain't 'bout to let this shit ride. So I rushes him. After 2 steps, he flashes his pistol and tells me to back up. So it wasn't nuttin I really could do but get blasted or watch. You know which one I did if I'm still here. I was so shitty though, I was about to cry. Finally, Tasha got up and got to taggin on him. Cooper couldn't even hang so he steps back and kicks her in tha stomach. Turnz around and starts runnin. I was about to

chase him because that was my limit, but Tasha was cryin too bad so
I held her. We go downstairs and her buddies come back in talking
'bout they seen Cooper runnin down the street. I couldn't take it, I
wanted to kill somebody. Her buddies was talking bad about me
anyway, plus they had to get some help for her. So I gave Tash a kiss
and all that, told her I loved her and all that and left. After about 3
or 4 hours, she calls me up. She had got back from the hospital. She
came to me wit all kinds of bullshit sayin she had twins, and they
gone and all this and all that. She also said when she see Cooper
again, she was goin pop him. I told her not to but she had her mind
made up. Anywayz, we had a long talk, about everything. Our whole
relationship and all that. So she finally decided to tell me that the
baby or babies weren't mine, that they was Cooper's. You don't know
what I felt. I cried my ass off. Not right then, but on the inside I did.
And after our talk, I cried my ass off. When she told me that I didn't
say too much else to her, but, why didn't you tell me, why did you do
it and how could you do it. After she fed me a bunch of bullshit. I
just hung up and cried and cried. I got played. My so-called true love,
we had so many plans and things to do. I couldn't believe it. She
called me and tried to give me her I'm sorry and sad voice. Talkin
'bout I didn't wanna hurt you, and I didn't know when to tell you. I
don't know I guess I was really in love cause I actually listened to her.
But I still wasn't fuckin around wit her no mo. So after a good 2 or 3
months, when she found out we was through, I mean really through,
she got to doin some silly shit. First it was prank callin. Then it was
prank callin, but actually talking to me, like "Fuck you" and "I'm
goin beat yo ass." Shit like that. Then she finally started playin games.
She'd call my house, wit a baby by her, it be cryin or somethin. Then
she'd either be like this your baby, 'lil Fred, Jr. or other times she'd say
it was 'lil Cooper. That shit really got to me. Even though the baby
wasn't mine, and she supposedly had a miscarriage, she still didn't
have to take it to that level. That really just hurt me. I tatted her
name on my arm. She didn't even get minez on herz. She was mad I
wouldn't holla at her, so she spread all kinds of rumorz and bullshit
about me, saying I was a pretty ass punk. I'm a hoe, I couldn't hang
wit her, she only wanted me for my looks and money. Bullshit like

that. Thatz when ladies wasn't nuttin, bitches, tricks, hoez, slutz, trampz, doggz, skeezers, skanks, etc. That's when I had my mind made up to dis any female (excluding family, but wit some exceptions to family) I could. My motto was, "Fuck 'em and leave 'em." I looked so old, I used to rap to older females, 20 and up. I used to have them take me places, and buy me stuff, then I'd just stop talking to them Tasha's T.A.S.H.. got re-razored over down the line. (But that's in a different story). Anyway, I ain't goin lie, down the line, it almost happened again, 1 and 2, ½, ½ times. The one is me and this girl (the glamour shot picture of the pretty coffee flavored female wit the red on) wasn't really planning to have a kid. But if we did, we did. The other 2-1/2, ½ (two halves) is girls I didn't love or really care about, but I got them pregnant. I can remember one time I met this 20 old lady at a V.P. at about 1:00 a.m. in da morning getting gas in my stolen Camry. She thought I had hella scratch. So I made sure she kept thinking it, along wit the Camry being my car. Her name was Kathleen and she already had a baby, a 'lil girl. I could tell what kind of female she was off the jump. So I dogged her. Not really dogged her, because her intentions were to dog me. That's what I told her and the way I acted. I portrayed myself as an innocent Northside, spoiled brat, at age of 18. I did and could get whatever. She figured she could hustle or get me to trade my lute on her. Boy did I clown. First I spent the night over her house a couple of dayz. To get comfortable (this was when I was on the run a while back). When she figured I was stayin wit her, I left. Then I got her to the point where she wanted me back. So I'd go, stay for a day and leave. She'd blow my pager up. I'd go and wouldn't even stay a day. So one day, she come to me wit some bullshit about she pregnant. She was talking 'bout she was goin keep it. So I had a plan for that azz. I set her up. First I told her how old I was. At that time I was about 15. Then I told her I'd have my mom press statutory rape charges if she didn't have an abortion. At first, she was like fuck it. We both goin to jail, me for child support I guess. But then she thought about it, and hated the fact she got played by a young ass nigga. So I forgot the time, but after 6 to 8 weeks of pregnancy (I think) it's $300 or $350. She wanted me to pay half, but I told her upfront. I ain't payin you shit, so I didn't. Even til this day, she says I owe her $150. The crazy thing about it is, she still be fuckin around wit me. She was like fuck it. I done already slept wit you, ain't nonbody else gotta know. James was and is the father to Kathleen's 'lil girl. So we still (or used to I don't know) be rappin every now and then. I almost got shot over her too. Same thing wit Kathleen, like Tasha. She had a dude named James, he was about 23-25. He was a killer, no bullshit. A big mutha-fucka. Anyway, one time when I spent the night he came over about 3:00 a.m. in da mornin. I was on the couch in my draws. She was in a shirt. So when she went to the door and opened it as far as the chain lock would let it, he seen enough to know what was up. A nigga in boxers on the couch sleep and his baby's momma wit a t-shirt on. He started rappin, but she was quick to slam the door in his face. I really didn't know what happened, because I thought that whole situation was a dream. It wasn't til that day that I found out otherwise. I don't know what James did, but he must've waited til we got up and left, so he could follow us. We was rollin in my Camry, just rollin around. After about 15 minutes, I noticed that the same canary yellow Buick was following me ever since we left. When we had got to a stop light, that's when I found out who it was. It was James. We both had our windows down (it was summer.) So he got to rappin. I wasn't trippin because this time, I had a 45 colt under the seat. So I'm sittin there at the red light in the turning lane. His buddy opens the door wit a bat in his hand, bout to walk towards me. Then James pulls outta strap too. So in my paranoia, I smashed. I told Kim about 10 times to grab my pistol. But she said she wasn't getting involved. I could've grabbed it, but I was too nervous because they was still following me. So I kept my hand on the wheel. Finally, they seen the police rollin beside us, so they vamped out. That including a couple other times explains why I always rolled straped. (But that's another story). Anywayz, those were a few examples and reasons, why I did some of the things I did to females. Especially all these young black ladies. All (damn near all) of them is horrorz. That's the way I've seen 'em, that's the way I treat 'em. So after a few rendevouz wit a couple femalez, all my niggaz gave me my nickname. My boyz, after they seen what I used to do and how I did it, they said damn, Fred, you straight be breakin bitches. So from then and that point on, I was Freddy Break-a-Bitch. Freddy B for short. Don't nobody know none of my names, but me and my niggaz. I really shouldn't have told you, I still don't know why. But if I ask you something, you better tell me if it ain't too personal. I was goin tell you a 'lil more about me, but that's about enough. I was goin write you some more, but you wanted to hear this so bad, so I told you.

Freddy B

4/28/97 – 7:45

Was up Ms. Martin? I'm still mad at you, that you weren't here Wednesday, Thursday or Friday. I'm still mad, because when Ms. Scott be bullshittin me, I know you there. But you weren't. I know you can't be there for me everyday, all day. But you didn't even tell me or nuttin. I thought you done jumped state or something or quit. You done been gone so long. I hope you be here today. I ain't goin lie, I kinda miss you. When I was shixxy that Thursday, everybody was like is it because you miss Ms. Martin? I did because I wanted to talk to you. But I feel better about that whole situation now. Not really better, but I'm cool. My weekend was cool, except for yesterday. I was 'bout to click on these boyz yesterday (staff and student). My parents came to visit me at 9:00. The visit was over at 11:00. We was talking 'bout our financial problems. So I'm goin have to getta job when I get out pretty quick. My social security runs out in September. I turn 18 in August, so I'm goin have to do some real good job huntin and try to getta job so I can help out. The thing is I'm still not ready to take that responsibility. But ready or not, I'm goin have to. We discussed a couple other issues, but it wasn't that important. Anywayz the way I almost went off was because after my visit, my parents got stuck up here. Their car wasn't gas in right so they was stuck. I didn't even know, because I had went straight to D-Hall. When I got through around 1:00, my folks was still here, but Sgt. Ellis had been out there tryin to help them. Ellis let 'em use the phone but AAA and all that other stuff was closed. So they called somebody else, and gave them directions. I don't know when exactly they left because the car is still out there, but I didn't know that at first. I was real worried and upset because I figured no one knew how to get up here. So I thought my folks was stuck up here. But when I finally found out they was gone, I started getting mad because I couldn't getta phone call. On the 4/29 I damn near cussed out every C/O on the unit tryin to use the phone. I was so worried, I didn't care about nuttin. I ended up usin the phone anyway, and tried to apologize to everyone after I found out what happened. I kinda felt bad a 'lil, but not really. My parents are first, and my first priority. I just didn't wanna handle the situation like that. Other than that, my weekend was fine. I slip damn near everyday though. It seems like something just something, 'lil or big always pisses me off, especially wit these new staff. C/O's come and go, like that. It's harder for me to adapt to them, and it's very hard for them to adapt or understand me. I think that could be a 'lil bit of it. Plus, the chargin rules. Wit this new superintendent, it looks like he's goin be changing a lot of stuff. So I gotta adapt to that. Then by the time I finally get to getting used to it, it all changes again. Or when I do adapt, it's goin be time for me to leave. And then I'm still goin be doin all this stuff in here, out there. I don't know, every soldier has troubles at the end. Wit 38 dayz and a wake up, I'm finding myself almost at the hardest point of my time, Stayin on my P's and Q's, knowin that if I mess up that, that's my summer, or 18th birthday. Or just anotha 30 dayz. I'm doin alright, but I'm struggling. Wit team comin up in less than 2 weeks, I'm getting worried.

I've done some things to where I could see why a staff gave me an UNSAT. I don't know, I'm just goin pray on it. I just hope that things can go the way me and my folks planned. *H.*

P.S. Oh my God. You still ain't here. I can't believe this. When are you comin back?

4/28/97

Momma, you still gone? Somebody told me you ain't comin back too. You can't do this to me. How can you leave me when I need you the most? I hope you ain't gone for real. I really can't believe this has happened. I don't even know what to say.

4/29/97

I heard that you would be gone for this whole week. I hope you come back earlier, but I don't think that's going to happen though. Ms. Pearce gave me your letter. It made me feel a lot better to know that you are comin back. But, I'm still kinda worried because from the looks of the letter it sounded like you were sick or in the hospital. I don't know though. I hope you aren't. If you are, I pray you get better. I've been so mad, because you ain't been here. Time is winding down, and I want you to be here til the very last day. I really appreciate you sendin me that card. I'm goin put that in my poetry book. See now my poetry book is goin be something like yours. Wit pictures, poems, stories all that. So I'm goin put yo card in there. I'm still goin write in here too. Ain't nuttin new really goin on, so I don't really have much to write about. But if something does, I'll be sure to write you. So, I hope you doin O.K. And I miss you. So come back soon. *H.*

4/30/97

Ms. Martin.... I'm in trouble. And yesterday was one of those. I damn near went to SEG dayz. This time I was saved by the grace of God. And even though I got saved, I still gotta major. My first major in like 5, 6, or 7 months. Let me tell you the story though. C/O Wilbur on the 4-12 came in yesterday in a shitty mood. I was goin to D-Hall, but barely got to work because he was goin put me on S.A.S. right before I went. But I bit my tongue and went to D-Hall. Now we (me, Bernie and M. Swenson) came out of D-Hall a little early. Me and Bernie was telling jokes the whole way down from D-Hall. When we went in the Day Room, Bernie made a little joke, so I laughed, gave him a little nudge and was like hell naw you a clown. Then Wilbur goin say, I'm on S.A.S. for horseplayin. I kinda laughed it off, but I didn't say nuttin. So, I walked over to him and told him "I accept," but I didn't do nuttin. So he tellz me, either go to S.A.S. for horseplayin or go to SEG for battery. So I say "Battery"!! You call this battery (I demonstrated on him what I did to Bernie, but I barely touched him). Then he sayz "Now you jus battered me. So you can go to Seg for 2 batteries, or S.A.S. for horseplayin. I said whatever you goin have to take me to SEG and walked off. (I know I should've just went to S.A.S., but I was too shitty. I had to walk around and do something before I cussed his ass out, or worse!) So he walks behind me (I'm thinking he goin do it right then, or try to P.R.T. me). He tells me to go down the hallway wit him. So I did. We get to the Time-out doors, and he tells me to put my hands on the wall. (See I was thinking I was either goin to time-out, or he was goin counsel me). I'm like man you got me Fxxd up, and walked back down the hall. I was tryin to get Wells before I went to SEG because I knew, he was goin try to take me. Plus I knew something was goin pop off, because he wasn't just goin let me walk off. I getz halfway down the hall, and he get to telling me to stop, and put my hands on the wall. But you know I wasn't 'bout to stop for that dude. So he grabs me. Now we face to face. His arms was on my biceps. He tried to turn me around, but I tellz him get up off me. Why you grabbin me. He tries again, but I tells him again you need to get up off me. I know he couldn't get me if he wanted to on his good day. Then he just grabs me holdin me wit my back against the wall. That's when I got too shitty. My voice got loud, and I got to huffin and puffin and ballin my fist. I was about to unload on him. I told him, "Look bixxx you betta get yo muxxxxxxxx hands up off me. So he didn't (and couldn't) do nuttin. But he did start talking shit all up in my face. Whatcha gonna do uh uh. So I letz him know I ain't like these kidz boy! You can't throw me around like them. I bet yo muxxxxxx ass bixxx! Now he scared, because he's powerless. I could've just let loose on him at anytime, and if he would've let go I would've beat his ass before he even hit his button. So he just holdz me waitin. And that last comment about beatin his ass, got Wells attention. So he told Wilbur to let me go. But he didn't. So Wells tellz him again, "Let Him GO!"!! So he does. Then Wells talked to me in T.O. Long or Butler wasn't there so he called Howard. After Wells explained it, Howard told me straight up, "You ain't goin to SEG Fred. So that was that. But Wilbur persisted, talking to Howard. My counselor and Wells and Howard all had my back. He was braggin to some kidz in S.W.

He swore to God that I was goin to and if I wasn't, I was goin be on S.A.S. and getta major. So since I didn't go to SEG, he wrote me a major for threatenin and intimidatin. Ms. Scott helped me a lot because she took me to her office for about 45 minutes. And it wasn't even my day. So I was cool because it was bedtime when I got outta her office. I didn't know nuttin 'bout the major till this morning til Coleman served it to me. I was so shitty. Wilbur didn't even write how he threatened me wit SEG first. He just wrote about when I went off. You know how Coleman is. I was afraid he was goin let me have it. But he was kinda cool. He said he hated to give me the major, but he had to. Plus he said, "It's still a chance that he would give me a SAT. But if I'm guilty, it's questionable. So I ain't had my C.A.B. (Community Advisory Board) yet. So there's still a chance. Sgt Corey and me had a talk too. She's on my side as well. So it's really 50-50. It all depends on the C.A.B. This is my first major in like 5 or 6 months. So I might getta 'lil lee-way. But, Sgt. Corey and Coleman let me know anymore trouble period til next week, I'm goin getta UNSAT. So at first my intentions was to tear it up. But I still gotta chance. So I'm just goin wait and see how my SAT's lookin. Plus, just cause I get an UNSAT don't mean I getta extra 30. I only need 3 SATS and I got 2. So if I get UNSAT this time, it really don't matter because I need to make my next one regardless. But they might try to give me a whole extra 30 dayz. That's when I might have to go on ahead and tear it up. I don't want to, and I know it will cause more trouble, but I've come too long to let a rookie ass wanna-be, punk ass C/O get me an extra 30 dayz. I damn near got all my women to have my back, you, Ms. Scott and Sgt. Corey. Now I just need Coleman, Long and everybody else. There's still a chance. Probably more than I think. I'm just over reactin. Everybody wants to see me go home, and they tryin to work me. So I think I can still make it. I really can't say what I'm goin do, or how I'm goin react if I getta UNSAT. The future's unknown. I say it now but be the next trip (or stroup) later. So I jus hope the future doesn't hold extra time. *H.*

5/5/97

Was up Ms. Martin. I'm really glad you back. It might not seem or look like it, but believe me I am. I'm just shitty today (for a lot of reasons), and a 'lil nervous, because tomorrow is my parole board. I'm cool I guess, I jus don't feel like talking to anybody. I've been a lil stressed this weekend. Thinkin 'bout all kinds of things. I got some more Ivy Tech books I've been lookin through. Plus, I finally went to my C.A.B. for my major, and I was found not guilty. So, that's good. But I'm still worried about my SAT and my parole board. And I'm thinking about a few things that I'm goin to do when I get out. Financial things, court things; it's a lot of stuff that's gonna have to be done when I get out. I'm just in my own lil thing right now, but I'm cool though. Jus thinking 'bout a few things. Thinkin 'bout the crib and my folks too. I'm sorry that I ain't in a good mood, or showing how glad I am to have you back, but I am real happy to see you. And hope you won't be gone like that again.

P.S. Here's my major and the verdict Ms. Sally Clark (the D-Hall Supervisor) came up wit. She said it was more of a "Refusal to Comply."

Mrs. Martin

Believe me – I am glad to be back! I didn't know that I was going to be gone, or I honestly would've told you ahead of time. I hope you can believe that. I had no intentions of making things difficult for you or leaving you with no one to talk with – had I of been available to trade journals or talk to you, I would have. I don't like not being here – you guys are what I do and love. I won't be gone like that again – that I know of but people do have situations that come up in their lives that have to be dealt with. It was necessary for me to be gone- even though I wanted to be here.

About your major – why were you so angry? Just the situation? Person? Time? It sounds like it could've been a real big problem situation had Ofc. Wells not been there and able to talk to you. I'm glad you were only <u>talking</u> and not acting – I'd like you to explore or admit about your anger a little more.

Meds – where are you <u>now</u> with them? I hope you do what you think is best for you to do – not what people threaten you with, but what is actually best for you now in your life and situation.

I'm interested about how you're feeling, with and about your counselor. What can I do? – What do you want her to do?

I know it seems like a long time before you leave – but look how far we've come – tomorrow will be fine – you will be fine. If you want to talk tonight after dinner, let me know. I have time – plus, I owe you quite a bit. Thanks for helping Mrs. Renlin so much!

5/7/97

Was up momma? I know you probably like nuttin pleases me. I find out I only got 1 month to go at Parole Board. Then I get my SAT today, and it still seems like I'm upset. Well, I really ain't shitty, I'm just playin it cool. I ain't tryin to get set-up, or in any trouble. So I'm tryin to refrain from talking, only when I have to. So far that part's been workin good, but all the times when I want to say something, and I don't, it makes me mad, and gets my blood to boilin. I ain't talked to nobody really, but I have snapped (just by raisin my voice) on a few people, because they like to play wit me. See it don't feel like I gotta month left to go. This is goin go by so slow too. I'm goin be thinking about the crib a lot. So every now and then I might look a lil down. And I can tell already from the way this day is goin that you probably gonna need to come over here for a lot more counseling sessions. I'm goin be so unstable, because I barely made it through this SAT (Thank the Lord). But regardless, my intentions are the same. I'm goin get my SAT regardless. And I will go home in June. I just don't know, what all obstacles and trials I'm goin run through. Oh, another thing is, last month I really didn't work on my main problem. But you already know it's time to work on my releasement and future plans. So if you still down, I want you to help me wit that. But before that, I gotz to work on my cards for Mother's Day. So don't forget, like you already did. *H.*

Mrs. Martin

Yes, I've noticed the mood and attempt to not talk – my response to that is – you may end up making yourself miserable and feeling like forever before you leave. I'd like you to think about the times when you were writing a lot – working in the A- Building – taking on other students to help – and dealing with conflicts and problems – time flew by – I can't even believe it. I don't think it's real healthy for you to keep all of this bottled up inside. As far as talking with you – I'll always make the time if I can. We can work on what_ you're ready to work on. You let me know what help I can give you – I won't bother you about any of it – you need to be ready and accepting to work.

I would like to see you do a Mother's Day card. I apologize I gave you the wrong date – my days have been off – since I was gone.

My momma, my princess, a black queen none the less A nurturer, a provider, a helping hand in distress

No woman, no female, no lady, no other

Can even come close, or compare to my mother

There's no way I can express, all the things you have done You went to so much trouble and pain, just to have you a son Even through the bad times, you stood by my side

Never embarrassed, or ashamed to say, "Frederic Harris is my son" with pride

And although I've put you through so much pain and sorrow Forgive my actions of today.

There's always a silver lining for tomorrow

So don't worry, it won't be long until we're back together I promise not to leave you again, we'll be together forever

So fear not, and don't trouble yourself, cast all your worries away I want you to feel great. So you can celebrate another

Happy Mothers' Day

By: Frederic W. Harris [May 1997]

<u>F. Harris – 5/12/97 – 9:00</u>

Was up momma? Man, right now I'm so shitty. It's over something petty. (the situation). But the overall reason of what happened and why it was takin. Tonight during laundry (I mean showers), Ms. Lockhart came to get some towels. I had already sent some to the south end, but she wanted some more. So I give her 2, she asked for some more, so I give her 2 more. Then she tells me stop being possessive and give her some towels. That made and always makes me upset. After about 8, 9, or 10 months of doin laundry my way, she comes and tries to tell me to run it differently. Plus, Wells is NW1 permanent officer. So sometimes she works our end when he's gone, but when he's here, I'm supposed to do stuff my way and keep everything in check. No extra or no shorts. But she always tryin to hand out everything. I'm not used to the rotation. Anyway, so (I was a 'lil sarcastic) I gave her all the towels, and in a sarcastic tone, told her here take everythin else in a smart alec way. Well, she got upset, and promised I wouldn't work laundry ever again. So I was mad about that. Then she worked in NW. The whole time it wasn't nuttin but arguing and bickering from Ms. Lockhart to students. I was writing in here and couldn't finish because it was so much commotion. So I walked out and began writing witout permission. So she got a 'lil upset, but she wasn't doin anything about it. Dirks (new C/O) saw her talking to me and called me down to his end so we could have a rap session, but she still wouldn't let me go. I begged and pleaded, but she demanded compliance to her d-mouth, but I hadn't said a word. I asked her a couple mo times, then just left. Before I got out the threshold, she called Long on a Signal 8. Long promised to give us hell if she had to call. So he was coming as I was leaving. I rapped to Dirks for about 20 minutes, waiting til Long came out and went back to the dorm. When I got back, they talking bout kickin me out to the Southside. Ms. Lockhart said I and 3 other students caused trouble. Long said write they names down and they gone. When I found this out, I left again to talk to Long. He was a 'lil mad because he had pleaded my laundry case to the Lt. and now my name was on the list. I begged and pleaded not to get moved, but he said nuttin's for sure unless it happens. So this looks like it might end up in a troublesome situation. How will I keep occupied or relaxed or maintained witout laundry? Or how will I maintain wit the Southside ass hoez? I just don't know? *H.*

5/13/97

Today I gets put on S.A.S. Sgt. Coleman said I disrupted line movement, so I didn't argue.

Mrs. Martin

Good for you for accepting your behavior and not arguing.

5/13/97

Plus I really did disrupt the line movement, but I wasn't alone. It was other people as well and the thing about it is, is that I got set up. See Bernie and Pickett are both so very playful. I'm not sure if they intentionally tried to set me up, but they did. Afterwards, Pickett was jokin around, saying, 'S.A.S., S.A.S.' trying to make me mad. It was workin a 'lil bit too. But I wasn't goin let it get to me. And at first I was gone let this S.A.S. get to me too. But it"s petty.

Mrs. Martin

Best Ever

5/13/97

So I gotta look at the big picture of 20+ dayz left. So this other than yesterday is my first bit of trouble. But I don't even think Long is goin move, and I don't think Ms. Lockhart went through wit that laundry room thing. If she had, Sgt. Coleman would have confronted me about the situation. So I'm just goin go head be cool and get off S.A.S. *H.*

Mrs. Martin

GOOD CHOICES – You really have a handle on what's happening and what's important. I can't believe it's only 20 more days – it is going <u>fast</u>.

A small S.A.S. – I know you can deal with – you said yourself you were playing a little – you have the chance to get caught – the sneak get away with it, but eventually get caughtup.

I'm proud of the thought process you've developed – you really seem to be able to think through things logically – <u>before</u> making rash decisions.

AWESOME JOB ^(Sticker)

Fred Harris – 5/13/97

[Journel Entry To Ms. Scott] A straight up, that was some bullshit you did out in the hallway today. That was some petty stuff to be doin. You goin confront me about talking to Ms. Pearce and Ms. Martin. The way you came at me, was so fucked up. You goin try to talk to me like I'm some kind of little petty ass A.S. peon. You act like I can't talk to nobody else or nuttin. You might be shitty because you had to come in to work when you had a doctor's appointment. But don't ever in yo life come to me wit some petty ass bullshit like you did before. I swear to God, I told you from the jump if you ever try to play me false, or act fake, phoney, or petty, I'd straight up bounce. Then you pull some bullshit like this today. Talkin 'bout you done worked wit me on my problems for 11 months. Yeah, alright. You gave me my first journal in December and didn't really pay no attention to me til the new year. So from July til December or January ain't no 11 months. Matter of fact, we just started to work on job and future shit recently. Not 11 months ago. So don't be tryin to come to me wit no bullshit like that cause I ain't goin for the okie doke. You tries to confront me today like I'm some type of hoe. Why this, where that? None of yo damn business. You got yo own personal life like I do. It may not be that much in here, but I do still got my own personal shit. So if I want to go talk to elementary, high school, or middle school kids, I can. I don't need yo permission to do it either. You tell me to be honest wit you, so I am. Right now I think you actin like a medalin, childish, jealous azz tactics. But I never would of thought you'd be so jealous and hateful just because I talked to Ms. Martin and Pearce. I ain't doin shit else in this book, and you don't have to bother talking to me anymore. If you gone keep comin to me talking that 'ol sidewayz backward ass shit. Then you can save it, cause I can't fade you. So this is it will be the last assignment thing that you gone get from me. I ain't 'bout to put up wit no jealous azz player hatin.

F. Harris – Thursday – 5/15/97

[Journal Entry To Ms. Martin] Well it sounds like you already know what happened yesterday, but I don't think you understand it in full detail. So I'll just briefly tell you what happened. Yesterday on the bus a lot of people was disrespectin Ms. Jones. When we was about to leave, somebody kept sayin, "Bitch, She a bitch." So C/O Rogers made me and 5 other people stay on the bus. We stayed on because Rogers wanted to find out who said Ms. Jones was a bitch. So I was just sittin there quiet the whole time. Didn't say shit, I had nuttin to do wit any of it. So Ms. Jones snatched up a few people tryin to act hard in front of her husband. So she get all snappy wit me; I still didn't do nuttin though. Then V.A. (Venable) made a comment that whoever said "bitch" ain't gonna get away wit it. Then out the blue Ms. Kennedy goin say, "I believe that was Mr. Pickett." The whole time she knew but didn't say shit. And I'm tryin to be cool and accept all that bullshit, when it could've been all avoided if Ms. Kennedy would've said who did it from the jump. So I getz mad you know runnin off at the mouth. But nuttin really disrespectful, then Ms. Jones puts me on S.A.S.. I told her I ain't did shit. Then I was mad at Ms. Kennedy for not sayin shit. Then I told her I shouldn't even be out here if she knew who did it. V.A. had my arm behind my back because he already knew what was about to happen. So I was against the swearin to God; I wasn't goin sit on S.A.S. Then she said, well then you gotta go to W.2. I didn't wanna gonna to SEG, but I wasn't sittin on S.A.S., so I already knew and they did too what was about to happen. So they grabbed me. I resisted of course which tore up my wrist a 'lil bit. I struggled for a minute. Then C/O Wells, my dude, my ace grabbed me, took me down, choked me, then busted my nose. Even after my nose was bleedin he was still choking me. Talkin 'bout don't resist, I wasn't resistin. I was tryin to breathe. So they shackled and cuffed me, ready to take me to SEG. Sgt. Corey told 'em to take me to T.O. (time out), but Ms. Jones wanted me to go bad. So Wells and Corey tried to talk to me, but I wouldn't talk. So finally Wells put me in T.O. The whole day Wells was tryin to be cool wit me, and say he was sorry it's his job and shit like that. But he got some personal enjoyment or brownie points, because chokin me and bustin my shit, compared to just P.R.T.'n me is 2 totally different things. Sgt.Corey put me on S.A.S., but I didn't even know she did (I figured it but I was too shitty to sit there). So this morning I getz a major, my 2nd one in less than a month. Then I get all shitty wit Riddle because he putz me on S.A.S. for receiving a major. I get to cussin him out. Damn near probably 'bout to go to SEG again. So to stop from messin up I go to T.O. again, 2 for 2. So Riddle being the player hater he is, talks to Corey this morning. She's shitty wit me. She confronts the community about arguing about S.A.S. and when you getta major you will be on S.A.S., etc., etc. So I ask to talk to her privately. So she tellz me to wait while she calls Riddle for support. So as everybody lined up, I was in the Sgt. Office talking to Corey and Riddle. The reason I'm so shitty is because Sgt. Corey said I could and maybe get an UNSAT from her. The way things are lookin wit 2 S.A.S. and a major and not so good reports from a staff and a Sgt., it looks like I might be here for that whole year, plus. Man, my last month is a shamble. Sgt. Corey, who used to be my ace too, is now not lookin that way. Ms. Gardner called her and she was on the phone. She knew what had happened, so she wanted to see if Ms. Scott can get through to me. I told Ms. Gardner I was through with Ms. Scott but really didn't say why. So now if I really do follow through, I don't think I will have as much help from Ms. Scott. Corey and Scott are real cool. But if I fall out wit Ms. Scott like I'm gonna do today when I show her my journal, then I know for sure I'm gonna have to bite my tongue. Everything's goin wrong. 21 dayz and a wake up left, and I'm getting majors and S.A.S.'s and cussin my counselor out in my journal. Straight up Ms. Martin, I'm so stressed out I'm breakin out wit stress bumps. I feel like I'm goin go crazy. I feel trapped and lonely. I just wanna cry. I do sometimes, but I can't let everybody see it because it'll be used against me. Plus a lot of younger guyz look up to me. So I can't make it look like I'm givin up. But there is one thing, if I do or think I'm getting an UNSAT, I'm mostly likely goin tear it up. Too much work and pain, hard, hard work, I just can't let that happen. I don't know what to do or say. I'm tryin to maintain but have so much animosity on my chest. Feelings of resentment and hate. I fear for what's up ahead for me because it ain't lookin good. *H.*

Mrs. Martin

I am really sorry you are having such a hard time – but we need to evaluate why you are feeling this way and what's leading you there. I'd like for you to think about it for a bit and try to process it.

What can you do about the stress – my suggestion is to request to see the doctor ASAP – talking about it helps too.

We also need to explore your self-esteem – you've done a lot of work, and you should be proud of it – not set yourself on planning to fail and prepare yourself for it.

F. Harris – 5/19/97

Today has already started off on the bad foot. This past weekend, and last week I've been in the middle of everything. You know how bad my previous week was. Well my weekend was probably just as bad excluding my visit. My commissary got stolen, and it was a few students on the wing. When I confronted them, they acted nonchalant, like they didn't know what was up. But the next day (well really that night) their tape had got stolen. So I was the first suspect. I was threatened wit SEG 30 days, majors, etc. if I didn't get the tape. But I had nuttin to do wit it, and I explained that to Sgt. Corey along wit the fact that the people who were accusing me of stealin their tape were the same students who allegedly stole everybodys' commissary. So I got a whole bunch of witnesses. And they found out who did it, so they went to SEG. Now that they're out, they're tryin to set me up, sayin I said on the "6," G.D. 74-14 that if I get an UNSAT I'm goin smash 'em. Plus, they tryin to say I'm trafficking and all kinds of other stuff.

I didn't have enough time to finish writing. So I'm gonna briefly summarize what was poppin off yesterday. I was so upset because Barry was tryin to set me up as well as numerous amount of other students. He figured since he gotta do an extra 30 why not get everybody else. He was one of the main people involved in my stolen commissary. So he figured all of the people who got their stuff stole snitched on him. The reason why I was upset in yo class was because me and Royce was the onez who they tried to say was trafficking. So that's why I was hype because I wanted to know what was goin on. Then on top of that, it was rumorz and speculation that they was goin jump us, and we goin jump them. Them is Farling, Alan, Battles and Barry. They're all from G.I. and them areaz. I call 'em L.C.B. (Lake County Boyz. Then it was supposedly, goin be against NAP, me, Charles, Blair, my son, M. Cort, G. Cort and thatz about it. I was upset because I wanted to find out what was goin on if somebody was goin jump on my guyz, or if I was goin get any paperwork, etc. Well, it ended up ending in a mini-townhouse wit me and about 12 other guyz. They wanted to make sure that we wasn't goin have no riot or keep tryin to set people up, etc. So that's why we came to school late yesterday. We didn't get it all ironed out, but we pretty much got all of it covered. Now it's basically just personal issues. All that other stuff is straight. So that's all cool, and all that other stuff in the past is pretty much straightened out too. Recently, my medz have been reduced dramatically. I'm only takin a 1/3 of what I began wit. I went from 60 mg a day, morning, noon, night to 40 mg (morning, noon) to 20 mg a day to 10 mg mornin, noon. The reason for this is because I'm getting taken off before I leave. I ain't goin lie either. I really do need it (in here, I'm not sure about the outz). But I'm a person who always has to experience it for myself. So I gotta give it a try. I explained my med situation wit Sgt. Corey, and she said she'd have to verify it wit the nurse (about my behavior changes could be from my medz). So we (me, the nurse and Sgt. Corey) talked about it, so now she knowz I ain't just actin crazy for no reason. Then on top of that, last Sunday me and Ms. Jones worked out all of our differences. Matter of fact, she came up to me first, apologized, and stated that I was still one of her favorites. She said we both had dumb azz attacks and that we both heated in the moment. I told her about the apology letter and she read it (not until she went home though). So I didn't find out 'til yesterday, Monday. She said her and her husband loved it. I wrote it to Ms. Jones, but Mr. Jones was there, so I apologized to him too. So even though I still got that major, Sgt. Corey told me it was cool too, because me and Ms. Jones talked it over wit her in her office. So this morning I explained the situation wit Coleman. So he is supposed to speak wit her too, and if he approves it, I know for sure I'm cool and made in the shade. When I get in the shade, I'm stayin there til I leave. My major might be cool anyway, because I got it served last Thursday. So I think I got 7 dayz. Today is the 6th; tomorrow is my last day before it getz dropped. But knowing me, I'll have my C.A.B. right when I finish writing this story. Hopefully, it won't happen though. I pray it don't, and I can get up outta here on the 6th. This month has been the hardest month I've ever been through since I've been here. See even back in the day when I used to go to SEG, this is still harder because then I didn't care, and it ain't hard not to care about something. I didn't care about anything or time, but now I got 11 months of built up anger trying to get all out in my last month of my time. Now I do really care, so it's hard to control myself. One time me and Ms. Scott was discussing if I were to get an UNSAT what she could do or say before the team so they would reason wit her. The reason she gave me is totally truthful and valid. And it got another student up outta here who was here for a while (lil Leo Ward). She simply goin tell 'em that I've been recovered or rehabilitated long time ago, and that now I'm just goin plain nutz from bein here so long. I think I am getting worse or more worse than I was before. I think that's true because I'm getting nutz and real restless. *H.*

Mrs. Martin

I'm glad you seem to have resolved some of your situations – I hope they are finished! There isn't much time left so hang on to your self until then. How are your plans for the school presentation?

<u>Fred Harris – 5/22/97</u>

A was up Ms. Scott? I know you probably figured I'd never write in my journal again. To tell the truth, I really wasn't even going to. Maybe a little doodiling, but nuttin serious. Anyway the real reason I'm writing is to explain a few things. Everything I'm writing you, I'm writing the same or damn near the same thing to Ms. Martin. First off, I haven't been writing, or talking to you (or Ms. Martin) for a couple of reasons which (both reasons) is why I'm writing this. The first is simply because, of course, the incident wit Ms. Pearce, Ms. Martin, you and I. It ain't really the fact of me not trustin yaw, it's just that I'm not trying to start any commotion or player hatin. You know how me and Ms. Martin are, and you know how me and you are. I don't want ya to lose yaws relationship wit each other, or me, or lose everything because of me. I also don't wanna jeopardize your career here. Plus I feel guilty and responsible for anything bad that happens to you concerning your job. To tell the truth, I don't feel the same or as comfortable talking to you. Shit done changed so much. I don't wanna make it any worse than it already is. Even though you may not wanna admit to it, I know you real shitty at this whole situation. Even though you might not get in trouble, just the fact about getting confronted about it. I just don't like the whole thing. It's like now I gotta choose. Even though I don't, that's how I feel. You or Ms. Martin, I can't do it, I don't even want to. I know yo feelings done changed a 'lil bit about her. Another thing is, it feel like I'm being used as a puppet or something. Ms Martin and Pearce want to know everything about you so they can bank you. And you got me to writing shit and finding out shit in advance before it happened. I ain't sayin you or her doin that, I'm just sayin that's how I feel. It's like it ain't about me no mo, it's about getting in trouble and player hatin. This shits really startin to get ridicolouz. I know yaw both still care (I hope) and really are concerned wit my future, but I just don't feel that same support system like I did a while back. Now the 2nd thing has a lot to do wit my release. See, I ain't good at sayin good-byes. I never have and never will. But usually when I say good-bye, it be to a family member or close one or someone who I can see and visit again. But even then I still hate to do it. Ever since I was a child, I avoided situations referring to good-byes or ending relationships. So my way of handling those situations is by trying to avoid them or stop our close contact or relationship. What I mean is, especially people real close who I depend on. I try to avoid so I can get that feelin where I don't need to depend on them or care not to. If I just treat and act the same towards you and Ms. Martin like everybody else do, I won't feel that need to have to depend on yaw, or I won't have that extra feeling towards yaw (the I really care about yaw and appreciative for all yaw've done feeling) See you know I'm better at paper and pen than face to face. So if I was to leave, I wouldn't know what to say, or how to act. Plus I hate the pain of leaving people I really care for. So I try to avoid that feeling by just avoiding tha confrontation and situation period. I don't really wanna leave yaw hangin, but I ain't good at big good-byes, but now if I met you for about a day or 2 you know that's all good. But damn near a whole year. I just can't see it. So I try to leave things all on the normal level or basis. I just figured I'd write you a 'lil something to let you know what' up.

F. Harris

Fred Harris – 5/22/97

Boy it looks like my June 6th is about to turn into June 20th or up. I got involved in so much bullshit today. They tried to get me wit everything from trafficking, prohibited contraband, theft, etc. I bought a walkman for 2 bottles of grease and a box of Star Crunch, and now they tryin to stick me wit that. I really didn't getta chance to talk to Sgt. Corey about the situation, but she did tell me, that most likely I would be getting a major. This is goin be my 2nd major in this 4 week period and probably my 3rd in less than a month and ½. Plus, I got 3 S.A.S. and 1 L.O.P., 1 S.A.S. and L.O.P. was from my C.A.B. wit Ms. Jones' incident (which I did get found guilty of. So I got that major against me too. Plus all the other 'lil speculation, supposedly, sayin I'm the 6, and G.D. 7-4-14 all that shit. Even if didn't nuttin happen in that situation, I was still accused or brought up in the middle of it. I'm already settin my hope up for an UNSAT (Ms. Gardner said Mayfield wouldn't void somebody who has been here a whole year for a tape or contraband.) Regardless, I ain't really goin trip, but if I get a whole 4 weeks, then that's when I'm goin trip. June 6th til July 4th is a really, really long time at least to me. Even though 11's a lot longer, another month is too. I'm takin full responsibility for my actions, and I know if I get an UNSAT, I deserve one, but I think this is getting a little bit out of hand. Tapes and contraband ain't no UNSAT situation. Well, I mean it is, but I have come a long way to be getting held back for some bullshit like this. I really don't know what to say, or how to react, but I'm just real shitty at this whole situation. This shit is makin me so mad. All this 'lil petty punk bullshit. Hoe ass tricks goin try to hold me back for some bullshit. I'm just goin leave it alone, because if I don't, it's just going get me in more trouble. *H.*

Ms. Scott – 5/23/97

Fred –

So the way I understand this last part of the essay is that because June 6 deadline is so close – now you're going to screw up your behavior on the unit.

Basically, Fred – Knock it off. Get it together! Behave this weekend! Journal or write a poem!

Take care –

Ms. Scott

F. Harris – Friday – 5/23/97

Hello Ms. Martin. How are you doin today? I know you ain't heard from me in a while and been wondering what's goin on. So I figured I'd let you know what was up. I've basically been upset ever since that Ms. Jones incident. Then I was upset about that situation wit Barry and them. Then I getz caught up in a whole bunch of trafficking and tradin havin to do wit tapes and walkmans. Then we got put on that mini-lock down (Thursday). I just been so shitty lately, trouble after trouble, after trouble, then I getz found guilty on my C.A.B. yesterday. I only had 24 hours L.O.P. and S.A.S., and I'm already off of that, but I'm still scared that I'm goin get an UNSAT. The future and jobs ain't even a thought to me no mo. I can't do nuttin unless I get up outta here first. So all of this stuff is gangin up on me at once makin me fall apart. so that's a 'lil bit of the reason why I been so upset. Now the reason why I've kinda been to myself or not talking to you as much is for a couple of reasons. One is a little bit because of the situation between you and Ms. Scott. I ain't afraid to talk to you or worried about what she might say. It's just the fact that you went against my wishes about informing Ms. Pearce. I still trust you and all that; it's just now I'm a little hesitant. I'm not tryin to say I don't still care, because I do, and no matter how much I get mad at you, you still goin be my other mamma, and I'm still goin care the same about you.

Mrs. Martin

Now remember you are the one who told Ms. Pearce and showed her your journal. I have absolutely no bad feelings toward Ms. Scott.

F. Harris – Friday – 5/23/97

But I do feel a little weird. You told me if I ever had any problems wit that situation to tell you anyway. So I am. I really don't have a problem, but I'm just letting you know how I feel about it. I've forgiven you about it anyway. 1. I feel like I've jeopardized Ms. Scott's career and got you 2 in a feud. Even though that may not be the situation that's how I feel. Now the 2nd reason is gonna be kinda stupid, maybe not to you, but to me it is. I don't understand why I do this. Anywayz, I found myself over the last few years getting real hurt at sayin good-bye or losin someone I love or care about. Sometimes I can't really think about losing or leavin you or some of the other people. Like Ms. Pearce said, its getting close to that time and I need to find out a way to say good-bye. But, through the years, I haven't really seemed to find that way. So I usually avoid farewells by just plain avoiding them or the person. I don't really want to avoid or lose you, but that's the way I've been known to handle good-bye situations. I really can't think of actually leavin you after 11 months. It still don't feel like I'm leavin, but I am, and I need to figure how to prepare myself to leave, witout hurtin anyone of our feelings, or leavin on a bad note. The longer I try to avoid you or talking to you, the more independent I get. But I'm afraid I'll have a stepped-on heart when I leave you if I continue to act the same. See, back in the day, I would always get my heart broke whenever I lost someone like you. So in order to avoid that and those type of feelings, I just avoided the person period. It's not a good way to end a relationship, but that's been O.K. for me over time. To tell the truth though, I don't wanna leave you like that, but the problem is I'm so accustomed to my previous actions that I wouldn't (and don't) know how to say good-bye. Truthfully, I'm scared, upset, and a little nervous. I don't wanna leave you like I have before. But in any situation I don't want us to end like that. So I would like for you to help me get through this. I also wanna talk to you more (even when I'm shitty). I really need you through this last 2 week stretch, and I want you to be here helping me everyday and bit of it. This is really the end. The final chapter. No mo allz well that endz well. I want to spend my hopeful 2 weeks wit you the best way possible. So I do wanna apologize because you've done nuttin to me, and I forgave you a long time ago. I still care for you, and like I said want you to help me through these last innings. So when you getta chance, please write me back and let me know what's up. *H.*

Much Love,

Sincerely,

Fred Harris

Mrs. Martin

Fred –

Please know nothing you've done or said has made me feel any differently about Ms. Scott. I was concerned because you were so upset and angry at how she had acted toward you. That's all – She's a counselor and she knows her job – I'm a teacher, and I know mine. I am sorry that you were angry about my speaking to Ms. Pearce, but I have a job to do and sometimes that has to come before a "word," hurt or no hurt. I am also very sorry that it has caused a problem for Ms. Scott towards me – but that needs to be between she and I – don't you worry about it. As for your last 2 weeks my suggestion is <u>PULL YOURSELF TOGETHER</u>. Deal with things the way you need to, but in the most healthy way you can. I'm here and whatever way you're able to get ready to leave is what you need to do. I want <u>this</u> to be positive for you. Talk to me.

F. Harris – Tuesday – 5/27/97

A Ms. Martin? I'm glad you told Sgt. Martin to get my journal back on Friday for other reasons we couldn't come to school. Anyway, some of the stuff I wrote may have been confusing. Ms. Scott ain't got no beef, I don't got no beef, and I know you ain't mad at any of yaw either. I was basically implying that I didn't want yaw to have no beef against each other. Not that yaw already did. I really ain't trippin on her no way. She been bullshittin lately dickin me around. I really don't even wanna rap to her, but I gotz to be cool til team. We all gotta play the game. So it's all good. It aint hurtin me. The only thing I expect is the SAT I deserve. Nuttin else, nuttin more. Now please don't take this the wrong way, I'm just telling you what I'm going to do. So don't worry. Something wit my SAT. I feel pretty cool about SAT, and I hate to say it, but it's goin be from some major ass kissin. I hate to do it, but like I said before, we all gotta play the game. I've gotten real good wit Sgt. Corey, we say we a team now, sidekicks. We both be helping each other out. She helps me in my trouble situations, and I help her find out about dirt, stealin, contraband, fightin, etc. She knowz wit my seniority and plug-ins and resources, she knowz damn near all information comes through or to me. So in return, she tries double hard to get me home. That's why she told Ms. Timmons about my major. So, hopefully, my 9 dayz and a wake-up will be cool. But another thing that'll help me out is that I got put back on my 20 mg medz, and even took my evening dose back. Plus, I plan to let that follow through till I get out. I'll decide where to go from there. So I guess things are lookin decent, because ain't nuttin goin be better till I get home. You feel me. I hope you do. I know you do though that's why I talk to you. I know you understand and care for me. *H.*

Mrs. Martin

Well, I'm glad you explained that to me. I thought for a while that it was going to be a real mess with everyone being angry. Thank you for the clarification. My response to your "<u>ass-kiss-ing</u>" comment just to get your <u>deserved</u> SAT – I have a problem with that because if you really deserved that SAT, there would be no reason for any ass-kissing – think about that. I'm glad you've decided to take your meds to finish out your time – I wish you would consider taking it at home again. I'm not for sure that Sgt. Corey will be able to work again due to that incident, so you may have more of your own work to do than you planned, but I'm sure you can do it. Hang in there – not much time! **Mrs. H**.

<u>F. Harris – 5/30/07</u>

A momma. Today I damn near got put on S.A.S. or L.O.P. Me and this C/O are always goin back and forth at each other makin each other mad, pissin each other off. We basically be at each other's throats (verbally), trying to set each other up for failure. Today I woke up on the wrong side of the bed. Coleman didn't work today so Sgt. Riddle (Male) covered. Me and him don't get along. He be all over yo back early in the morning. Plus the officer I got into it wit, he's definitely on my case. His name is Fitzgerald. I don't know if you know him, but he's kinda like Long (personality wise). He has a dry, old fashioned, sarcastic type of sense of humor. He makes jokes and comments sarcastically all the time. He usually refers to me as a pri-madonna, the General, The Chief, little jokes referring to my senior-ity here. He knows that pisses me off. So, in return, I piss him, make his job a lot harder. Instigatin, aggrevatin, doin stuff I know that intentionally makes him mad. So we usually go at it everyday he's here. Well today, (like every other day) I wore my blue shorts to din-ing hall. Riddle being the nitpicker he is, accompanied by Fitzgerald, being the playerhater he is, were trying to bank me for it. But, Lt. Egger gave me permission (he really did give me permission, but he said since you been doin it, keep on). So I told Riddle and Fitzgerald what Lt. Egger said. I was the only one wit blue shorts on. So I stuck out like a sore thumb. Egger came up to breakfast and Riddle started mixin up words that I had said. So he was still tryin to bank me. I avoided it for the moment, but when we got downstairs, he got to talking indirectly about me. He was talking bout me but he jus didn't say my name. So I told him I knew what was up, why he still tryin to front me out. Then he get all mad talking 'bout he goin write me a major for improper dress. He really couldn't do that though. So he got all mad cussin, callin me a primadonna and I think I'm all that, etc. So I let him know, "Fuck You, I ain't shit." He still doin it though. So I tellz him again, but realize 6 could turn into 36. So I chill, but I was still getting paperwork. However, I talked to Lt. Egger and he covered for me, but I think he did that because I told him I only had 6 dayz left. So he was really tryin to look out for me. When I got out of that they was still P'H'N (Fitzgeral and Riddle). So then they wanna give me a minor for disrespect. I was so shitty I wasn't goin go off, but I jus wanted to cuss 'em out, cause they got to botherin me first. But Fitzgerald's conscience told him what was up. He felt bad because he knowz I'm tryin to go home, and he wants me to because I ain't like some of these other kidz in here. Plus, he knows how I react to his name calling, so he knew I was goin to respond to him like "Fxxx You." So he apologized, and we made an agreement. His part was no more frontin me out or name calling, and mine was full respect, don't try to tell him how to do his job, and try not to get everybody's head hyped. So I resolved it wit no paperwork, S.A.S. or nuttin. I was in the wrong wit my comments and responses, but he was too. That's why I tried to keep myself together to see what my consequences was, instead of jus goin off. I think I was a little upset partially because of everyone actin a fool yesterday and it jus stayed wit me. Even though the day has started off kinda bad, I should be cool. I just gotta put up with Riddle for another 2 dayz then I should be cool. So I'm sure I can maintain. *H.*

Mrs. Martin

I like to see that in you again. It's been a long time since you've sounded very sure of yourself. It sounds like you've worked it out. Please be patient with staff. Some are just as stressed as you. I apologize for not getting over to see you yesterday evening – I had something that was unavoidable come up. My schedule doesn't always run how I want it to. Keep working.

PART III

FINAL THOUGHTS

So, I came to grips with reality, I had to change and stick with it. I could not think of living day to day by the orders of a Correctional Officer.

Among the list of reasons and causes of my mistakes, I would have to say that being disobedient was probably one of my worst problems. At the ages of 15 and 16, I was into things most teens were not or should not have been into, having large amounts of money, driving highly expensive cars and staying out from dusk until dawn.

I was doing things I had no business doing. I thought I was slick trying to come up with excuses to my parents for my actions. My parents were not stupid, they had their suspicions; however, they played the less assertive role. Just let the cards fall in place. If I messed up I paid the consequences. When we used to pass the Juvenile Center, my dad would always say, "You had better straighten up, boy, before you end up there on that hill with the rest of those boys." It looks like he predicted correctly. He would tell me which friends were right and which friends were wrong for me and how by me stopping to go to Church, that the world and Satan were the only things waiting for me; and how police were trying to crack down on the law; and how arresting a black teenage male would probably just make their day. But, since my parents played the less assertive role, they let me make my mistakes. All the times my dad talked to me, I figured it would never happen to me (getting caught up in the world, bad friends, and jail). I thought I could handle myself. Boy was I wrong. Everything my father said came about as a prophecy; right before my eyes! I stopped going to Church, started going out causing trouble and making a ruckus. Gangs, money and drugs were before me day by day. The streets had taken over my life. I even ran away from home just to be with my so-called friends.

When I was with my friends is when I started getting locked up. Things from there on went downhill. I began to get locked up on a frequent basis. After so long, I was too deep into the streets I really could not escape it if I wanted to. I finally came to the conclusion that what my parents had said was really true. I did not find that out until it was too late. Even what my dad had said about my friends. They were the main people hurting me, and on top of that they snitched on me to get themselves out of trouble. That is crazy, but some people learn the hard way. I guess I was one of those people.

I did learn that straying away from God is moving closer to sin. In the Bible it says, "Honor thy father and thy mother..." which I had no concept of. I could not expect to abide by the word of God, if I could not listen to my parents words or the words of the law. Being disobedient causes nothing but trouble, and I found that out the hard way.

When you are growing up, there is always that one kid who is worse than everyone else or that one group of people that cause the most trouble all the time for no reason. When I was younger, those guys used to be my best friends. With those best friends, I only caused more problems and a lot of commotion. We would go to the club to fight and steal for fun, get high and drunk until we passed out. There were no good things about hanging out with those guys because it got me jumped on two or three times, shot at on numerous occasions, and expelled from school. Why did I hang around those guys? It was for a few reasons: (1) anytime I was in trouble I knew I had somebody to watch my back for me no matter what, (2) another reason was because I wanted to be part of something or belong to something to help make me feel needed or have a purpose, and (3) lastly, I just plain and simply thought it was cool. However, it did not just happen like that! There was major peer pressure involved. I was somehow persuaded that being bad or a thug was the cool thing to do. Afterwards, I found out the only thing my friends got me into was trouble and jail.

In the final analysis, I found out that part of my downfall as a teenager was my age and immaturity. Being young and inexperienced can make a person vulnerable to unproductive experiences. It is also like there is no concept or understanding of things being done. When I was younger, I had a lot of excess energy, and no direction into which to channel it. So I guess I directed that energy into negative things. The thing I was not looking at was the fact of how immature I was being by not doing something positive or productive with that energy. Instead of getting involved in a hobby or sport, I got involved in gangs and gang banging. I feel that I was too young to really realize how grave a mistake I was making with my life. I knew I was doing wrong, but I do not think I understood the consequences of what I was doing. Everything was just fun and games to me when I was younger. At 15 or 16, there was no looking at things too seriously.

I would like to say that every action has a reaction. If someone does something wrong, they will get punished, and if someone does something right, they will be rewarded. In my case, I did something wrong, and although getting locked up was not fun nor great, I needed it. The time I spent being locked up gave me a chance to really think about what I got locked up for and then why. I took responsibility for my actions and acted upon them by changing. To me, one of the best ways to learn is through experience(s), which I have a lot at this point in my life.

Incarceration is an experience and feeling that no one would ever want to go through. Knowing that one has been stripped of most of his/her freedom and rights and is serving a sentence for a crime can be very painful. Such things like working and physical activity are small rewards for good behavior or good work done as an inmate.

Before anyone thinks of doing anything stupid like committing a crime, realize that the price you must pay if caught is incarceration which is something no one truly wants to experience or go through. Plus I did a complete 360 degree turnaround when I got out. If I had not gotten locked up, I would probably be into the same stuff I was into before – the streets. Nothing has impacted me as much and made me change like me getting locked up. My being locked up was not what I anticipated. I figured I would not be able to get a good job or that everyone would look at me differently. I also felt that I would be outdated; meaning, I would be a year behind everyone else, and that it would take me forever to get back to where I was or catch up.

Fortunately, I was totally wrong. People accepted me just as I was – everyone! Everybody was just waiting to see me when I got out that they totally overlooked the fact I was even locked up or what I was locked up for. When I got out, I got my driver's license and my car. I got a job pretty quick too. I didn't keep it for long though.

I got a job at Federal Express and got a new car. On top of all that I went to college for a year too. Everyone doubted me and thought I was going to get locked up again. But I'm proving everyone wrong. I've finally earned respect. So I feel that I had a positive effect of a lesson well learned from my incarceration.

PART IV

WORKS BY FREDDY B

Alone

I'm all alone in this world, It seems like no one can feel me
And when people try to get closer, I don't want no one near me
Nobody understands or comprehends the problems that I face
Sometimes I don't even wanna live, delete Freddy 'B witout a trace
Because I did not ask to be here, so why am I on earth
I've been causing trouble, havoc, & chaos ever since my birth
All the talks wit family, friends, & doctors, they don't realize
All the things I've done & seen, through these scanless niggaz eyez
I'm trapped alone in this world, when will the madness end
And will God hear my prayers & give me a companion & a friend
Because I'm getting to the point, where I'm like Fuck It! I Jus Can't Take It!
No ones here wit me anyway, so It don't matter If I make It
But I Love God, & He's here wit me, I think I can make It home
But for now I gotta make It through this shit, but I still feel all
Alone

By: Freddy B

Untitled

Now pay attention to these words that I teach
You ain't gotta be Barry White, but practice what I preach
Cause I'm a player, an O.G. from way back
I used to sell dope, gang bang, and bust caps
But now I'm through wit that
Cause being in the game gives you knowledge
Not tha kind from goin to high school or college
You see all of my knowledge and wisdom
Is from being locked up so long in this dirty system
That's why I fear no man except for God above
I trust no one in tha world, for the world I have no love
I'm 17 and I done seen so much
Kids gettin shot and stabbed – my boyz, brains and guts
That's why I play Ashes to Ashes and Dust to Dust in God we Trust
But now all of that's in the past
I wanted to live life grown as a teen way too fast
But I ain't trippin, I'm just sittin remenissin
About those wrong choices I made along wit dem wrong decisions
I can't complain for the choices that I have made
And doing 6 to 9 for my crimes is the price that must be paid.
So all you so called thugstas and you hustlas pay attention
Don't be a busta, think through and make the right decision.
But now I got plenty of time to think things through my mind
I'm in the Department of Corrections serving 6 to 9
And as time rolls on jus giving up is on my mind
But family, friends and Bible verses help to keep me trying
Cause I can't complain for the choices that I've made
And 6 to 9 for my crimes is the price that must be paid
That's why I'm down on my knees thanking God for my blessings
Cause through the rough life that I've lived, I finally learned my lesson
So all you so-called thugstas and you hustlas pay attention
Don't be a busta. Think things through and make the right decision.

By: Freddy B

Who Am I?

I am Freddy B, that's who I am. Who are you?
What gives you the nutz to question me?
I am 17, young & black, grew up in tha hood wit my boyz.
Some people say I'm a risk because I'm strong, young, black, & smart.
I'm marked by the government because I oppose a threat.
But you don't know me, & they don't either, so why do they all oppress me?
What do you expect a man to do, If you never give him a chance?
I'm not blind, I can see who's the fakes & phonies.
Who's out to help me & hurt me
I'm not bad, I'm just misunderstood, unable to be comprehended.
Just need a friend every now & then who I can relate to.
I can be soft, & gentle, the sweetest thing you'd ever meet.
But I can be crooked, & real scandalouz, If you hoez are out to get me.
But I am human, I have feelings, & make mistakes like everyone else.
So why Is It when I mess up, you come down so hard on me?
Is It because I'm 17, young, & black?
Or Is It because I'm Freddy B?
You don't know.
So I don't either.
Yaw tell me to be good,
Shit – how do you figure?
I have no love fo tha system, or no man, they have no love fo me.
So don't question yo'self why I do the shit I do.
I choose to live my life fo me. Not fo none of you.
So If you still don't seem to comprehend, I guess yaw just won't know.
But yaw can't understand ya'selves, so why yaw question me?
Until yaw learn about yaw'self, don't even question Fred B.
Because all yaw need to know, Is that I'm Fred B til I die.
So all yaw chumps who question, & oppose me, that's the answer
to yaw question.

By: Freddy B

Untitled

My destiny is testing me,
Why me?
Why is the Lord stressing me?
My mind's unstable, so why you question me?
Professionally.
An ex-con, ex-thief, ex-thug as you know it,
Rearranged ex-gang banger now a funky poet
Blow it.
Off, like ya ain't listenen
Knowin ya payin attention,
Cause I'm wise, young, smart not to mention
Hella heart
From the start.
Participate, and take part
Of the lessons and wise teachings from an O.G.
Who me?
Yes me.
Freddy B
Nap
Old hoods, no good.
H.V.P.?
Probably.
My mentalities 'bout to explode.
Unload.
Of my shit that's untold.
So let me reload and unfold,
Grab a hold
To the knowledge
Learned no where else.
Just from Freddy B's "Thug College"
Holla if yaw feel me.
I know yaw hear me.
Just prepare yo mind,
To bump and grind,

Relax.
Don't think about time
Listen to what I spit, and find
Your mind boggled, and mixed you see,
Somewhat like an unsolved mystery,
Who could it be?
But Freddy B.
Again and again.
Spittin the real like a sin
Or a drunk man, sippin gin.
Why you spit the real?
Shit, that all depend.
Defend.
And protect yo mind, from the world.
It's a terrible thing to waste, just like a pearl.
Yo mind's in a quarrel.
Mentally do a 360 twirl
Prepare for the worst.
First things first.
Your mind's dyin of thirst.
Mess around, end up in a hearse.
But don't trip, I know the truth hurts.
A villain or a vandal?
Don't matter.
The world's a big scandal.
Plottin and skemin, Niggaz best believing,
The crazy shit a nigga do when he feinin.
Oh, by the way,
Fuck the president,
Don't forget the government,
Them hoez sittin on a mint.
Act like a penny of it, can't be spent.
People's homeless and dyin, can't yaw take a hint.
Seen hella crazy things.
The funk, and pain's what I bring.
The gangsta hymns what I sing.

In and out like a one night fling.
I see the evil in your eyez.
Jealous niggaz, I despize.
Wize.
But to my surprise,
I still don't know what the future holdz, and liez
A mental 187
Who said all thugz go to heaven.
Graves open like 7-11.
A yeah that mental 187.
Let your mind marinate,
Listen to what I narrate.
How much can your mind take?
Be real 'bout your shit don't be fake.
Hear those niggaz tell war stories.
Claimin money, fame, and glory.
Fuck them fakes and them phonies.
In this world ain't no homiez,
Aint much more that I can spit,
But that I'm tired of all this shit.
But I still gotta represent,
Thankin God, my knees bent.
So through my struggle and my strain,
I've felt good, I've felt pain.
Feel like I'm goin go insane.
But I chill and try to maintain.

Because the wisdom, that I earned,
Is that 'ol shit, that I learned.
So fuck them imitators and player haters,
Who's oppressin me.
Lord knows my destiny's testing me.

By: Freddy B

Mom of Moms

Let me take the time to praise the Lord up above,
for givin me a mom as great as you, who gives me so much love.
You've always been there when I needed, until the end.
Your not only my mom your my best friend.
You always try to sit me down talk to and lecture me,
I should've listened, but I had my own strategy.
Cause since I've been getting older I just have'nt been the same,
but don't trouble yourselves, because your not to blame.
I understand that you try and do all you can,
to raise me in the right direction to become a man.
When you try to help me I'd just argue and fight,
but I thought I was grown and everything I said was right.
But after time it didn't take me very long,
to find out everything I planned and did ended up goin wrong.
Cause everytime I'd just end up getting incarcerated, and bein seperated,
from family, just made me frustrated.
I guess I really should've paid attention,
cause now all I see are bad choices, and decisions.
And at the same time flushin, my hopes and dreams down the drain,
while you and dad at home in pain, goin insane.
Now I've had some time to think, and I've been reminissin,
on all the wrong things that I've done, and I'm wishin,
That I could take back all the bad, the crimes, and the felonies
and thought of how ya care, and how much you both mean to me.
Cause over all these years, it wasn't long to discover,
that not many women in the world, are as great, as my mother.
And through all the arrests, and trials in court,
you always back me up with your 100% full support.
And when I can't tell, talk to, or trust no other,
I'll know who'll always be there for me, and that's my mother.
Whenever I have a problem, you haven't let me down,
and over all these years, there's one thing that I've found,
that whenever I feel down and out, like no one's there,
you always prove your love, and show your tender lovin care.

So now that I'm locked up, I've thought it out, and realized,
that I still have a life up ahead, just clear my mind, and open up my eyes.
So when people ask me how'd I make it, I won't be embarrassed to say,
I wouldn't have made it through my life, without Fred & Yvonne Harris.
Oh well, I might not be a writer or a famous poet,
but everything I wrote, is from the heart, I hope you know it.
And I hope you like this card, but I must end it and say,
that I want you to have a happy, and very special (56th) BIRTHDAY!!!!!

HAPPY BIRTHDAY MOM!!!

By: Freddy B

APPENDIX I

Frederic Walton Harris, Sr. Birth Certificate

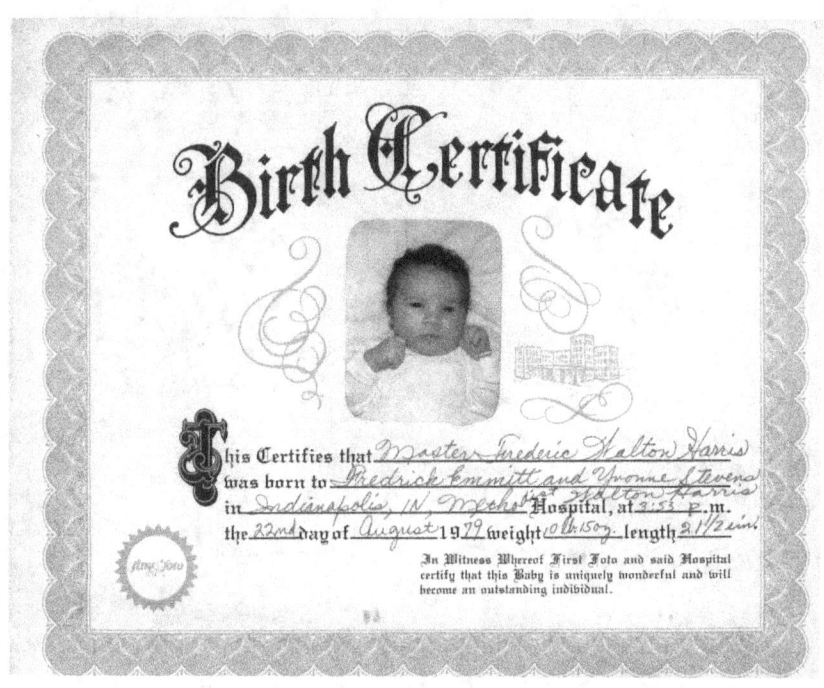

APPENDIX II

The Harris Family

THE
HARRIS
FAMILY

APPENDIX III

Freddy, Family & Friends

Precious Memories

APPENDIX IV

Frederic Walton Harris, Sr.

Frederic Walton Harris, Sr.

Sunrise: August 22, 1979
Sunset: June 1, 2002

APPENDIX V

Freddy's Parents

Frederick Emmett Harris Sr. & Yvonne Stevens Walton Harris